EGALITARIAN COMMUNITY

EGALITARIAN COMMUNITY

ETHNOGRAPHY AND EXEGESIS

ROBERT A. ATKINS, JR.

WITH A FOREWORD BY MARY DOUGLAS

The University of Alabama Press

Tuscaloosa and London

∞

The paper on which this book is printed meets the minimum requirements of American National Standard for Information Science-Permanence of Paper for Printed Library Materials, ANSI Z39.48-1984.

Library of Congress Cataloging-in-Publication Data

Atkins, Robert A., 1949–
   Egalitarian community : ethnography and exegesis / by Robert A. Atkins, Jr.
     p.   cm.
   Includes bibliographical references and index.
   ISBN 0-8173-0513-0 (alk. paper)
   1. Church—Biblical teaching. 2. Sociology, Biblical. 3. Bible.
N.T. Epistles of Paul—Criticism, interpretation, etc.
4. Equality—Biblical teaching. I. Title.
BS2655.C5A75   1991
227'.067—dc20   90-38665
                                  CIP

British Library Cataloguing-in-Publication Data available

For my parents:
Robert and Dorothy Atkins

Contents

Figures

Foreword

Mary Douglas

The title alone suggests the usefulness of the book to students of religion. Egalitarian communities have been unduly neglected in the social sciences. This is partly because they are thought to be the simplest kind of community, as if they were the obvious, primary kind of society from which all others are unfortunate deviations. Archaeologists tend to think of hierarchy or individualism as late arrivals on the paleolithic scene. Sociologists tend to think of the egalitarian community as the most obvious, the type of social bonding that does not need special explanation or theory. That very assumption needs to be explained: what sort of community would it apply to? Would it work for a community of adults, no children, both sexes about the same size and weight, so that differences can be fairly fought out and equality restored after the fight? Or does it imply a crypto-theological idea that humans are naturally peaceful and able to live together without special ordering, until some serpent sneaks along, tempting with wealth and power? Or does it imply a community that would normally be harmonious until the strains of overpopulation test it beyond virtue?

Another widespread assumption teaches that fewness of numbers guarantees peace and equality, and so implicitly the first communities, being small, would have been egalitarian. There is no evidence and no argument to support the popular bias, against which theory and experience suggest that an egalitarian community is a remarkable achievement, to be wondered at and not at all to be taken for granted.

The likeliest explanation of the bias that gives primordial rightness to the egalitarian community is that the world has listened to its own dissenting sects: "When Adam delved and Eve span, who was then the gentleman?" There is perhaps a dissenter inside each of us. The rhetoric of equality stirs us all. We have heard the protest against artificial social distinctions, against exclusiveness, against contempt of the lowly. It is a protest that we can use ourselves at any time. We have taken at face value the dissenters' claim that by embracing equality they are returning to a primitive church. The really interesting thing is that though equality is often worth achieving, it is a very difficult condition to realize and even more difficult to sustain over a period. It needs constant vigilance and the application of complex rules of distribution. In the most egalitarian commune or kibbutz, hidden hierarchy is apt to lurk. Equality does not come naturally; it needs discipline and foresight and intricate regulation.[1] If this is surprising, the surprise demonstrates the bias towards thinking of equality as natural and easy.

Another aspect of egalitarian communities that is commonly underestimated is their fragility. They tend to break apart, often in anger. The ones that have the best record for survival tend to have anticipated this weakness in their constitution, and have legislated for a principle of regular subdivision. Their fragility accounts for the association between egalitarian communities and smallness of scale. This is another source of weakness in religious sociology. The idea that harmony is threatened by increase in size is misleading, because it carries the implication that increase of scale in itself produces a tendency to set up hierarchical denominations. Underneath this reasoning is the idea that social harmony is easier to achieve in small groups, which is very far from true, as any experience of small groups will confirm.[2] Egalitarian forms of society are very important. We should be analyzing egalitarian community structures, and tracing their variations, distinguishing the numerous ways of instituting equality, checking which kind sheds members at the fringes, which kind splits in half, and asking how friendly and effective are relations after splitting. Is the local harmony of the small group bought at the cost of larger disharmony between the separated groups? This range of questions is interesting academically for religious sociology and the history of religions, and important practically for those who have to try to design constitutions for religious orders and communes. Unfortunately, instead of systematic study, our concern for a valued principle is blocked by uncritical assumptions of the primacy, naturalness, smallness, and stability of egalitarian communities.

In this book the author addresses the topic directly by asking whether the communities to which Paul addressed his letters were egalitarian. The question needs a method of comparison. What criteria can assess the spirit of equality? In what institutions is it enshrined? How was the Pauline community constituted? How much authority were members being told to accept, how were they supposed to settle their disputes, how should they deal with non-members? The author's survey of the subject shows that the ground has already been well tilled. The Pauline churches would seem to have had fluid rules and poorly defined categories of leadership. As to the boundaries separating them from other religions, there are contradictory signals: It is not clear from the information whether these were strong (in the light of the reiterated contrast between slaves and free) or weak (given that members pursued their normal professional or artisanal avocations in the outside world). The Pauline terminology of adoption needs exegesis in the light of these questions. In what sense were new members adopted into a community at all? Was it a purely spiritual change of status, or was there to be an earthly community into which adoption gave a secure place? Robert A. Atkins, Jr., takes this as the starting point for an exercise in cultural analysis. It would be useful to set up criteria for sifting such meager details as exist, and to make them so explicit that the research could become comparative. If the method is good, it would be possible to compare the religious communities converted by Paul with those administered from Jerusalem or Rome.

Atkins describes why something like cultural theory is needed. Given the present anxiety about the possibility of objective interpretation, he is recommending a tool. It is difficult to be aware of the other without being conscious of self. The problem is to lend our ears to the cross-cultural conversations that are being held in our own culture. The tool he employs does not claim to pick up more detail, but on the contrary to select and classify information according to a theory; it is not a photo enlarger that brings more of the subject matter into view, but a light that beams selectively, making the user aware of personal prejudices at the same time as it lights the corresponding parts of the community being observed.

A large part of this book is taken with a technical discussion of two dimensions of comparison. One dimension measures the extent to which the social unit has borders closed to the outside world. For thinking about the meaning of adoption the question of exclusivity is prime. Following the model presented by Gross and Rayner in *Measuring Culture*,[3] Atkins develops criteria for comparing the strength of members' mutual commitment to a community. One might belong formally to a particular group but in practice spend very little time with it. A high degree of full-time presence in one community and a high degree of absenteeism in another would, if it could be accurately assessed, cause us to estimate the strength of the first community's solidarity higher than that of the second—a possible basis for predictions on how such groups will behave as a community under crisis. Or, one might be a member of a group but know only one or two of the other members. Reflecting on the solidarity of a group in which all members know each other, as opposed to one in which they all know the leader but know each other hardly at all, would cause us to rate the first stronger than the second, and base predictions on our assessment. How much do the members of a group participate in group activities, what proportion of their available time do they allocate to the group? How sensitive are they to the pressures of fellow members? How much do the individual members share a common background? If we can find a way of assessing these signs of a life in common, signs of investment in common purposes, we can put more meaning into the other signs of a strong group, such as the existence of a separating boundary, a badge, a group name, a ritual of entry.

The other dimension is structure, ("grid" in the jargon). The more a community is structured, the less it can be counted egalitarian, unless the structures are mainly rules for preventing members from creating inner coteries, corners of control and influence, informal pecking orders. The latter are the insulating rules, such as those in an egalitarian community of Carthusian monks, very different from the functional and institutional distinctions on which a hierarchical community is built.

The theory on which the author is drawing is that all social units vary along these two dimensions; investment in either or both is decisive for the quality of the community life; the two dimensions are very powerful predictors of the commitment of the members to a specific pattern of cultural values. Most of the theoretical work is concerned with inferring from the pattern of organization the kind of values that would be needed to sustain it. There are costs for each type. If members want to have a strong community, they will be committed to a certain amount of exclusivity in their dealings with the outside. If they want an entirely open community, they must be quick to censure discrimination. If they want clear decision-making, they must be prepared to concede some authority. If they are against authority as a diminishment of egalitarian ideals, they must be reconciled to ambiguity and weak leadership. Ways of distinguishing distinct cultural types is at the center of the theorizing. This is where Atkins has placed his contribution.

In the effort to make precise comparisons, great care is needed to make sure that other variables are under control. The two or three communities that are selected have to be sufficiently alike in the general condition of their lives. If the Pauline communities are very different from those in Jerusalem, the differences should ideally be visible and able to be taken into account. If the data is based on letters in one community, so it should also be in the others. Rather strictly limiting himself to Paul's correspondence, the author develops criteria for deciding the extent to which these communities are being advised to organize themselves in a hierarchical or an egalitarian style. The results of a toothcomb search for clues are tabulated according to the principles expounded in Gross and Rayner's handbook.

In one sense this project ought to be part of a larger research scheme that would apply the same tests to the community of Jerusalem and to those other communities organized from Jerusalem. Then the extraordinary diagrams would have their full value. Without comparison it is difficult to interpret the diagram of network connections to Paul (see pages 106–7). Every line is centered on him, and few lines connect other members of the communities to each other. This strongly centered diagram must be largely an effect of the sources: letters by one person would tend to show up that pattern. In a hierarchical system the leader would write to all the heads of sections; there would be letters from them to each other, but if the research kept to the same kind of sources, the lateral communications would not show up. It is important to recognize the limitations of the material in order to be able to point out the value of the technique. Gross and Rayner's book on methodology used the example of information gained by face-to-face fieldwork. Atkins's work is perhaps the first attempt to use those prescriptions rather creatively on written texts, from which the calculations which are at the heart of the method cannot be carried out. Another example is Aaron Wildavsky's cultural analysis of Moses as a political leader.[4] The method has also been applied to fiction.[5] If the full method could be tried out by fieldwork among living communities, the result would show the typical shape of charismatic leaders' networks. For some kinds of communities the networks would be dense and replete, for others more paradigmatic. We would have a method of comparing the structure of communities with the structure of their ideas about the world.

The other diagram is more startling (see Figure 5). When he has assessed the values for each criterion of group and structure, Atkins does admittedly impressionistic calculations and maps the community on the diagram of cultural bias. Perhaps the most important result is that he has made his analysis open to checking at every point. Anyone who wants to disagree with him can go back to the list of group criteria and grid criteria with the Epistles in his hand and give reasons for making a different assessment. Furthermore, it will not be difficult to do this exercise again, using more richly contextualized sources, and to compare quite precisely the organization of the Pauline with the other churches.

The diagram shows the Pauline Church squarely into the right bottom quadrant of the Grid-Group map. It will take more familiarity with the background of cultural theory than this book provides to make plain what this implies. The implications of a church falling plumb into the bottom right quadrant are very rich. Such a form of organization, characterized by weak authority, much ambiguity between members, and a strong boundary against the outside, is prey to its own factions and very fragile. Its internal problems may stem from its position of dissent from a larger ambient community. Anything that makes defection easy and loyalty costly to the individual weakens the authority structure. No rules can be applied, no punishments threatened, when all that will happen when the community good is in conflict with perceived individual interests is that the individual members will melt away. Easy defection pushes a community to adopt the egalitarian form of organization that makes a virtue out of lack of authority. This is one of the lessons that comes out of Rosabeth Moss Kanter's beautiful comparative study of the longevity of communes.[6] She showed that those American communities that had somehow made their external boundary secure, so that they did not have to worry about their members walking out, were also the ones which instituted some degree of hierarchy—and these were the communities which managed to survive after the death of the founder. All those that achieved some degree of community security had a rule for holding property in common.

Paul did not require his congregation to pool their possessions. Jerusalem did. In a community whose members have signed away their right to private wealth it is much easier to make the impulse to further solidarity effective. It is more than likely that if Paul had tried to impose community of possessions on Antioch or Thessalonia or his other churches, he would not have kept the congregation for as long as he did. These reflections lead us to ask about the special conditions of his mission to the gentiles. Something about the long lines of communication from his base, weaknesses of funding, or other problems of organization, would explain a lesser expectation of commitment and a more ambiguous attitude to authority, a particular type of solidarity which Atkins has captured on his diagram.

From this point old theological issues can be reexamined. For the author, one upshot is that he is able to give a particular Pauline meaning to the idea of adoption. Or rather, he is able to signal that adoption into an unstructured family is bound to mean something very different from adoption into a structured one. Words will have different meanings and doctrines will be different according to the cultural bias of the church, and the cultural bias is an aspect of the lives of the people. As he puts it well: Paul did not exist only on a level of ideas.

If this kind of research were to be continued and the methodology developed and refined, a different conversation would be possible about religious doctrine and pastoral concern. It might be assumed that the millennial trend in early Christianity, as elsewhere, drove the congregations of believers to adopt their egalitarian form of common life. But if the two are generally found together—egalitarian community and millennial expectation—their relation could be more complex. It would be good to look for the conditions under which it is impossible to set up a dissenting community of any other kind. Then the eschatology would be part of being reconciled to a situation in which internal organization cannot be reasonably expected, in which practical promises cannot be implemented—a community in which solidarity is always apt to evaporate for lack of institutionalizing, where the only stable expectation is for continuing uncertainty until the millennium.

Preface

When we attempt to explain the cultural artifacts and remains from another people quite different from our own, we are about the business of interpretation. The task of interpretation is twofold. It is both descriptive and critical. Both tasks are part of the interpretive process.

Description requires observation. Participant observation is the standard of ethnography—the art and science of writing about human culture as it is found. Historical and literary criticism is the standard of biblical exegesis—the art and science of writing about the literary artifacts of several ancient and foreign peoples.

Criticism requires awareness. Awareness of the diversity of human culture is the standard of anthropology. Social consciousness is the standard of the hermeneutical task undertaken by the biblical interpreter.

The two questions of the biblical interpreter—What did the text say? What does it say?—are but specific examples of the descriptive and the critical tasks. The problem for the interpreter, whether of the Bible or of society, comes when we attempt to factor in the effect of the cultural bias that informs both our observations and our critique.

There is no unbiased or scientific position open to the interpreter. There is only the more or less successful attempt to converse across cultural boundaries.

Mary Douglas has proposed that we accomplish this conversation across cultural barriers by selecting a methodological tool to open up description and critique. If we describe patterns of behavior and response related to a specific concept or experience within both our own and a foreign culture, then this concept or experience becomes a "tool" for opening conversation. We can examine patterns of behavior and responses in relation to our own. We compare and contrast.

This text explores one means of providing for cross-cultural conversation. By frankly admitting a western European—even an American—bias, and proposing a methodology conversant with that bias, we hope to prepare for self-critical reflection *on the part of the reader*. We will systematically examine several aspects of the experience of the individual within society. We will examine the side-effects of the choices individuals make as they participate in the Pauline church in order to describe their experience. We do not propose that this focus on the individual comes from Paul or Paul's own cultural experience. It is ours.

By examining evidence of several sets of decisions, and by pooling the results of these examinations, we hope to mitigate the effect of our distance from the communities that supported Paul's mission to the Gentiles. Such is the tool we will use to open conversation between Paul's ancient and very foreign world and our own.

This text is intended for those interested in biblical interpretation. We find that Paul's letters reveal a social world that has the bias of an egalitarian community. We find that adoption terminology used by Paul in his letters to the churches of Galatia and Rome is appropriate to such an egalitarian community. We find that rethinking the exegetical task in terms of ethnography is helpful in opening our conversation with Paul.

This study began as a doctoral dissertation done at Garrett-Evangelical Theological Seminary and Northwestern University, Evanston, Illinois. Professor Robert Jewett was the faculty advisor. Without his support this project would never have seen completion. Professor Mary Douglas graciously offered assistance and direction at an early stage of this research. The opportunity to make presentations in the Section on Social Sciences and New Testament Interpretation at the annual meeting of the Society of Biblical Literature in 1988 and 1989 helped develop and hone the argument. Professor Bruce Malina of Creighton University, who cochairs the section, offered much encouragement and helpful comment.

I must express my gratitude to those who have supported me and my work for the past decade: my family and the people of my churches.

Marlene, my wife, and Christina and Matthew, my children, have given up family time so I might finish yet another rewrite. The churches I have served as pastor in Malden and Rockford, Illinois, have allowed me the freedom to pursue these scholarly interests.

Interpreting the text Sunday after Sunday requires getting to know the people. I hope this study demonstrates that it is imperative for the one who preaches to work at knowing both the modern and the ancient audience of the text. The art of the preacher/interpreter makes us hear the critique of the ancient with the ears of the modern.

For how shall they hear apart from one who proclaims?

EGALITARIAN COMMUNITY

1

The Study of the Social World of the Apostle Paul

The Apostle Paul lived in the middle part of the first century. He traveled about the eastern end of the Mediterranean basin, visiting cities and towns heavily influenced by Rome. He wrote letters to small groups of people in these urban areas of the empire. These people, who regularly participated in small group meetings, identified themselves as differing from others in their society because of their participation in these groups. At least some of the letters written by Paul to them have been preserved in the canon of the New Testament.

When we read the letters of Paul in the New Testament, we should remember that Paul was involved with his social environment, not just his theology. His letters, being situational, reflect his involvement with the people around him. That is, the letters of Paul reflect the supportive interactions as well as the conflicts Paul had with other people. We read of the small groups he founded and visited as well as something of the interactions he had with others in groups he did not found. Paul did not exist on the level of ideas set apart from his life experience.

The language of the letters of the Apostle Paul—their form and their content—derive in large measure from the social context in which they were written. Paul's letters—and indeed Paul himself—were shaped by his social environment, at least to the extent that he responded to others around him. This shaping process in areas of human interaction outside the Bible is studied in the disciplines of rhetoric, sociology, and anthropology. Biblical material, at least that of the Pauline letters, is available for research by the rhetorician, social anthropologist, and social historian.

The social context of Paul and the Pauline church is not a general concept like "the Hellenistic world" or "Pharisaic Judaism." Though heuristically useful, these general concepts exist only in the mind of the historian of ideas. Social context has to do with the specific patterns of behavior and of social interactions that made up Paul's life experience, including his travels, his letters, his preaching, his conflicts, and his interactions with others both within and outside of the churches he founded.

When we begin to think of Paul's letters as culturally conditioned examples of epistolary communication—as examples of Paul's patterned behavior—we begin to think like social anthropologists. We begin to see that the letters themselves are raw data that will help us to understand the bias that Paul's experience of his culture lends to his witness.

Sociological Descriptions

Some interpreters of Paul would examine epistolary style and cultural conditioning for the purpose of being able to separate out these very human aspects of Paul's message. By skimming the dross from the metal, they would refine the treasure of God's pure word through Paul. They would remove the impurities of cultural bias. By way of contrast, the social historian appears to treasure the dross, the bias that results from being embedded in a particular culture. Norman K. Gottwald has observed in his groundbreaking study of the social history of Old Testament Israel: "What the social scientific approach contributes is the recognition that all ideas, even the highest and most encompassing, have social matrices and are . . . shaped in the dynamics of cultural and social development."[1]

The world we see and the world with which we interact is not a shadow of some real world of universal ideas. The cave in which we exist provides our context, our culture, and our language. Without these, there is no communication. We exist in the particular, not in the universal nor the ideal.

Understanding the particular begins with a process of categorization.

Unique and identifying qualities or characteristics are used to separate or distinguish phenomena. Similarities are used to group or type specific examples. The process of categorization involves identifying and describing both that which distinguishes and that which types, that which separates and that which groups. We intuit recognizable patterns and use these patterns to interpret new experience.

This process of categorization does not sit well with those Christian theologians invested in identifying the uniqueness of the Christian message and the action of the divine. Categorization implies both uniqueness *and* similarity. Sociological study of New Testament communities has been understood to "explain" the unique Christian message with reference to universal or culturally bound laws of human social behavior. The fear is that this explanation—in that it is used to group social phenomena like the early Christian community in the context of similar social phenomena displayed by other communities, religious and nonreligious— explains away the role of God and the unique message of the church. The fear is that sociological descriptions of religious phenomena, especially Christian phenomena, are reductionist.[2]

Sociologists do tend to look for something other than the manifest or expressed function of observed behavior. In looking for a latent function of behavior—a purpose for behavior not apparent to the participants involved—sociologists set themselves above or apart from the participants, as knowing more than they do about that in which they are involved. This "higher position" may result in explanations of religious phenomena that focus entirely on nonreligious categories. Religion has been explained (psychologically) as a projection of social needs, identity, or conflict, (functionally) as a social mechanism for group identity or as compensation for real or perceived deprivation, or (materialistically) as a means of social or class dominance.

Sociological explanations of religious behavior are not entirely comfortable to the believer because they tend to focus on latent functions of belief and symbolic behavior. The religious community is more comfortable with discussion and even dissection of the manifest or expressed function of belief and behavior within the community. This is the province of theology, liturgy, and ethics, properly and traditionally the concern of the faithful. Sociology and anthropology are suspect disciplines within the religious community.

Sociology or cultural anthropology, however, does not have to resolve the question of the latent function of religious or symbolic behavior without regard for the manifest function or expressed intent of the religious community. Moreover, because the sociologist studies human behavior, the "truth" of a religious value is not necessarily evaluated. It is at the juncture of ideology and dispassionate observation that conflict arises. Neither sociologists nor theologians are free from ideological bias.

Sociologists and anthropologists are interested in identifying patterns of behavior and belief. Random behavior, if it exists, is neither interesting nor useful. Identifiable patterns of behavior express socially the identity of the participants. These patterns of behavior are complex and must be categorized experimentally in order to be described in any useful way.[3]

Bruce J. Malina offers a verbal simulation game that gives insight into the reasons why social anthropology is important to understanding the writings of the foreigners we meet in New Testament communities. In this game he also demonstrates the complexity of interpreting observed data.

> Chances are that if other people only knew your name, your social rank, some of your statements, and some geographical information about you, you would say that they really cannot understand you yet. What more would they have to know? What more would you have to know to understand a foreigner? Just as you get to know yourself by comparison with others, by comparing how you are similar to and different from others, how you are just like others and unique relative to others, so you might now move on to asking the same questions about our hypothetical group of foreigners. How are they similar to others in their area of the world and period in history; how are they different? How are they just like other people in their time and place; how are they unique relative to others?[4]

In this simulation game the question is asked, "What more would they have to know?" For example, the extent to which our identity is informed by the persons who happen to be president, governor, and mayor during our lifetime is determined by our social interactions and our social involvement. To the extent that our identity is contingent upon our social experience, in order to know and understand who we are, one has to know about the type and form of contacts we have with others in our society. It is the same with the people of the first century: the social interactions of the individual are reflected in the way the individual identifies himself or herself. The pattern of social interactions—the transactions an individual has with others—are reflected in the way the individual explains or justifies his or her behavior. These explanations and justifications include manifestly theological statements.

Christians find it quite easy and have become quite facile at moving from manifest statements about belief and behavior made by participants in the early church to the application of these observations in contemporary twentieth-century situations. But what do we really know about someone who, like Paul, lived in the middle part of the first century? How might we find out how he is similar to others and how is he unique? How might this information inform or affect our ability to interpret the things Paul says?

We answer these questions with observations of Paul within his social context. We begin—insofar as we are able—by observing Paul, his behavior, and the behavior of those around him. We are fortunate to have some help in this endeavor. Several scholars have described facets of the social world of the Apostle Paul. The work of Gerd Theissen, Abraham Malherbe, Howard Clark Kee, Edwin A. Judge, Bengt Holmberg, Bruce J. Malina, John G. Gager, Ronald F. Hock, Martin Hengel, John Elliot, Jerome Neyrey, Norman R. Petersen, Robert Jewett, and, in particular, Wayne Meeks exemplifies the usefulness of the discussion of the social history of New Testament, especially Pauline, communities.[5]

John G. Gager's book *Kingdom and Community,* published in 1975, brought popularity to the concern for the social world of early Christianity. A working group of the Society of Biblical Literature as early as 1973 took this theme. At the same time, Jonathan Z. Smith set out the working definitions and preliminary scholarly history in an article titled "The Social Description of Early Christianity" in the first volume of *Religious Studies Review.*[6] Carolyn Osiek has summarized these efforts in her very readable study *What Are They Saying About the Social Setting of the New Testament?*[7]

In this study we will use a specific method derived from an interpretive model of human culture developed by Mary Douglas. The primary goal will be to better understand and interpret Paul's letters. The secondary goal will be to adapt the method in an informed and rational manner for use with the evidence available to the New Testament interpreter. The first two chapters seek to raise the reader's comfort level in the use of sociological methods on New Testament materials, first, by reviewing the most comprehensive study of Paul that uses these methods and interpretive models—that by Wayne Meeks—and second, by rethinking biblical exegesis as a specialized form of ethnography. The second chapter also reviews the parameters of the available evidence by rethinking the common language of ethnography—functionalism—in terms appropriate to a study of Paul's social world.

Paul uses a special word in his letter to the Romans and in his letter to the Galatians: *huiothesia* in the Greek, "adoption" in literal translation (the RSV uses variously "sonship" and "adoption"). The final chapter of this book offers a demonstration of the interpretation of Paul's use of this special word employing the results of a "grid-group" analysis. We find that this word embodies the two conflicting concerns of the egalitarian community: limited differentiation between participants together with a significant differentiation between participants and nonparticipants.

Grid-group is the interpretive model described by Mary Douglas.[8] It also names the specific anthropological method derived from her model. Chapter Three describes the model. Chapter Four describes the method and makes the adaptations required to use the method on the historical-literary evidence we have available. Chapters Five and Six do this work, and Chapter Seven draws the interpretive conclusions. First, most of us— at least those who work with the biblical text—need to become more comfortable with the tools of sociological and anthropological research.

A Functional Analysis of Paul's Church

Meeks, in his *The First Urban Christians* and later in *The Moral World of the First Christians,*[9] has given us a look at the social status of those who participated in the Pauline church and at the way these early Christians behaved. He provides us with a look at the social context of their belief in a resurrected messiah and the ethical decisions they made as a result of their belief. By bringing together so much of the evidence and focusing the discussion on the function of belief in sociological terms, Meeks has set the agenda for this discussion.

Meeks's study of the Pauline church offers a systematic attempt to describe the social situation of the participants in the Pauline church and correlate this description with elements of their ideology. He identifies his approach as that of a "moderate functionalist."[10] He emphasizes the integrating function of ideology for participants in the Pauline church who experience stress related to social status.

Meeks looks for the social environment of the individual local churches with which Paul interacts and finds them to be in urban areas of the eastern empire. These urban areas were heavily influenced by Rome. He develops what he calls a prosopography of the Pauline church as represented in the letters of Paul and in Acts. He examines the social structure of the Pauline church; he identifies its boundaries, describes its ritual, and discusses its governance. Finally, he correlates theological statements in Paul's letters to his sociological findings. He is looking for the integrating *function* of Paul's manifest theological statements.

Meeks begins by offering what he calls a *functional approach* to the study of Paul and his relationship to apocalyptic thought.[11] Since Schweitzer, we have understood Paul to have grounded his thinking in apocalyptic thought.[12] Yet the connections between Paul's apocalyptic world view and sociological studies of millennial movements have proven difficult to clarify because we have difficulty correlating evidence of social behavior with manifest statements of ideology. There must be some interpretive medium to link ideology and social description. For example, Gager uses the functional effect of conflict to describe "phases" in the development of the early church.[13]

Meeks approaches this issue by asking the functional question. He asks about the social purpose of apocalyptic language and allusion found in the letters of Paul.[14] The functional approach that Meeks proposes is parallel to that of anthropological studies of millenarian movements. The problem is one of categories of evidence—he needs an accurate description of the Pauline church using sociological and not theological categories. This concern for empirical evidence—insofar as it can be reconstructed—brings Meeks into a new area of study. There are few roadmaps to guide him, so he organizes the material as it seems best to him from the perspective of his view of the evidence itself.[15]

In order to accomplish his task, he sets out to describe the social world of early Christianity in his study of the Pauline church in its urban setting and then find the "social function of its beliefs." In order to make his comparison, he also needs a clear description of the cultural setting of apocalyptic thought and *its* social function. He settles upon a synthesized anthropological description of millenarian movements to provide the pattern for recognition.[16]

The Social Environment of the Pauline Church

Meeks begins to present a sociologically informed view of Paul with a description of the environment of Paul's mission. Paul chooses to go to the city, to the urban areas of the eastern provinces. "The Pauline world was one in which, for urban and mobile people, Greek was the lingua franca, but upon which the overwhelming political fact of Rome was superimposed."[17] The mission of Paul that we hear of in the letters was a mission to urban areas that were connected by sea or by Roman roads.

Meeks describes the social level of the individual Christians within this larger social context as they are represented in the letters of Paul and in Acts. He identifies the status and the level of integration into society of each of the participants of the Pauline church as available data allows. He considers multiple dimensions of status because this is the way the individuals "crystallize" their status in society.[18] He assumes that signs of stress, withdrawal, or political action, just as in contemporary societies, indicate low status crystallization: "these kinds of behavior, some sociologists believe, show that a high degree of status inconsistency produces unpleasant experiences that lead people to try to remove the inconsistency by changing the society, themselves, or perceptions of themselves."[19]

A Prosopography of the Pauline Church

Meeks's key tool for working with the data he has collected is the prosopography. A prosopography—in this case—is simply a gathering of the names of the people associated with Paul together with as much biographical information about their life and social status as is available. Meeks begins his examination of Paul's churches with this structured and empirical approach to the material because he wants more clues to the multiple dimensions of their social status than can be provided by a general classification according to the traditional categories of class, *ordo*, and status in Roman imperial society. He draws up a list of eighty people who are mentioned in relationship to Paul, either in the letters or in Acts. About thirty of these have some indication of their status attached to their name. For most, about fifty, there is little information available except the provenance of their name or their ability to travel. There is, however, enough evidence to infer some characteristics of those whom Paul mentions.

> The levels in between [the highest and the lowest levels of society], however, are well represented. There are slaves, although we cannot tell how many. The "typical" Christian, however, the one who most often signals his presence in the letters by one or another small clue, is a free artisan or small trader. Some even in those occupational categories had houses, slaves, the ability to travel, and other signs of wealth. Some of the wealthy provided housing, meeting places, and other services for individual Christians and for whole groups. In effect they filled the role of patrons.[20]

The Christians located by Meeks in the Pauline church are frequently identified by divergent economic ranking and social status. They are upwardly mobile urban people.[21] "Although the evidence is not abundant, we may venture the generalization that the most active and prominent members of Paul's circle (including Paul himself) are people of high status inconsistency (low status crystallization)."[22]

Theissen's study of the Pauline Corinthian church has confirmed the view that the church was made up of people from a variety of social levels.[23] The local churches to which Paul writes are not homogeneous, but are made up of people who do not share social station and indeed may be socially mobile. This fact poses the question of the social organization of this pluralistic church for Meeks's study.

Organizational Models from the Ancient World

Meeks looks for a model to illuminate the organization and situation of the Pauline church. The options include: the household model, voluntary associations of the Hellenistic period, the Jewish synagogue, and various philosophic or rhetorical schools.

The household model[24] is attractive because Paul says the church met in houses of its members and that he baptized a household, and because several of the people he mentions in his letters are identified by the households to which they belong. The structure of the local church was at least linked with the household in the house church meeting form.[25] Apparently, membership could come simply by association with the householder. Consequently, the "new group was inserted into or superimposed upon an existing social structure," yet this existing social structure is not represented in patterns of hierarchy or power relationships within the house church.[26] The existence of the itinerant apostle, fellow workers, and charismatic leadership in the church based on "spiritual gifts" runs counter to the hierarchical patterns of the Roman household—especially the power of the *paterfamilias*.[27]

Voluntary associations were common in the Hellenistic world of the early Roman empire and may be used to describe Christian associations.[28] Membership was by free association and depended upon the support of wealthier patrons.[29] Yet the purpose of association, fellowship and conviviality, was not the purpose of Christian association. Pauline Christians were involved in a much wider and more inclusive social interaction.

In retrospect, the synagogue was the most natural example for the Pauline church to follow. The Pauline church and the synagogue had much in common, from writings to organizational beginnings in the household. But the synagogue is not mentioned by Paul. Membership and entrance to the fellowship is different, the role of women is different, and the ritual is different, as we have come to identify the synagogue in later centuries. It is simply not clear what the form and the purpose of the synagogue was in the first century either in Palestine or in the Diaspora before the destruction of the temple in Jerusalem.

The philosophic or rhetorical schools resemble the Pauline church because they take the form of the household or of voluntary associations.[30] There are differences (for example, the Christians' concern for salvation), but the ancients outside the church fellowship and familiar with classical schools could easily have confused the Pauline church with one of a number of philosophic schools.

None of these proposed models offers an exact matching pattern for the organization of the Pauline church. Yet each one offers a helpful analogy. Although each could have been considered by contemporaries to have similarities with the Pauline church, it is not likely that anyone within the church would mistake its form for one of these organizational forms. The similarities type the Pauline church as part of the same social world, but the distinctions between it and each available option suggest that the Pauline church should be put into a new or different category.

The task is, then, to describe this new category. Meeks studies the literary remains—the letters of Paul—to analyze the social structures of the Pauline church. He observes the texts without preconceived or rather with unintentional order. The texts are dissected not according to any systematic organization from a sociological, theological, or anthropological method, but simply as the evidence appears to Meeks.[31] These texts are used to identify or provide a new category: the Pauline church faction.

The Social Structure of the Pauline Church:
The Importance of Belonging

Using evidence from the letters of Paul, Meeks first turns to the issue of identifying the social boundaries of the faction. Are participants encouraged to identify themselves explicitly or implicitly as a person who belongs to the group? Are outsiders distinguished from insiders in the fellowship?

He observes that the language of the Pauline groups as revealed in the letters of Paul is full of references to the family: brother, sister, children of God, and the like. Baptism—a rite of entrance—is related to adoption into the faction.[32] Meeks makes reference to the formalized "putting on Christ," the "new man" the "son of God," and the ecstatic cry all as part of the incorporation of the new member. These are signs of the strength of the social boundary around the Pauline church faction. The participants are aware of a distinction between themselves and outsiders. "Whatever else is involved, the image of the initiate being adopted as God's child and thus receiving a new family of human brothers and sisters is a vivid way of portraying what a modern sociologist might call the re-socialization of conversion."[33]

Meeks identifies three descriptive statements that encouraged group coherence and identity within the letters of Paul:[34]

(1) You turned to God from idols. You are different from the gentile who do not know God. Don't be like them.
(2) Revelation of the spirit and special beliefs are made available only to believers.
(3) The Gospel: Jesus, the Christ who died, was raised. This pattern of parallel antithetical statements is common to Christians. It is "in-group" talk.

These distinctive statements of the Pauline church encourage separation from society because they imply that there is a special status available only to believers. This status is reflected in special signs of participation in "in-group" talk. The participants are encouraged by this language to identify themselves as members, set aside from the rest of the population.

This group is separated from the rest of society by its speech patterns. This special language includes terms to distinguish those who do not (yet) belong. Paul uses language, especially in the earlier letters, that encourages group identity distinct from outsiders. Meeks cites the "children of light and children of darkness" language from 1 Thessalonians and compares it to the Essene writings from Qumran. Although this comparable Hellenistic context is available from Qumran, the Pauline use is distinct, as it is informed by a concern for persecution. This concern strengthens group identification by emphasizing the danger from without.[35]

There is evidence, then, that the participants of the Pauline church distinguished themselves from others in society. There is also evidence from the letters of Paul that they were encouraged to identify themselves as belonging to this Pauline faction of the followers of Christ. There is, therefore, an identifiable social boundary useful for determining who is and who is not a participant. Meeks goes on to quote Mary Douglas—a social anthropologist—to say that attitudes toward the body reflect understandings of society. Though "obvious" examples of Mary Douglas's dictum exist in non-Christian groups contemporary with or slightly later than Paul, Meeks notices that the Pauline church is instructed that there are no distinctions between Jew and Gentile.

> Yet by abandoning these rules, the Pauline Christians gave up one of the most effective ways by which the Jewish community had maintained its separate identity in the pagan society. That was the practical issue at dispute between Paul and his opponents in Galatia, although the complexity of Paul's theological and midrashic arguments has often led later interpreters to forget this simple question. *Would the abolition of the symbolic boundaries between Jew and gentile* within *the Christian groups mean also lowering the boundaries between the Christian sect and the world?* The Pauline Christians answered this question with a significant ambivalence, illustrated by two cases discussed in Pauline letters; the issue of idolatry and rules for marriage and sex.[36]

Meeks offers the explanation that because the Pauline church faction threw out the old legal structures of Judaism, it had to define purity of the community in more "social" terms.[37] A case in point is 1 Cor. 5:9–13, where Paul takes great pains to remove any doubt about what he meant in his last correspondence. Paul says that he did *not* mean that the Corinthians should have no truck with those outside the fellowship.[38] The social boundary of the Pauline church faction, though strong, is not impermeable. Ambiguity results.

Evangelistic activity is the reason Meeks offers for the apparent permeability of the otherwise strong social boundary of the Pauline church faction. He finds a tension between the separation of the participant from aspects of pagan or Jewish society and the drive for missionary activity. This tension results in ambiguity.

> One of the most obvious facts about the movement associated with Paul and his fellows was the vigor of its missionary drive, which saw in the outsider a potential insider and did not want to cut off communication with him or her. . . . There is a tension in the literature of the Pauline groups between measures separating it from the larger society, and the intention to continue normal and generally acceptable interactions with outsiders.[39]

Similarly, there is an ambiguity in the boundary of the local church faction as it relates to other church factions. The individual churches associated with Paul were part of a larger body. The reference to the church in Judea, the collection for the saints, the sharing of apostles' visits, the ability to visit other church settings and share news, all reinforced this connectedness. The rituals, baptism and eucharist, portray a unity among those of the Pauline church in every city.[40] The boundary of the local church faction is open at several levels to several others who identify themselves with Jesus. This ambiguity results in organizational conflict, as witnessed in the letter to the Galatians.

Authority in the Pauline Church Faction

The identification of ambiguity and conflict in the description of the boundary of the Pauline church faction brings up the question of conflict resolution. To what type and form of authority does Paul appeal? How is the Pauline church faction governed? Meeks makes some assumptions about group process and development as he begins to answer these questions. "No group can persist for any appreciable time without developing some patterns of leadership, some differentiation of roles among its members, some means of managing conflict, some ways of articulating shared values and norms, and some sanctions to assure acceptable levels of conformity to those norms."[41]

Meeks suspects that the organization of each local church required some structure of authority. Bengt Holmberg—a social historian of the Pauline church cited by Meeks—describes a complex relationship of power and authority in the earliest church at three levels: the relationship to the saints in Jerusalem, the relationship with coworkers, the relationship with local church leaders.[42] These concern the several levels at which the Pauline church faction is open to others who identify themselves with Jesus. Meeks's work follows this pattern but begins with a discussion of the middle level. "Foremost among the techniques that the Pauline mission invented were return visits by the missionaries to the groups they had planted and, when a visit was not possible, letters."[43]

Paul is never unequivocally successful in resolving the controversies that surround the ambiguity of social boundary and identity. He seeks to have those to whom he writes recognize the "correctness" of his position. He attempts to communicate with them. Rhetorical forms, especially deliberative, demonstrative-epideictic, and ambassadorial, are important to him.[44]

In his discussion of the question of authority Meeks refers to two works on the structure of authority in the early church: one by John H. Schütz and the other by Bengt Holmberg.[45] He begins with a discussion of leadership terms and of various controversies and the process for handling them. Using 1 Thess. 5:12 as his key, Meeks identifies three categories of leadership: apostles, fellow workers, and local leaders. These are all functional, not ecclesiastical, offices. He suggests three "warrants for authority:" (a) a common ethos—informal modes of control, (b) specific warrants—commonly accepted ethical behavior, and (c) rules—traditions handed down.[46]

Given a common ethos Paul can offer advice and arguments, and he can be persuasive because he shares with all participants some common presuppositions. For example, he frequently reminds the new Christians of their beginnings. This is an informal mode of social control.

Paul also uses rational arguments to form a consensus about the behavior expected from the communities. In these cases Paul does not use his position or status to provide a warrant for heeding his advice. There is no appeal to norms of legitimacy in Paul's conception of authority.[47] Others could and did appeal to their position within the church. The citation of special revelation, the appeal to scripture and tradition, and the appeal to the experience of the Spirit, all are used as arguments for authority by Paul. These are special warrants. Special warrants are apparent in the lack of an appeal to power external to rational argument. In his letter to Philemon, Paul says he could make such an appeal but will not. One example of this attitude at work is his appeal to the paradoxical pattern of the reversal of power. The relationship with Christ is revealed in weakness.[48]

Paul does appeal to rules for behavior and to the tradition for the authority to make statements concerning the patterns of behavior of participants in the Pauline church faction. The traditional norms of the fellowship, however, are not frequently stated as rules in Paul's letters. Even when we have the appeal to authority in tradition or in the sayings of Jesus, the statements are general and suggestive, not prescriptive: "the two most striking features of Paul's application of these rules are the remarkable freedom of his interpretation and the flexibility of decision apparently required of his readers. . . . The impression is one of great fluidity, of a complex, multipolar, open-ended process of mutual discipline."[49]

After a review of various examples of conflict within the Pauline church faction and the letters sent to respond to those conflicts, Meeks describes the primary means of conflict resolution as informal. Letters, emissaries, and face-to-face meetings are the means; advice, persuasion, and argument are the mechanisms. Paul does not order the new Christians around out of a hierarchical sense of power or authority. He builds a case for his position and asks for acceptance.

Ritual Practice in the Pauline Church

Ritual is a difficult category with which to work in attempting to interpret the relationship between ideology and social culture.[50] The way one views the rituals in cultic practice determines the results of the study of those rituals. There *is* an interrelationship between the ritual of the cult and the self-understanding of the individuals who participate in it. This is another way of saying that the mechanism by which individuals justify their actions and the actions themselves are intertwined.[51]

Mary Douglas notes the difficulty in her own work of moving too succinctly from religious categories and ritual patterns to an understanding of belief structures:

> I now see that the problem of understanding foreign beliefs is distorted by the concentration on great moments dramatically enacted. The very category of religion, focusing, as Victor Turner puts it so well, on rites of life crisis and of affliction would be a distraction to the task I should have in hand. It implies that a scanning of the grand affirmatory points in social experience will always turn up the corresponding catalogue of rituals of affirmation, separation, and healing, and thus map in advance that part of the culture which corresponds to religion the world over.[52]

Meeks uses the language and work of Victor Turner to describe and even reconstruct the ritual patterned behavior of the participants in the Pauline church faction:

> The unity symbolized by the Lord's supper, I have suggested, can be seen as a reminder or re-presentation of the liminal transcendence of societal oppositions that was declared in baptism. Now it is commonly asserted that this baptismal unity and egalitarianism is "merely sacramental," that is, as a purely symbolic leveling it signifies an ideal state, perhaps a future eschatological state, but has no effect upon actual social roles . . . in the case of a group that maintains a strong identity distinct from the larger society, some aspects of liminality may linger in its daily life.[53]

It is already difficult to move from observations of ritual or symbolic behavior to a definition of the ideological concerns of a society. In the Pauline church we are one step removed from direct observations of ritual practice. We simply do not know what the major ritual moments of Pauline church life were like. Victor Turner's work on the ritual process is used by Meeks both in the reconstruction of the ritual practices *and* in their interpretation.

In examining the ritual of the Pauline church, Meeks identifies *(a)* minor rituals, as regular meetings with prayers; *(b)* baptism, as an initiation rite; and *(c)* eucharist, as (1) a common meal, (2) an imitation of

Jesus' last meal, (3) a ritual enactment of vicarious meaning of Jesus' death, and (4) a focus on the eschatological coming. These categories of ritual patterns and statements of the manifest meaning of the eucharist are discussed separately in Meeks's work. We will examine only the process of interpretation of baptism and the eucharist.

Referring to Gerd Theissen's work,[54] Meeks sets the social tension in the Corinthian church into the larger arena of the "eschatological drama" known as the eucharist. The taboo of 1 Cor. 11:30 places behavior related to social stratification under the ban in the context of the cultic practice. This ban is related to the baptismal rite, which replaces the old stratified society with a new homogeneous one built upon socially functional gifts of the Spirit.

In other words, the patron and those of the patron's social class are asked to wait for the entire church population to arrive before beginning the ritual meal. The old measures of personal worth in the larger society do not supersede the new unity within the church. Roles are achieved according to the ability to accomplish them within the Christian community, not according to any preexisting or external social standing.

The conflict for Meeks comes when this functional idea of unity in the Christian cultic practice is transposed to experience within the rest of society. He finds ambiguity. For example: in 1 Cor. 7:22 slaves become the Lord's freedmen and free men become Christ's slaves. In Philem. 16 the returned slave is no longer a slave, but a beloved brother. Yet Paul does not ask for all slaves to be freed. Or in another example, there is the equivalence of rights and duties in marriage (1 Cor. 7). Yet Paul objects to "*symbolic* disregard" for sexual differences in dress (1 Cor. 11:2–16). Meeks proposes that this ambivalence is caused by those who, though they are a part of the fellowship, have not yet fully incorporated these social functions of the ritual practice into their lives.

Meeks also refers to a similar ambiguity when attempting to interpret "the social ramifications" of the "baptismal reunification formula."[55] Although we have Paul's own statements about the purpose and meaning of baptism as an initiation rite, we do not have a description of the actual practice.[56] Reconstructions must be based on assumptions about the relationship between ideology and behavior.

The Christian converts were baptized naked. . . . What confirms the fact for Pauline groups is the variety of metaphorical allusions to taking off and putting on clothing that we find in those parts of the letters that refer to baptism. Those allusions are of two sorts, as we shall see: the mythical notion of taking off the body, the "old human," and putting on instead Christ, the "new human"; and the rather common ethical figure of taking off bad habits and putting on virtuous ones. The convergence of both types in the baptismal reminders of Pauline paraenesis is most easily accounted for on the assumption that the candidates from the beginning took off their clothes to be baptized and put them back on afterward, and that these natural actions were given metaphorical significance.[57]

Meeks reconstructs the structure of the Pauline baptismal rite using oppositions in motifs that he has noticed in his analysis of the Pauline texts.[58] This reconstruction uses the imagery of a descent into "liminality" and assent to "communitas"—terms that come from the work of Victor Turner.[59] This ascent into communitas differentiates this reconstruction of the Pauline church ritual from the initiation ritual defined by Turner. The new Christians are not reunited with their preexisting society with a heightened sense of humility and social place. They are instead connected to a new social group marked, itself, by the new patterns of communitas or profound unity and equality.

In both the rites of baptism and eucharist Meeks encounters the problem of interpreting the ritual patterns he has reconstructed. He consistently finds ambiguity in the relationship between the ritual patterns he discovers and the social patterns he observes. "The relation between the symbolic reality presented in the rituals and everyday reality, both in the inner life of the group and in interaction with the larger society, remained an area of controversy and ambiguity."[60]

Interpreting Patterns of Behavior and Relating Them to Patterns of Belief

Meeks has difficulty interpreting the ambiguity and controversy he finds in social and in ritual behavior patterns in the Pauline church faction. This difficulty is made more acute because he has not selected a specific sociological or anthropological method with which to work. When he goes to examine the data, he has decided not to have a systematic method for arranging it into categories of evidence concerning the church.[61] Rather, he has arranged the data as it occurred or presented itself to him. Consequently, he is left with a methodological problem when attempting to identify the functions of Paul's ideological statements. He finds it difficult to integrate manifest ideological statements with the empirical evidence he has found. He must look intuitively for patterns of belief as they relate to patterns of life. Because he has not selected a specific sociological or anthropological model, it becomes difficult to confirm or refute the results of his study objectively. His intuition is his intuition—it must be correct. Falsifiability of the results—one test of their usefulness—is lost.

For example: in his concluding chapter Meeks says: "We might guess that people who have advanced or declined socially, who find themselves in an ambiguous relation to hierarchical structures, might be receptive to symbols of the world as itself out of joint and on the brink of radical transformation. They might be attracted to a group that undertook to model its own life on the new picture of reality. Of course it is impossible to prove this, and if such a correlation between social experience and symbolization did exist, it would be hard to tell which was cause and which effect."[62]

He examines the environment of the local churches of Paul and finds them to be uniformly urban areas of the eastern empire, areas heavily influenced by Rome. He examines each name cited in Paul's letters or associated with Paul in Acts for clues to their social station and outlook. He examines the church in relationship to the Hellenistic models available. He looks at its boundaries, its ritual, and its governance in an attempt to describe the Pauline church. But, when he comes to drawing conclusions concerning patterns of belief and their relationship to patterns of life in the Pauline church, he has to operate intuitively. He offers brilliant observations concerning the social world of the Pauline Christians, but he ends his statements of correlations with question marks.[63]

The most useful findings Meeks has given us are derived from empirical observations. He demonstrates that the Christians who show up in the texts related to Paul are: *(a)* urban, *(b)* upwardly mobile, *(c)* of a high level of status inconsistency—people who have not crystallized their status in their own and others' expectations, and *(d)* most often free artisans or small traders—although all levels of society except the very top and the very bottom are noticed.

The church is made up, therefore, of people of "mixed strata and ambiguous status." It meets in the households of patrons. It sets itself apart from the rest of society with language of belonging and with injunctions against signs of participation in any other religious cult.

The problem is that the method Meeks uses does not distinguish between implicit or hidden and explicit or overt social controls by allowing the evidence to be organized by the implicit bias of the interpreter's own observation and inference.[64] What is needed is a sociological or cultural anthropological model for understanding culture by which the observed data may be organized explicitly.

The Methodological Definition of a Concern for Categories of Evidence

The methodological issue is, how does one organize the observations one makes of the Pauline church? The available evidence is fragmentary. It is gleaned from the limited literary remains of only one part of its leadership. The problem is how to find a mechanism by which the data may be observed and by which the various categories of evidence can be kept separate. The difficulty in moving from observation of behavior, especially symbolic behavior in ritual patterns, to the function of ideology is apparent when reading Meeks's work. Without at least an experimental or provisional model for observation, it is difficult to refute his findings objectively.

This problem of keeping literary evidence in separate categories so that manifest and latent functions may be distinguished is solved only with a clear working definition that offers specific categories for interpreting the inferred behavior. Since the data is fragmentary and not reported by disinterested trained participant observers, distinguishing the categories of evidence is most important to the social historian. We cannot rely upon intuition.

One of the difficulties noted by Meeks as he begins his work is the selection of a theory of human social behavior. He opts for a "pragmatic" approach in which he uses various theories of social organization as he sees they are needed.[65] His organizational principle is, in fact, negative: avoiding theological categories as interpretive frameworks.[66] The difficulty with this approach is that—in the very process of collecting evidence—the cultural bias of the researcher asserts itself in unseen ways to color the interpretation of the evidence. The other option—selecting a specific, even experimental or provisional method to organize the evidence—results in the possibility of falsification.[67] This possibility is a risk that allows us to understand and use the results of a study.

Moving from observations of social behavior to statements about the functions of ideology requires an explicit statement of the mechanism by which behavior and ideology interact. Only if the researcher's assumptions (concerning the processes involved in social interactions) are expressed may the reader realistically evaluate the conclusions. There is a danger in moving too succinctly from observations of social behavior to statements that are ideological or theological. These categories of evidence must be kept separate and distinct in order that we may keep track of the operation of the expressed assumptions of the observer concerning social processes.

Chapter Three identifies the anthropological model that informs the present study. Chapter Two attempts to provide crossing links between biblical studies and anthropology. Meeks has defined the issues for us and provided a functionalist approach. Chapter Four redefines the method that results from the model for use with the letters of Paul.

2

Cultural Anthropology and Biblical Criticism
Ethnography and Exegesis

Cultural anthropology is the social scientific study of human culture. It is difficult, however, to get behind the term "culture" with a clear definition of the interpretive process. Differing definitions of the term "culture" have resulted in differing methods for the social scientific study of human culture. The late-nineteenth-century consensus—that observable patterns of behavior represent social adaptation to the environment through an evolutionary process similar to Darwin's conception of biological evolution—has been eclipsed.

Social Darwinism met·strong reaction in the early part of the twentieth century among anthropologists who rejected the attempted unification of human culture under the guise of European ethnocentrism. It was completely discarded as an interpretive theory following its abuse by the Nazi movement in Germany. They justified their crimes as social engineering on a massive scale that—they claimed—only furthered the natural process of cultural evolution. The rejection of Social Darwinism in the first half of our century has taken the form of cultural relativism and functionalism.[1]

From the earliest colonial period, explorers and missionaries collected and returned to Europe and Great Britain the exotica of foreign places. This practice resulted in great museums full of artifacts and libraries of colonialist reports—the largest of these in London. Functionalism developed within British social anthropology as a mechanism or set of guidelines for anthropologists to think about and record their experiences in the field. Ethnographies written by anthropologists preserved primitive culture in the face of colonialist expansion and global westernization.[2]

Ethnography remains the centerpiece of cultural anthropology. Ethnography is descriptive. It has its roots in the travelogues of colonialists but it has an enlarged purpose. The anthropologist, undertaking to do field work, becomes a participant observer in a foreign culture, observing, recording, and describing patterns of behavior. Ethnographic field work is the cornerstone of an anthropologist's career. Ethnography—the social scientific description of a culture on the basis of observation—is the foundation of the social scientific interpretation of culture.

Bronislaw Malinowski, in the period between the world wars, established the modern procedure of ethnography and became a leading proponent of functionalism. He identified the elementary problem facing the field worker: "When he first takes his residence among people whose culture he wishes to understand, to record, and to present to the world at large, he obviously is faced with the question of what it means to identify a cultural fact. For, clearly, to identify is the same as to understand."[3]

An anthropologist who attempts to understand and interpret the behavior and expressions of people of another culture makes assumptions concerning the ability to perceive or make sense of foreigners and their behavior. This is the epistemological problem. Is it possible to make sense of witchcraft belief when the anthropologist denies that witches exist?[4] Unbiased, empirical observation of another culture is not possible, or if it is, it is useless. Even if it were possible to record events and behavior without cultural bias, such a record, by itself, would be without purpose. The rest of us—mere mortals—would have to find a way to interpret the record so that we could understand it.[5]

Interpretive Ethnography

Robert Ulin, following Clifford Geertz, recognizes the parallel difficulties of the anthropologist doing field work and of the literary exegete interpreting a pericope. "Both the textual scholar and the anthropologist are confronted with the difficult task of appropriating that which is alien or not one's own . . . the process that characterizes the comprehension of human actions and cultural products is not essentially different from the interpretation of a text as a life expression."[6]

The anthropologist interprets foreign statements and behavior when the meaning of these statements and behaviors is not immediately apparent *in his or her own culture*. Interpretation begins with the task of recording the observations of the field worker. Once data have been entered in the canon of observation, the task of translation begins. Though we know that culture is not text, there is an appropriate analogy between the task of the translator and that of the ethnographer. The task of translating from one culture to another begins in the attempt to answer the questions raised by the process of cross-cultural interpretation: How is it possible to understand—from my cultural perspective—culturally embedded phenomena from another time or another place?

Clifford Geertz defines "ethnographic thick description" as a means of coping with the problem of interpretation in ethnographic writing. Thick description attempts to place a cultural phenomenon into sociological categories by describing it fully, making it rich with illustrative detail *for the culture of the ethnographer*. Interpretation of the subject cultural phenomenon is communicated not as a depiction of a "real world reality," but for a specific audience with varying degrees of approximation and open-endedness.[7]

James Clifford and George E. Marcus have put together a collection of essays under the title *Writing Culture: The Poetics and Politics of Ethnography*.[8] This book is a reader in the issues confronting those who would interpret foreign culture. These essays were prepared for an advanced seminar on the subject held in 1984. The title contains three words central to the issue of cross-cultural interpretation: "writing," "poetics," and "politics." Ethnographic writing is an activity quite distinct from the activities of the actual people being written about. The ethnography itself—as an object of writing—is judged as better or worse, as a more or less felicitous description of foreign experience *in the cultural setting of the ethnographer*. The political agenda of the ethnographer includes the dominant role of the stronger culture *into which the ethnographer is translating*. The present power structure with its asymmetrical role relationships makes itself felt in faraway places as it acts as a control on the ethnographer.

Talal Asad's essay, "The Concept of Cultural Translation in British

Social Anthropology,"[9] is especially helpful on this point. Asad develops the image of the translator of texts from one language to another. As the differential between the languages grows, the requirement that the translator use artistic license in communicating meaning rather than literal wording grows. The language into which the translator is translating is usually the "stronger" language. The original is forced to adapt its images to the new context—it is the "weaker" of the two. Hearing the challenge of the "weaker" text is impossible if that challenge has been translated away. Textual translation is useful as analog of the process of ethnography and of exegesis. We seek a translation that opens our ears to hear the critique of ourselves to which we are deaf.

The literary exegete is in no better position than the anthropologist to interpret cross-cultural meaning. The anthropologist sees and hears what has not been seen and heard before in his or her experience. It has not been seen or heard because it is not part of his or her own cultural experience. Yet new experience must be described and recorded. New experience is not only interpreted by categorization, it is also perceived in comparative categories: New experience X is like known experience A. The process of observation and the identification of cultural facts is, therefore, informed by the depth and breadth of the experience of the ethnographer in the field. The exegete is similarly vulnerable to experience in making her or his observations and to ethnocentric imaging in interpreting them.

This vulnerability to ethnocentric misinterpretation is most deeply felt when one attempts to understand the cultural role of ideology and symbolic behavior. We will return later in this chapter to this question of interpretation, but for now we are interested in providing some connections between the task of the biblical interpreter and the ethnographer. Perhaps we may find ways the biblical interpreter can be informed by the social sciences.

Four Perspectives on the Function of Ideas and Values in Society

The cultural context of a social organization includes the manner in which the ideas and values espoused by the organization—explicitly or implicitly—serve to support and enhance the distribution of power, privilege, and prestige.[10] Just how this supporting function is understood to occur depends upon the perspective of the researcher. There are four basic theoretical perspectives: the conflict, the functional, the symbolic interactionist, and various synthetic theories.[11] These four perspectives for interpreting the functional processes described in an ethnography have parallels in exegetical studies of the New Testament.

In other words, twentieth-century exegetical analyses of biblical texts may be reclassified according to the categories of cultural anthropology. First we will outline the basic categories of sociological interpretation and then offer examples of the way New Testament scholars may be reclassified. By this process it is hoped that those who identify themselves as biblical interpreters may become more comfortable with the language and patterns of comparative sociological research.

In laying out the basic categories of sociological interpretation, we have followed the work of Vincent Jeffries and H. Edward Ransford in their *Social Stratification: A Multiple Hierarchy Approach*. This text focuses on the individual—not the family—as the basic unit of stratification.[12] Their analysis—together with the multiple hierarchy approach itself—coincides with the central location of the individual in Mary Douglas's grid-group methodology. This textbook, with its focus on the interactive effects of power relationships, is therefore a helpful preparation for grid-group work.

The conflict perspective for understanding the structure and dynamics of social systems is historically identified with the work of Karl Marx. "From the conflict perspective, society's predominant bent is toward instability and change. Society is composed of groups with conflicting interests in continual but varying degrees of opposition."[13] The unequal distribution of power, especially access to the means of production, leads to conflict. The role of ideology is to enhance the ability of the ruling class to "exploit the working class." Ideology is, therefore, the creation of those who, wittingly or unwittingly, would support the existing unequal distribution of power, privilege, and prestige.[14] Ideology, the beliefs and values that support the position of the dominant few, is a weapon that keeps lower classes from recognizing their true interests.

The functionalist perspective for understanding the structure and dynamics of social systems is historically identified with the work of Emile

Durkheim and Herbert Spencer.[15] "Functional theories of society say that there is a predominant tendency toward order and stability in societies. Commonly held values and traditions form the basis for the integration of society."[16] The unequal distribution of access to rewards is seen as making a positive contribution to society and social order. The role of ideology is to justify or integrate the unequal distribution of rewards, thereby assuring that vital positions are filled by qualified people.[17] Ideology and the social hierarchy related to it, therefore, directs the activity of individuals toward socially desirable goals. Ideology is seen as systemic, not class-ist; integrative, not repressive.

The symbolic interactionist perspective for understanding the structure and dynamics of social systems is historically identified with the work of Herbert Blumer.[18] "Symbolic interactionist theory assumes that society and culture constitute the effective environment of individuals. . . ." Further, "interactionist theory holds that the study of human behavior must deal with two basic kinds of data, that pertaining to individuals and that pertaining to society and culture. In order to analyze and explain structure or process on either level, both individuals and cultural data must be taken into account."[19]

Through the process of socialization, the individual incorporates the values of society into the choices he or she makes. Interaction theory focuses on the individual who actively makes choices that reflect the result of past choices and available options. The interaction of the individual personality and the "sociocultural" system is dynamic. That is, the "values, norms, and beliefs of society are cultural definitions of reality with which individuals must deal."[20]

The synthesis of the conflict and functional perspectives has resulted in a more "empirically based theory."[21] This synthesis recognizes that the conflict and consensus interact, that they are inseparable. The synthetic approach is historically identified with the work of Max Weber.[22] "Two of Weber's major interests in the sociology of religion center on the effect of religious ideas on economic activities and the relationship between religions and social stratification. . . . These three religious ideas [predestination, individual calling, and religious asceticism] fused into an ideological system that had profound effects on the development of capitalism and its attendant system of class stratification."[23] Ideas and empirical data are merged in this synthetic perspective. The results combine

the valid insights of both conflict and functional perspectives while delet-
ing the "moral evaluation with respect to the existence of social inequality."[24]

Parallels between Sociological and Biblical Interpretive Perspectives

The conflict, functional, interactional, and synthetic perspectives represent various ways of understanding the role of ideology in culture.
These patterns of interpreting the interrelationship of ideology and
culture are helpful in describing the work of researchers in other fields.
The work of New Testament scholars can be reclassified according to
these same patterns.

The basic motivation for organization and for change in society may
be seen as an interest in unity, or as the result of the pressures of conflict.
For example, Hans von Campenhausen understands the basic motivation
that drives the early church to be the memory of a primitive charismatic
unity. Helmut Koester, on the other hand, sees the presence of an early
controversy as the primal motivating force behind the organizational development of the church. These two motivational options are described
in sociological categories from the conflict (Koester) and the functional
(von Campenhausen) perspectives.

Helmut Koester connects together three historic recollections of the
church that, taken together, strongly suggest a very specific conflict in the
Jesus Movement (the first-generation church). These are Steven's martyr-
dom (Acts 6:1–8:5), the Apostolic Council (Galatians 2), and the incident between Peter and Paul at Antioch (also Galatians 2).[25] This conflict
is between those whom he calls the "Hellenists" and those of the circle of
Peter and James (the "Circumcision Party"). Koester sees the early
church as developing in an environment of internal controversy that
caused change within the church.

Hans von Campenhausen focuses not upon the force of controversy in
forming the church but upon the process of "institutionalization." The
message of Jesus was the pure energizing force around which the church
formed. This primitive charismatic message was, in his (translated)
words, "impaired, trivialized and distorted."[26] The function of the continuing cult was (and is) to grasp or reconstitute the primitive original, a

conclusion that leads von Campenhausen to propose an original unity among those of the earliest generation. They were the closest to the source and were led by "charisma" rather than derived authority. According to von Campenhausen: "The decisive factor, however, was not one of the importance of particular offices or of the competence of ecclesiastical authority. That which in spite of everything held the primitive church and its 'apostles' together was not the unity of an organized Church, but the unity of their witness to Christ and of their vocation."[27]

There are those who see the ultimate unity of the Christian message as the energizing force behind the formation of the early church and those who see controversy and disunity as the motivation for the development of the early church. Other examples exist, but these are sufficient to illustrate the point that both conflicting and integrating forces are used to interpret the early church and its literary remains.

The symbolic interactionist and synthetic perspectives for understanding the role of ideology also have parallels in studies of the early church. Examples are found in the work of Ernst Käsemann and James M. Robinson as they examine the theological concerns of the earliest church and its literary remains.

Ernst Käsemann operates from a symbolic interactionist perspective in defining the motivation of the early church as it made the transition from the ancient church to "early catholicism." This was the movement from an imminent expectation of the Parousia, through various modifications, to the final "extinction" of that expectation.[28] The categories that define this conflict were ideational but they responded to the interaction of the expectation of Jesus' imminent return with the experience of continuing life. In other words, the primary force for the development of the early church was the cross between theology and experience: the delay of the Parousia. Käsemann: "This by no means occurs everywhere at the same time or with the same symptoms and consequences, but nevertheless in the various streams there is a characteristic movement toward that great Church which understands itself as the *Una Sancta Apostolica.*"[29]

This "necessary" development of nascent catholicism comes directly from the experience of the delay of the Parousia and the unfulfilled expectations of Christians like Paul. The mark of this development, in Käsemann's terms, is the incorporation of Paul's apocalypticism into salvation history. The church became an "integral factor in the salvation event." The church functions to integrate the experience of the believer.

This represents a perceived conflict in the realm of theology and its resolution in the development of an institution.

Käsemann finds evidence of the movement from the Pauline apocalyptic view to the nascent (second-generation) church in Ephesians. The movement is made visible in the issue of the identification of the disciple, "so that becoming a disciple of Jesus is no longer the basis but the consequence of being a Christian. . . . The decisive factor here is that men do not act on their own but are passively joined to the salvation event. . . . The drama of salvation is not concluded with Easter."[30]

The impetus for this development into nascent catholicism comes from the pressure of enthusiasts. The two powers standing to either side of Paul, identified by Käsemann as enthusiasm and legalism, conspire to force the new and developing church into the arms of a new ecclesiology under the pressure of the delay of the Parousia. "The *necessity* of new orders is conclusively demonstrated by the struggle against enthusiasm. Historically speaking, it was only in this way that the Christian Churches were able to repel the assault and survive as churches of Christ."[31]

The force of this new and developing enthusiasm came from the success of the Gentile church. The "fiction" of the authority of the apostles was the means used to combat these enthusiasts. The emphasis here, for Käsemann, is that this argument with the enthusiasts forces the church by necessity to adopt an "illusion of demonstrable continuity immanent in the Christian realm."[32] The interaction of the new cultural situation with the individuals who carry the traditions of the church results in new options.

Käsemann's conclusions parallel those we have seen of von Campenhausen. The shift to the early church environment from the primitive experience brought with it an "impairment, trivialization and distortion" of the original word and message. For Käsemann, that original message is found in the work and word of Paul conceived in an apocalyptic environment. The delay of the Parousia was a historical fact that came from outside the church and that challenged both the ideology and symbolic practice of the early church in its new cultural environment.

A parallel to the synthetic perspective is the trajectory theory of J. M. Robinson. Robinson offers another vision of the force that transformed the early church. He finds the energy for the development of the early church to be a by-product of the trajectory of the theological ideas themselves. The opponents of Paul begin by misunderstanding the "eschatological reservation" (a term borrowed from Käsemann) and move on to a realized eschatology. The dying and rising in the baptism litany were for Paul a *present* dying and a *future* rising. The opponents couple these to form their own already realized eschatology. Robinson calls those who unite the dying and the rising into an event already accomplished in the baptism of the believer "protognostic fanatics."[33]

The missing links to later enthusiast theologies are found in Eph. 2:5–6 and Col. 2:12–13. The later gnostics appeal directly to Paul for support in the baptismal resurrection. The opposing school, found in the pastorals, reject this view (2 Tim. 2:18). Polycarp in his letter to the Philippians (7.1) attacks the same heresy, as Robinson sees it, and he follows the trajectory of the pastorals.[34] Conflict and its resolution are the trail that Robinson follows. He describes theological ideas as if they have a character or a personality of their own. Their life begins in a moment of conflict, and they are played out upon the scene of history to their resolution. This is a synthetic pattern identifying the interaction of conflict and function.

Although there are conceptual correlations between sociological categories and exegetical studies of the literary remains of early church communities, there are also glaring differences. Exegetes focus their work on the ideas and images, the communication and the form, of the text, whereas sociologists focus on behavior and social forms of the society.

Sociological Categories in Contemporary Biblical Research

The traditional focus on ideas and theological constructs in biblical research leaves out the motivating role that sustaining and changing multiple social hierarchies have in defining ideology.[35] John G. Gager describes the problem with reference to the Apostle Paul: "previous efforts to explain Paul's use of justification merely by showing his dependence on a line of tradition reaching from the canonical prophets to first century Jewish apocalypticism, is really no explanation at all."[36]

Gager is describing the genetic fallacy. The question remains: even after identifying possible historical antecedents, do we know what motivated Paul to select one and not another portion of the history of ideas available to him? The historical and critical study of ideas and their situation in life allows us to identify their uniqueness. The sociological study of Paul's church allows us to identify those aspects of Paul's ideology comparable with the ideology of others in similar social situations.[37] Comparison and contrast permit us to translate and to interpret for our time the patterns of preference in the early church. Sociological research tools have become more acceptable among New Testament scholars in the past few years.

Those who place emphasis upon the interaction of the culture with the eastern religious cult groups later known as Christianity have focused their work on the relationship of ideology and behavior. This perspective on the forces that shaped earliest Christianity suggests that various trajectories of development were energized less by the inner forces of theology and ideology of the primitive church than by the interaction of the participants in the church and its development within the context of its surrounding culture. Gager is especially concerned about the "adequacy of certain traditional assumptions about the study of early Christianity."[38] He proposes a new paradigm that will see "old facts in a new light."

The new light is the appropriation of the tools of sociological research into the study of the New Testament community. The important shift in this paradigm is in the focus of the research. Sociological studies are less concerned with the unique in the primitive church than with that which the new movement has in common with other movements through history. For example, Gager says this about comparisons between contemporary cargo cults and the early church: "Recent discussions of millenarian movements have focused on two fundamental issues: *descriptions* of the cults themselves—constituencies, leaders, beliefs, history, and environment—with an emphasis on isolating common elements in different cults; and *explanations* of their similarities and underlying causes. Although the two issues are by no means identical, they are inevitably interrelated."[39]

Similarly, Theissen identifies the period in which great changes in the ideology of the church took place as a key for understanding the development of the early church. The force that led to change, however, was not ideological, but sociological: the questions of boundary and participation are related to cultural patterns and preference selection. Theissen discusses the interaction of behavior and ideology in the breakdown of the boundaries of Palestinian Judaism:

> Once the stage had been reached when birth and descent were no longer acceptable as the criteria for membership of true Judaism, the next step was not far away. In principle, why should not anyone participate in the privileged role of the true Israel? Just as inter-cultural segregation inevitably led to schisms within a culture, so this development of schisms led to the universalization of Judaism. This universalization inevitably broke through when the intensification of norms became the relaxation of norms, and when it was recognized that even an elect remnant within Israel could not satisfy these intensified norms: all, Jews and Gentiles alike, were directed towards grace. The breakthrough happened in the Jesus movement, though it was only with Paul that its final consequences were drawn.[40]

In recognizing the sociological pattern at work, Gager confirms the importance of the delay of the Parousia in the development of the millennialist cult known as primitive Christianity. His method, sensitive to conflict and resolution in a social environment, finds that the success of Christianity depends upon the form of institutionalization and theological understanding adopted by the movement. This contrasts with the conclusions of Käsemann, who finds only theological corruption in the process of institutionalization.[41] It also contrasts with the description provided by J. M. Robinson's trajectory studies, that the ideological content of the struggles marking the transitions of the Jesus movement into the nascent church and then into the early church is preceded by the process and form of that development. Gager: "At the very least, we may be certain that ideological struggles between kindred communities ought never to be taken at face value and that such struggles play a role in the formation of ideological and institutional structures of which the participants themselves are but faintly aware."[42]

Many of those who have undertaken a self-conscious reworking of biblical exegesis along sociological or comparative lines criticize those who are not so aware of cultural context. For example, Malina says:

> Most New Testament study takes place in terms of verbal and literary analysis, historical description of persons and events, as well as some geographical and archeological information, all of which serve to clarify the

meaning of the texts. All such information is certainly of great value for making the Word of God intelligible. However, most of the time Bible students take all such information and conceive it as operating in much the same way as it would operate in our own society. Such unconscious shuffling of cultural contexts might make the Bible immediately relevant to the student, but at what cost to the meaning intended by the sacred author, the meaning most Christians would hold to be intended by God?[43]

There are differences between the interests of a sociological study of the early church and theological-historical studies of the New Testament. Gager's discussion makes this clear in pointing out that sociological analysis looks to describe the similarities between various religious groups in their development whereas historical, theological analysis looks for unique attributes. The one seeks to describe by similarity, the other by difference. But precisely because of these differing perspectives, there are areas where each method of study may inform the other.

Conclusions about theological concerns drawn from sociological analyses alone may not give full weight to unique aspects of a particular theological development. For example (in response to Theissen), even though the intensification of norms and intracultural segregation may have marked the Jesus movement, reading a universalization of the movement implicit in schism back into the theology of the movement *without textual evidence* requires a leap of faith. We have no historical basis for claiming that a theological tenet that only becomes realized in practice with Paul preexists Paul. On the other hand, the texts that form our historical record were not written for our purpose, but for people who lived in a very different social world with a very different world view. Conclusions about the content of the text that do not take into account the foreignness of the social world from which they originate similarly require a leap of faith.

The Problem of Interpretation

We return now to the problem of interpretation left hanging at the beginning of this chapter. Though we can begin to see the essential similarity of the two disciplines—ethnography and exegesis—we must confront the problem of cross-cultural interpretation.

In the present poststructuralist period, all language has become suspect as it has been found to encode the ideology of the dominant culture in hidden and subversive ways. The conventions of language are the means of ordering thought and therefore behavior. Cross-cultural interpretation is itself suspect because of this encoding barrier. The process of interpretation rephrases encoded meaning into the encoded ideology of the interpreter.

This hegemony of the dominant culture is manifest in the one-way pattern of social critique: "They are not as sophisticated as we"; "They are not as technologically advanced"; ". . . as scientific"; and so forth. So there have come various proposals for "demythologizing" the text. The contemporary response to this hegemony has led cultural interpreters to emphasize the diversity of culture out of a concern for an egalitarian social justice. Each voice is allowed to be heard—the voice of the interpreter but one of these. In this egalitarian world with equal access to authority, all interpretation becomes misinterpretation, or, alternatively, each and every interpretation is correct. Relativism replaces fixed meanings; subjectivity replaces rationality.

Susan Garrett has criticized Bruce Malina's *Christian Origins and Cultural Anthropology* on the grounds that it lacks awareness of contemporary shifts in the anthropological paradigm.[44] The work Malina has done—his awareness of cultural theory—prepares the way for the interpretation of ethnographic information by emphasizing the distinction between ancient, foreign cultural patterns and our own. In her review of Malina's work Garrett refers to an analysis of twentieth-century trends in cultural anthropology by George E. Marcus and Michael M. J. Fischer, both of Rice University.[45] Their study, *Anthropology as Cultural Critique*, is subtitled *An Experimental Moment in the Human Sciences*.

Marcus and Fischer propose that the complex internal criticism which has led the field of cultural anthropology into experiments in ethnographic writing has parallels in other human sciences. Indeed, in the field of biblical criticism, Malina's work reviewed by Garrett is just such an experiment. But Garrett misreads Malina, or at least his intentions. The paradigm he develops—in response to his own idiosyncratic and perhaps naïve reading of Mary Douglas—is not about "real world realities" but about a simplification, an approximation, an abstraction of the rich and concrete particularized world.[46] The goal is not to describe the historic Paul, but to come into dialogue with him, reflexively aware of his critique of our own culture. This is not a different goal from that of contemporary experiments in ethnography as described by Marcus and Fischer.

The issue of the cross-cultural interpretation of ideological statements and/or symbolic behavior is exceedingly complex. Grid-group analysis—as created by Mary Douglas—is a method for interpreting *ethnographic* data. The grid-group model—as created by Malina—is useful for interpreting meaning communicated through texts within a social context.[47] There is a difference. These two should not be confused. There are different agenda at work. Malina seeks to challenge the ethnocentrism he perceives in the work of biblical interpreters. Douglas challenges those who would detach "culture" from living human beings—and thus provides a ground for western interpretation in her focus on the individual.[48]

The real difficulty with Malina's work is that he does not go far enough in preparing an ethnography of Paul's community before attempting to interpret artifacts of that community—the letters of Paul. Malina's agenda is a challenge to the authority of unintended ethnocentric bias in biblical interpretation. It would seem that he leaps upon grid-group theory fully developed *as a model without bias*. Garrett is correct in identifying this weakness. "Malina's omission of any discussion of the theoretical and ethnographic underpinnings of Douglas's model fosters an impression of the model as absolute—as somehow untainted by the ethnocentrism that it aims to circumvent."[49]

Garrett goes further in this line of critique in reviewing the work of Jerome Neyrey concerning "witchcraft accusations."[50] She accurately describes the opposition of the "positivist" and the "interpretive" perspectives among anthropologists and the contemporary bent toward interpretive ethnography. But interpreting a text is not the same as interpreting culture. The text may be "mined" or scanned for bits of ethnographic information. It may be subjected to literary analysis to determine the author's point of view and narrative function. But the text alone cannot provide the feedback necessary for the communication model to operate.

Marcus and Fischer describe the contemporary "experimental moment" as a time between dominant patterns of research. Opposing perspectives in anthropology result in the critique of each. The experimental moment responds to each perspective: "We distinguish two trends. . . .

One trend is a radicalization of concern with how cultural difference is to be represented in ethnography. . . . The other trend of experimentation . . . tries to find more effective ways to describe how ethnographic subjects are implicated in broader processes of historical political economy."[51]

The point is not that one vision of ethnographic writing is inherently better than another, but that every ethnographic endeavor is contextual; Marcus and Fischer:

> The motivating spirit of experimentation is thus antigenre, to avoid the reinstatement of a restricted canon like that of the recent past. Individual works have influence on other writers of ethnography, but are not self-consciously written as models for others to follow, or as the basis of a "school" of ethnographic production. Particular tests can be judged as awkward, or even as failures in terms of the goals they set for themselves, but they may be interesting and valuable nonetheless for the possibilities they raise for other ethnographers.[52]

Neyrey—and Malina—probe the discontinuity between the cultural bias of the interpreter and that of the interpreted. They interpose a "Formal Tale"[53] in order to radicalize the representation of cultural difference. Like it or not, there is no "third language" of reality that provides us with an opportunity for correct interpretation across cultural barriers. Even an interpretive ethnography of an ancient narrative—one that is deeply aware of both the ancient cultural setting and literary context—relies upon modern rationality to convey the assumed coherence of the ancients' thought. Ernest Gellner describes this conflict in his essay "Concepts and Society."[54] Garrett's work is brilliant. She successfully explores the interpretive question: finding more effective ways to describe how ethnographic subjects—in her work: the narrative subjects Luke introduces—are implicated in broader processes of historical political economy—in her work: the divine economy and the cosmic struggle of God and Satan.

In using grid-group as a model for opening our ears to the critique of our own culture from the people of a nonwestern culture who wrote and preserved the biblical text, Malina and Neyrey are also very successful. They ask the alternative experimental question: how to find more effective ways of radicalizing the concern with how cultural differences are to be represented in ethnography. Our bias is that of the "strong" language—we expect the biblical message to be translated into our context. We need to hear and experience the context of the "weak" language as a challenge to our own.

We need to go even further than Malina's model, and as employed by Neyrey, in developing the methods we use to redescribe literary texts in sociological terms. The model describing human culture we use for interpreting cultural artifacts defines our perspective and orders our observations. Interpretive ethnographers in the field have the luxury of repeated exposure to ritual patterns and behavior. They can ask about the manifest meaning of patterned behavior and cultural artifacts. The literary critic cannot. When we ask interpretive questions of ancient texts, our modern assumptions concerning human culture reign unchecked. Our focus on the world of the native is not enough. We do not have enough ethnographic information; only selected portions of elite and privileged ancient society are represented in the corpus of literary data.

In this study we use a restrictive set of formal operations to question the text over and over. In being precise with the questions asked, we provide the means by which both the text and other interpreters may offer feedback. We offer the opportunity for critique of assumptions and observations on a question-by-question basis. We offer the opportunity to observe the process of conclusion and to gauge the importance of each bit of ethnographic evidence in drawing that conclusion.

When we proceed using a formal tale—or specific model of human culture—to tell the story of culture, we put on display the political agenda of those who would use the model.

In this regard, we note that Bruce Malina—a white American male educator—defends his use of the grid-group model by pointing out its development in the work and person of Mary Douglas—a white British female in a white male-dominated educational system.[55] Interpretation of literary texts, if it is possible to do at all, requires us to define our terms and our agenda.

The issue is not the elimination of bias, but the self-conscious selection of one over another within the interpretive process. Jürgen Habermas claims, for instance, that "the ideal speech situation requires equal access to and possession of resources." Thus an egalitarian bias is selected as better and more ideal than a competitive or privileged cultural ideology.[56]

We need to do our ethnographic rewriting with intentionality because the art of writing—the poetics—influences our observations. Before we interpret cultural artifacts, we need to observe *their* cultural context as well as our own cultural context. The common language of anthropological observation—even in experimental ethnographic writing—is moderate functionalism. This is not the functionalist perspective that informs many models of human culture following Durkheim. Functionalism remains the language of ethnography as cultural relativism is the basis for ethnography. By exploring functionalism, we shall seek to develop a common language for exegesis using the patterns of ethnographic writing.

Ethnography and Biblical Exegesis

The problem with writing an ethnography of a historical social entity like the early church faction associated with the Apostle Paul is that you cannot use the basic tool of ethnography: participant observation. It is not possible to enter into actual dialogue with those involved in order to prepare an ethnographic thick description of any part of the ritual or organizational patterns of the early church. In other words, our problems as biblical scholars go beyond even those of ethnographers in the field. Our data base cannot even pretend to be either unbiased or detailed. Biblical scholars can enjoy neither objective, dispassionate, participant observations nor ethnographic thick descriptions. The discipline we follow must create another option for writing an ethnography of a historical community.

If ethnography is the centerpiece of cultural anthropology, and if biblical criticism is comparable to cultural anthropology, and as exegesis is the centerpiece of biblical criticism, then ethnography must be comparable to exegesis. The interest in describing both what the text said and what it says represents the two functions of cultural anthropology: the descriptive and the critical. One result of biblical exegesis is the interpretation of the sacred text for people today. This interpretation implies a cultural critique of the social environment of the exegete. One result of cultural anthropology is critique of the cultural patterns of the anthropologist. There is a parallel in these results.

All ethnography is interpretive unless its purpose is solely to display curiosities and exotic artifacts from strange places. Just so, all biblical exegesis is interpretive unless its purpose is solely to preserve the inerrant word of the Authorized Version. Although this interpretive activity may be suspect because of the fascist effect of language, it remains the only process for the critique of our own culture and behavior. By exploring the patterns of functionalism, we hope to identify some of the characteristics of ethnography and make them applicable to exegesis.

The common language of ethnography that sounds like ethnography is functionalism. In order to ensure that the whole culture being observed is available, functionalism mandates a semiformal series of questions to be answered. Malinowski's list is found in his 1939 essay "The Functional Theory."[57] We will look at a standard description of functionalism to find a set of guidelines for the exegesis of biblical texts in sociological categories. In this way the biblical scholar's method will be conversant with ethnographic methods. The hope is that patterns for the work of the biblical exegete will be found that will enable the development of canons for attempting an ethnography of biblical communities.

Functional Analysis and Biblical Exegesis

Some years ago Robert K. Merton offered a "Paradigm for Functional Analysis in Sociology" in which he attempted to "codify" functional analysis as it had been practiced.[58] The eleven points of this paradigm outline both the requirements of a method and an attitude in ethnographic description. "The paradigm presents the hard core of concept, procedure and inference in functional analysis."[59] He constructs this paradigm from elements found in his study of research and theory in the field of functional analysis. His paradigm is helpful in defining the requirements of a consistent method for use in working with sociological data in the New Testament. The primary issue to be addressed is the process of observation. In the handling of the evidence, what are the appropriate categories in which it may be viewed? What are the means by which those categories may be kept separate?

This paradigm is a method for the *interpretation* of sociological data as observed by the field worker.[60] It has three purposes: (1) It is a codified guide for functional analysis. (2) It reveals the postulates and assumptions underlying a particular functional analysis of sociological data. (3) It sensitizes us to the ideological or political concerns of a particular func-

tional analysis and makes us aware of more narrow scientific implications in sociological study.[61] What follows is a point-by-point overview
of Merton's paradigm with some discussion of implications for the study
of the Pauline church.

Point 1: The Item(s) to Which Functions are Imputed

It seems obvious when one puts it down this way, but the selection of
data to be analyzed determines the results of the study. Simply recording
a list of facts as in ancient Near Eastern "Mesopotamian List Science"[62]
does not get western Europeans any closer to an interpretation or understanding of those facts. There *will be* a protocol to the selection and
categorization of observations. The issue is defining that selection process. Merton puts the question this way: "What must enter into the protocol of observation of the given item if it is to be amenable to systematic
functional analysis?"[63]

Functional analysis is interested in understanding the ways in which
observable behavior *functions* in a society. One basic definition of observable behavior is that it is repetitive. That is, observable behavior has
a visible pattern to it. Random behavior is not useful to the observer and
therefore is ignored.

This first statement of the paradigm reveals the primary concern for
using sociological tools to interpret Paul and the Pauline church. *The
data in which we are interested are evidences of repetitive or patterned
behavior.* As Merton lists them, these include "social roles, institutional
patterns, social processes, cultural pattern, culturally patterned emo-
tions, social norms, group organization, social structure, devices for
social control, etc."[64] By developing a description of these repetitive, patterned, behavioral evidences, we move toward the understanding of the
cultural patterns of the Pauline church faction.

The description of patterned behavior should include five categories of
observations:

(1) the location of participants in the pattern within the social structure—
differential participation;
(2) consideration of alternative modes of behavior excluded by emphasis
on the observed pattern (i.e., attention not only to what occurred but
also to what is neglected by virtue of the existing pattern);

(3) the emotive and cognitive meanings attached by participants to the pattern;

(4) a distinction between the motivations for participating in the pattern and the objective behavior involved in the pattern;

(5) regularities of behavior not recognized by participants but that are nonetheless associated with the central pattern of behavior.[65]

Most of these categories are self-explanatory. They give direction to the process of the observation and the selection of information. The first category is a description of the roles of the participants who "differentially" choose to exhibit the patterned behavior, their social status, and their group affiliation.

The second category, excluded behaviors, is exemplified in the identification of the group boundaries of the Pauline church in its urban setting.[66] The third, the meanings of observed behavior given by the participants, is given by Paul himself in his letters. We must be careful here, however, because the context in Paul's letters is either motivational or didactic. The meaning Paul imputes to patterned behaviors may not be clear if his purpose is motivational. All three of these categories taken together offer clues to the "imputed" functions of patterned behaviors.

The fourth category of description lists the psychological rationale for either conformity to or deviation from the observed behavior. A psychological function is not the same as a social function, nor is it an objective behavior in itself. Describing the array of motives the participants have for their actions is "slippery." It is included in functional analysis because psychological functions offer clues to the way observed behavior functions for the group or society. In the letters of Paul we find clues to the social function of patterns of behavior in inferences of psychological motivations for membership and participation in the fellowship, but these clues are extraordinarily difficult to keep straight.[67]

The fifth category, patterns of behavior not recognized by the participants, is especially powerful in interpreting the meaning of behavior. In New Testament research, however, we do not have available to us independent observation of the earliest phenomena. We have only the observations of the participants themselves. *Unwitting regularities*[68] or patterned behaviors are very difficult if not impossible to discern. They must be inferred from the form of the letters themselves, our only directly observable patterned behavior.

Point 2: Concepts of Subjective Dispositions (Motives, Purposes)

The second point of Merton's paradigm for functional analysis concerns the need to keep observation of the motivations of participants in a social system separate from the "objective consequences of attitude, belief and behavior." Identifying subjective motivations through a description of psychological functions is not the same as describing the meaning that patterned behavior has for the social system. The objective consequences of repetitive behavior *may* indeed coincide with the subjective motives of the participants in the social system; then again, they may not. By expressly examining the subjective motivations of the participants, the observer can separate and identify these motivations.

For example, Paul's own explanation of the baptism ritual in Romans 6 may not correlate with the way the ritual actually functioned in the Pauline church. The unexplained reference to Christians' "being baptized on behalf of the dead" (1 Cor. 15:29) suggests that baptism functions for inclusion of deceased relatives into the group in a way that is, at best, tangential to Paul's description in Romans.[69]

Point 3: Concepts of Objective Consequences (Functions, Dysfunctions)

The third point of Merton's paradigm carries the weight of the distinction "between conscious *motivations* for social behavior and its *objective consequences*."[70] If the second point of the paradigm is compared with the third, the distinction between that which the participants say and the behavior they exhibit is revealed. Merton cautions us to be careful to include in our observations behaviors that are both functional *and* dysfunctional for the social system. There may be more than one consequence of an identifiable repetitive behavior. Further, some of these consequences may act as positive contributions and some as negative contributions to the social system under study. Finally, there may be confusion when we go to interpret functions because any observable repetitive behavior may have either or both manifest and latent functions.

Manifest functions are those objective consequences contributing to the adjustment or adaptation of the system which are intended and recognized by participants in the system;

Latent functions, correlatively, being those which are neither intended nor recognized.[71]

Though semantically obvious, the distinction between manifest and latent is difficult to grasp in practice. Merton goes on to describe manifest functions and latent functions by distinguishing between them: "the first referring to those objective consequences for a specified unit (person, subgroup, social or cultural system) which contribute to its adjustment or adaptation and were so intended; the second referring to unintended and unrecognized consequences of the same order."[72]

Distinguishing between the objective consequences of behavior and the motivations of the subjects involved in the patterned behavior is difficult. In his letters Paul makes no attempt to distinguish between the motivation for any behavior in which he asks the church to participate and the objective consequence of that behavior. The social function of the collection for the poor in Jerusalem and the motivational discussion in 2 Cor. 8–9 are not the same, but Paul does not make that distinction. It is left to the researcher to distinguish between them.[73] Merton's categories of manifest and latent functions seek to make the examination of intended and unintended consequences systematic and so to distinguish them from subjective motivations.

Point 4: Concepts of the Unit Subserved by the Function

Merton asks us to identify and separate those people for whom a particular behavior or pattern functions to make a contribution from those for whom the pattern dysfunctions. The consequences of a given behavior for people of different status or of a different subgroup may be dissimilar. Separating these corresponds to the identification of the *range* of functions and dysfunctions in point three of the paradigm.

Certain behavioral patterns of the early Christians caused difficulties for the Pauline church and for individuals of higher social rank. Meeks has demonstrated that the Pauline church was made up of people of differing social rank and station having in common ambiguous status in the social system.[74] He discusses the ways in which belief and behavior function to support these participants. Stephen Benko discusses several patterns of Christian behavior observed by pagan critics and the ways these dysfunctioned in pagan society. For example, the holy kiss functions both as a sign of participation emphasizing group unity and as a sign of the cost of membership.[75]

Point 5: Concepts of Functional Requirements (Needs, Prerequisites)

The requirements of the social system or subgroup under study determine the relationships among various objective consequences of behavior, intended or unintended, functional or dysfunctional. Survival alone, interpreted narrowly, is not necessarily the primary requirement or objective of a social system or subgroup. The Pauline church faction is just such a case in point. It has parallels with other cargo cults.[76] The concern for the survival of the cult within society may be replaced by concern for survival in the expected coming crisis. The conditions for survival that determine whether any pattern functions or dysfunctions for participants in the Pauline church faction may be controlled by an unexpected or unusual sets of factors.[77] The rules that govern behavior in cultic practice will be based on a new, all-encompassing beginning for society.

This point of Merton's paradigm, as well as the next two, demonstrates the greatest difficulty for those working with ancient sources to find information in sociological categories: There is no chance for experimental validation.

BASIC QUERY: What is required to establish the validity of such a variable as "functional requirement" in situations where rigorous experimentation is impracticable?[78]

It is possible for explanations or justifications of behaviors voiced by Paul to be interpreted differently by different interpreters from various cultural perspectives. Sacred texts no longer speak as author-to-audience, but as text-to-audience. This hermeneutical fact provides Protestant clergy, like myself, with an intellectual excuse for constant employment in reinterpreting the sacred text week after week. The social scientist, on the other hand, does not approach the text in the same way. The exegete as cultural anthropologist attempts to discern the "functional requirements" of the subgroup, "the Pauline Church," in order to understand the ways in which various behaviors and ideologies functioned or dysfunctioned. This is the descriptive task.

What is necessary to establish the validity of a variable as a functional requirement when considering the literary remains of an ancient factional group is careful description and attention to method. When writing about the cultural patterns of the Pauline church faction, the researcher is reconstructing an ethnography. By clearly describing the cultural theory and assumptions underlying the reconstruction, the writer presents the reader with the final responsibility for validating the results. Does the dialogue make sense from the perspective of the reader's cultural bias? Does the dialogue make sense from the reconstructed perspective of the ancient writer? Is there validation of the dialogue using an alternative method?

The "sheer description" of rites, rituals, and patterned behavior goes a long way toward identifying their function when it includes the identification and social context of the individuals involved.[79] Sheer description is different from ethnographic thick description in that it is not itself in conversation with the ethnographer's audience. Sheer description is dependent on method and discipline. It does not delve into slippery areas of motivations or intentions. It allows for reflexive social critique, which it does not produce. That is the interpretive task.

Point 6: Concepts of the Mechanisms through Which Functions Are Fulfilled

"Concrete and detailed" accounts of the social mechanisms of the Pauline church are impossible to construct. Our observations are limited to the inferences we can make from the actual letters of Paul and, perhaps, related sources. Social mechanisms[80] are the means by which the behaviors under study achieve their function or dysfunction. Cause and effect are *very* difficult to demonstrate in social environments where we can interview participants; they are impossible to demonstrate histor-ically. Still, Merton's categories of applicable social mechanisms are useful for describing the requirements of the method used by the social historian for identifying and ordering the available evidence. The method must incorporate both categories for patterned behavior and categories for social mechanisms.

Point 7: Concepts of Functional Alternatives (Functional Equivalents or Substitutes)

BASIC QUERY: Since scientific proof of the equivalence of an alleged functional alternative ideally requires rigorous experimentation, and since this is not often practicable in large-scale situations, which practicable procedures of inquiry most nearly approximate the logic of experiment?[81]

New Testament research may be able to substitute an examination of the functional equivalents or alternatives for particular social structures for participant observation. Substitution is necessary for the study of his-torical phenomena. When changes in the social patterns of the early church are examined, the function of specific repetitive behaviors at spe-cific times and places are highlighted. No social mechanism indispensably fills a social function; other behavioral patterns are always available. The function that any social mechanism fills will demand to be filled by some other mechanism through transfer if the first social mechanism is no longer available. This thesis gives life to the concept of "trajectories" in theological thought.[82]

The institutionalization of authority in the early church may provide an example of this process. In terms described by John H. Schütz, active power is interpreted by authority that is itself, in turn, interpreted by legitimacy.[83] This process of the formalization of authority from charis-matic spiritual leaders to legitimate bishops and elders may be traced in the transfer of the function that orders or organizes the common life of the community at each stage.[84] The delay of the Parousia causes changes in the social patterns of the early church.[85] One might suppose that the substitution of a functional alternative caused by the delay interprets the pattern that goes before.

Point 8: Concepts of Structural Context (or Structural Constraint)

The changes caused by intervening conditions, as in the delay of the Parousia, are limited in their possible variations. For example, the concepts of authority and power are not ultimately isolatable either from other social structures or from the cognitive containers, the theological ideas, that sustain them. "The interdependence of the elements of a social structure limits the effective possibilities of change or functional alternatives."[86]

Interpretive images of the social unit include a living organism, as Merton has it,[87] or a dynamic ecological system, as Mary Douglas has it.[88] Another image, and one I prefer, is that of a tensile structure like a geodesic dome. This is a mechanical construct in which, at equilibrium, each part is both supporting and supported by every other part.

Point 9: Concepts of Dynamics and Change

Change occurs when stress on one part of the body—the dynamic system, the tensile structure—causes other parts to shift or compensate for that stress. The idea of dysfunction is suggested by Merton as a mechanism by which stress, instability, and consequent change may be analyzed and its effect studied. The objective consequences of a social mechanism dysfunction when they materially lessen the adaptation or adjustment of the system.[89] In other words, the pattern dysfunctions when unrelieved stress results for the participants.

Change in the social system is reflected in changes in the ways the participants explain or justify themselves. Change in ideology reflects changes in the social system just as changes in behavior reflect changes in ideology. Neither culture itself nor subgroups of a society remain static. Merton notes that "functional analysts *tend* to focus on the statics in social structure and to neglect the study of structural change."[90] Functional analysts are not alone in this tendency.

Point 10: Problems of Validation of Functional Analysis

BASIC QUERY: To what extent is functional analysis limited by the difficulty of locating adequate *samples of social systems* which can be subjected to comparative (quasi-experimental) study?[91]

The difficulties of working with sociological categories when examining the early church are manifold. The evidence is inferential. We have only documents whose purpose is something other than the conveyance of sociological information. We must infer the evidence from the data. Therefore, functional analysis, by itself, is not possible. A full description of the social mechanisms involved is not available without an intervening social theory.

The problem with Wayne Meeks's self-description as a "moderate functionalist"[92] is that in interpreting the data he has gleaned, he sometimes proceeds in a circle. Theological statements are subjected to interpretation to infer behavior that then is used to infer a context for theological statements. Theological statements are not sheer description. The important methodological concern is not that observation of one must precede the other, but that theological and behavioral categories must be kept distinct.

Writing letters is a part of the patterned behavior of the Pauline church. The letters themselves are evidence of patterned behavior. But, inferences can be made from the content of those letters only where information about the Pauline church is provided incidentally to the purpose of the letter. Prosopographic evidence is a case in point.[93] It carries useful sociological data because of its literary situation-in-life, which is personal greeting or introduction. It is, therefore, extremely valuable because it carries useful data incidental to its purpose.

More difficult to obtain and interpret is the data that must be inferred from Paul's theological statements. For example, Meeks describes the Christian rite of baptism. We do not know what the ritual looked like when Paul baptized new Christians; "we have to rely on inference to answer the simplest questions about what happened, and we will remain ignorant, however clever our detection, of many details that might, if we knew them, alter our total picture of the ritual."[94]

It is difficult in the best of circumstances to move from a sheer description of rites and practices to an understanding of their *function* in the society or subgroup. The task at hand for functional analysis is to infer the manifest and implicit function of patterns of behavior. Actual statements from participants concerning the purpose of ritual or patterned behavior is only one evidence that is useful. But in the case of Meeks's description of cultic initiation in the Pauline church, ritual behavioral patterns have been inferred largely from the motivational literature of the fellowship. Keeping motivations and functions separate is, therefore, impossible. To advance the inference of evidence from the data, other tools are required.

Mary Douglas's grid-group analysis as described by Gross and Rayner[95] provides an appropriate paradigm through a multivariant model into which the data may be categorized. Neither functional analysis nor synthetic analysis by themselves can avoid the problem of circularity for the social historian.

Point 11: Problems of the Ideological Implications of Functional Analysis

Ideology affects the way the researcher perceives the evidence and even the way he or she selects the data collected. In the case of New Testament scholarship, the theological traditions of the researcher determine not only the questions that are of interest but also the manner in which those questions are addressed.[96] Functional analysis provides a form of ethnographic "common sense"[97] to pattern or test various methods.

There is "no *intrinsic commitment* to an ideological position"[98] in functional analysis. Yet the interpretation of data and its collection are symbiotic; they are part of the analyst's understanding. The researcher *may be* sensitive enough to the cultural bias of the social unit in question to provide a telling collection of the data. The reader should be careful to note the organization of the evidence before it is interpreted.[99]

Summary: The Paradigm for Functional Analysis

Merton's paradigm for functional analysis identifies the requirements of a method that categorizes the evidence useful for an ethnography. For the Pauline church faction, these are remains of repetitive or patterned behaviors found in the letters of Paul. These evidences must be kept distinct and separate from motivational or didactic descriptions offered by Paul. An experimental ethnography of the Pauline church faction must carefully place the evidence into appropriate categories according to these canons of the method.

Following a discussion of parallels between interpretive patterns of sociology and biblical exegesis, we have reviewed the "common language" of ethnography—functionalism. What is required is for biblical scholars to rethink exegesis as ethnography when attempting to use sociological categories. This completes the circle. Ethnographers—following Clifford Geertz—have begun to use the concepts of literary analysis to inform their interpretation of foreign beliefs and practices. The problem of interpretation is common to both these endeavors.

Making the Connection between Sociology and Ideology

Although there are important insights found in a functional or a modified functional analysis of the Pauline church, there still exists the need for a method that makes the connection between ideology and the categories of sociologically observable behavior. This method must keep the categories of evidence ordered and clear. It must be verifiable and falsifiable. It must provide a theoretical basis for correlating patterns of behavior with specific theological statements. It must state explicitly the understanding of social interactions assumed to be operative. Finally— and most importantly—it must function to interpret the ancient cultural patterns in terms appropriate to the intended audience of the interpreter. Reflexively, the dominant culture of the interpreter must be prepared to hear the critique of the ancient. Lest we be too optimistic about our ability to accomplish our goal, we should remember the situation of ethnographers who attempt to make sense of what they have never seen before.

Our western world has a new-found awareness of the deep contextuality of meaning. The two tasks of the human sciences—the descriptive and the critical—have been challenged by this new awareness. How is it possible to come to know and to understand people from another culture? Our awareness of this central epistemological question is heightened by our developing appreciation for the value of diversity of human culture.

Deep contextuality stands as a barrier to shared meaning and to the interpretive process. The very presence of the participant observer—clearly differentiated and separated as an observer from those observed—demonstrates the stronger-weaker cultural dichotomy. One cultural representative—typically one with a western industrialized cultural bias—will assume a dominant role in the interpretive process. All meaning will be "translated" into the terminology of the dominant culture. The subservient or weaker culture is observed and made into raw material to be transformed into information useful to purposes of the dominant culture.

So: How is it possible to come to know and to understand people from another culture if yours is typically the dominant cultural bias? How can we come to hear what we cannot see? Is it possible to reverse roles? Is it possible to become the weaker culture? Is it possible to provide for an egalitarian interpretation—reflexive in its critical task, inclusive in its descriptive task?

This "crisis of representation" in anthropology is reflected in a new awareness of the deep contextuality in the interpretation of ancient texts like the Bible. Biblical interpretation has been concerned for the past century with the exegetical and the hermeneutical questions: What did the text say?—What does it say? These concerns are parallel to the descriptive and critical task of the other human sciences. We have discovered that the "situation-in-life" of an ancient text is sociological as well as ideological in its deepest sense.

Biblical critics are newly concerned with defining the relationship of writing within the ancient culture in the descriptive task and with defining the relationship of descriptive and interpretive writing within our own culture in the critical task. We can no longer leave or suspend our own place within the dominant culture under the guise of an impersonal scientific method because we have then allowed the experimental scientific model of our dominant culture to define the terms of meaning.

The alternative is to suspend the deep contextuality of foreign belief and symbolic behavior by selecting a methodological tool for ethnographic interpretation. For example: E. E. Evans-Pritchard's attention to misfortune, or Victor Turner's attention to the ritual process, or Aaron Wildavsky's attention to risk, or Mary Douglas's attention to dirt. Each of these offers a mechanism by which we may suspend—and I mean suspend, not eliminate—the deep contextuality of meaning and provisionally answer the "crisis of representation." "While the initial problem is posed by the difference between 'our' kind of thinking and 'theirs', it is a mistake to treat 'us' the moderns and 'them' the ancients as utterly different. We can only approach primitive mentality through introspection and understanding of our own mentality."[100]

Grid-group analysis uses a model of human culture informed by a symbolic interactionist perspective for correlating observed behavior with ideology. The next chapter describes this grid-group model, including an explicit statement of its social accounting approach to the study of social interactions. Though we recognize that grid-group is not the only available anthropological model[101] with a corresponding method that fulfills the requirements outlined above, grid-group analysis has the advantage of clear working definitions and a paradigm that is adaptable for use by the social historian.

Grid-group does not escape cultural bias. Indeed, its strength is in its ability to interpret diverse, foreign cultural patterns with a model appropriate to western Europeans. Grid-group can assist us in making distinctions among various cultural artifacts, while affording a cross-cultural context to interpret cultural phenomena and providing a critique of western patterns of thought and social behavior.

3

The Grid-Group Model
The Relationship of Cosmology and Behavior

People make choices every day. They choose one behavior over another because they prefer it that way. These preferences, taken collectively and observed in repetitive patterns, are the side-effects of human culture. Culture is not itself observable, but its effects—in the sum of choices made—are.

We will use one theory of culture concerning the relationship between cosmology and behavior—that of grid-group analysis—to try to understand Paul and the Pauline church better. In using this theory of culture, we will focus on the side-effects of culture found in the social behavior of individuals to visualize the effect of cultural bias on their preferences.

This model for understanding the various forms taken by human culture has been described by Mary Douglas in a series of books and articles published over the past two decades.[1] The model has been used by various writers in the past decade to better understand cultural patterns of leadership,[2] preference selection,[3] risk,[4] editorial bias,[5] and symbolic behavior.[6] The model is a result of the conjunction of the experience of Douglas as an anthropologist and her reading of educational theories developed by Basil Berstein. There is a happenstance in this conjunction—nothing in the model is ontologically necessary. The model simply helps western people describe and interpret what we see and hear around us and in so doing helps us to bring foreign experience into conversation with our own.

The model depends on a perception that people make choices—decisions—each day as they go about daily life, that somehow these choices reveal the preferences of individuals, that these preferences are the side-effects of culture, that these side-effects will reveal the bias of each culture. In other words, the study of the side-effects of culture is a proxy for the study of the invisible culture itself. The grid-group model is uniquely western in its focus on the individual and in its vision of culture as a dynamic process interacting with each individual, producing bias or preference. The hegemony of the individual is the essence of western culture—it occupies, therefore, half of the communication model. Grid-group provides for cross-cultural dialogue.

Cultural Theory and Biblical Interpretation

Grid-group begins as a model or theory of culture. Cultural theorists do not describe social reality as would natural scientists describing a physical phenomenon like rain. E. E. Evans-Pritchard admits, "I do not believe there can ever be a science of society which resembles the natural sciences."[7]

The grid-group model makes the connection between descriptive ethnography or social scientific observation of culture and its interpretive understanding by finding the common denominator of all human cultures in the individual. Mary Douglas, the anthropologist who has initiated and defined the theoretical basis for grid-group analysis, claimed her place in western culture, as her 1980 review of the work of E. E. Evans-Pritchard makes clear.[8] The alternative to an approach like Douglas's—a claim of neutrality in cultural perspective—makes interpretation impossible. A cacophony of voices leaves us as foreigners. Interpreters make dialogue possible. Reflexivity—the ability to hear critique as well as observe the exotic—leads to insight even as cultural boundaries are respected.

Cultural theory is a "socially constructed reality," to use the phrasing of Peter Berger and Thomas Luckmann.[9] In this "constructed reality" lies the interpretive power of grid-group model. Grid-group analysis trusts in the ability of the model to bridge the barriers the dominant culture imposes on interpretation. The juxtaposition of the foreign with the native culture within the model enables the native to commend and critique the foreign. Cultural theory enables communication.

Four powerful streams of British and French social thought converge to make grid-group analysis work as an interpretive tool.[10] These are represented by Emile Durkheim, E. E. Evans-Pritchard, Claude Levi-Strauss, and Basil Bernstein. Social realities have social origins (Durkheim). These social realities must be studied and explained from within their indigenous setting, and they can be interpreted only by provisionally suspending or containing social scientific observation (Evans-Pritchard). Social realities are the visible forms of the deep architecture or internal structures of culture (Levi-Strauss). These forms of culture are revealed in the way the individual interacts with the social pressures of society and are available for categorization in the context of these interactions (Bernstein).

Douglas shapes the confluence of these streams into a cultural theory that interprets social realities by placing them in a social context. Grid-group analysis results in a graphic social accounting of the choices individuals make. "Social accounting" is an important term. We will return to it later. For now, we want to understand this graphic depiction or "mapping." A two-dimensional grid map defined in a social accounting ethnographic method enables us to predict the typological "cosmology" of that society or social unit because there is a correlation between a grid-group mapping and cosmology. The correlation between the grid-group mapping and the cosmology of the social unit under study is relevant to New Testament interpretation because theology is a part or subdivision of the individual's cosmology.[11]

"Cosmology" is the old term for what today is studied under the label "physics."[12] This is both a field within the natural sciences and a field of philosophy. Cosmology is simply the way we understand our world to be put together—our understanding of the way all things work. Now, it becomes very complex and messy when we try to delve into manifest ideas and thoughts about the origins and meanings of the universe and to understand and interpret these cross-culturally. It becomes completely impossible when we attempt to have a conversation between ancient or primitive cultures and a highly developed technological culture concerning the beginning and purpose of all things. The dominant—technological—culture refuses to be vulnerable to the weak—"prelogical" or "prescientific"—culture.

Since we are interested in interpretation and cultural critique, we are primarily interested in the way cosmology, either primitive or sophisticated, interacts with the individual in preference formation. The grid-group model is interested in the side-effects of cosmology that are found in the way the individual explains or "justifies" his or her behavior. Grid-group intends to provide for our reflexive conversation across cultural boundaries.

In other words, it should be possible to observe a correlation between a social accounting of the transactions of an individual as he or she interacts with society and the theological assumptions from which he or she proceeds. Mapping Paul and the Pauline church according to the grid-group model provides a cultural context for a modern, western interpretation of theological concepts used by Paul and *therefore allows for a discussion of our own cultural bias.*

The way the individual makes sense of the myriad of transactions that make up life in society is to *justify* his or her actions with a pattern of beliefs and values. These beliefs and values may be described without reference to the cultural context, but they make sense to the individual only within his or her own context. This concern for context is roughly comparable to the concern in the historical–literary critical method to define the "situation-in-life" of the biblical text.[13] Grid-group analysis defines the cultural context of the individual by using observations of individual actions to map a context for the social unit or society under study. The cosmology or theology of the cultural unit is interpreted by reference to the correlation between this mapping and the patterns of values and beliefs that justify behavior.

The Connection between Sociology and Theology

The ethnographic and programmatic work Wayne Meeks[14] has done—and which was outlined in Chapter One—identifies the social context of Paul and Pauline theology. He begins with a question: "What are the connections between the central beliefs and symbols of a group or movement and its social context?"[15] He proposes to study this connection by describing the social status of the members of the "Pauline groups" and "calling attention to the possible social functions" of their belief in a crucified and resurrected messiah.[16] In other words, he examines the social status of the people he can identify in the Pauline church. He then studies the theology of the Pauline church as revealed in the letters of Paul. Finally, he relates these two by looking for the function that central beliefs might play in integrating the social situation of believers with their world. This program of interpretation requires that the researcher have some understanding of the way theological belief and social situation are related.[17] Meeks is looking for the sociological function of a system of belief.

Grid-group analysis answers Meeks's concern for a connection between social context and theology with a method for visualizing the effect of culture. The grid-group model proposes a definable correlation between Paul's theology and an accounting of the interactions that make up the cultural situation of Paul and the people in his churches. It does not, however, begin by looking at his theology. That is, it does not begin with a discussion of cosmology or even the side-effects of cosmology in the way an individual explains or justifies his or her decisions. Grid-group begins by observing behavior.

As required by the canons of functional analysis reviewed in the preceding chapter, the protocol for examining data is defined by the requirements of the ethnographic method. The data to be examined and the order of examination are defined by the method. In using the grid-group model to develop our ethnographic-exegetical method, we must first complete a social accounting of the behavior of the participants in the Pauline church. Only then may we correlate the function of theological images with Paul's social situation. But we are getting ahead of ourselves in discussing methods. First, we need to understand the model itself.

The Causal or Interactive Hypothesis

The hypothesis that there is a connection between social situation and theological principle is more exacting than, though roughly parallel to, the requirements of historical–literary criticism for describing a "situation-in-life." Historical-critical biblical study sifts through the cultural and literary context of a literary work to offer an intellectual "background" for the development of its thought.[18] Meeks and others propose a causal or interactive relationship between a social context and the theological principles that may be found in a literary work.[19] This social context exists not in the world of ideas, but in social and cultural categories, the ways in which people relate to each other and their environment.

Douglas, as a British cultural anthropologist, is critical of those who would limit research to theological categories without reference to sociological categories:

> Many scholars spend a life-time on the analysis of cognitive categories without attempting the harder task of relating them to social experience. They can justify their neglect of the latter by a belief that spiritual forces, the structures of the mind, move by their own autonomous principles to which the grosser social forms are either subject or irrelevant. But I would argue that only their withdrawal from the dust and hurly burly of heavy responsibility allows them to indulge in a philosophical attitude which separates spirit from matter, exalts the one and debases the other.[20]

The general claim of an interaction between social environment and theology is unavoidable. One thinks of the effect of the black plague on medieval theology or the effect of World War I on European liberal theology. Making that claim specific, however, is not easy. What is the exact relationship between attitude and environment? How are signs of culture—for example, philosophy and religion—affected by events? How can one determine the bias that culture contributes to the behavior patterns and beliefs exhibited by people in a society? Wayne Meeks points us to Mary Douglas for a discussion of this symbolic interactionist question.[21]

Observing Cultural Bias with the Grid-Group Model

In an unassuming monograph published two decades ago, Douglas proposes an elegant definition of the correlation between social environment and "cosmology."[22] She is concerned about the problems incurred by cultural anthropologists when research on one culture is limited by the use of a theoretical framework derived from another culture. There is, seemingly, no universal framework with which the results of the study of one culture may be used to understand another.

> Here to Cambridge many researchers come whose work in New Guinea suffers from this lack. For years they have been rumbling in complaint about the inadequacy of existing theoretical frameworks for interpreting this cultural region. Rebuking each other for taking over African models of

society they are clearly casting around for an interpretive scheme that will fit better to the Melanesian ethnography. But are the disconcerting forms of behaviour specific to Melanesia? It could be that a general theory is needed that will explain both the favoured African model and a Melanesian one, as well as some examples from Africa, North America and the Mediterranean, Asia and even from industrial society.[23]

Douglas wants to *construct*[24] a model for understanding human culture that seeks to reveal the interaction or relationship of the theoretical framework—the cosmology—of a culture and the observable patterns of behavior—the mapping—of the society itself. The context of her work on the "natural symbols" or "cosmology" of societies leads her to look for a correlation between the results of a "social accounting" of a culture and its "cosmology."[25] This correlation is the basis of an overall or general theory of culture that she proposes. This theory begins in the search for a systematic explanation for behavior. For example, the issue of the avoidance of dirt:

> As we know it, dirt is essentially disorder. There is no such thing as absolute dirt: it exists in the eye of the beholder. If we shun dirt, it is not because of craven fear, still less dread or holy terror. Nor do our ideas about disease account for the range of our behaviour in cleaning or avoiding dirt. Dirt offends against order. Eliminating it is not a negative movement, but a positive effort to organize the environment.[26]

Grid-group is the model Douglas proposes. It is not in itself reality. It is only one way of interpreting or understanding the reality of culture by the observation of the side-effects of culture. Douglas refers us to Basil Bernstein for the basis of her grid theory and to E. E. Evans-Pritchard for the standard of ethnographic writing.

We will find, in Chapter Eight, that adoption terminology serves to integrate ideologically the experience of the participants in the Pauline church. Paul uses the concept of adoption to offer a positive explanation of participation without supporting a strong social hierarchy. This is a functional description of the correlation of cosmology and behavior. When we interpret and understand this correlation, our own cultural patterns and biases are called into question.

Douglas seeks to observe universal principles in her study of cultural patterns in differing social and physical environments. This search has led her to emphasize the place of the individual in society.[27] She understands society to be the amalgamation of the behavior of individuals. There are two assumptions behind her work. The first assumption is that society is composed of interactive forces that at any moment may have achieved the state of equilibrium. They only appear to be static because they are in a state of equilibrium. In reality, however, they are dynamic forces in balance—in my language, a "tensile structure."[28] She says that any universal explanation of culture must attempt to plot these tensions as they exist at one moment in time. This is the reason for using the principles of accounting. The second assumption concerns an understanding of the individual's relationship to group process and social hierarchy. It proposes that, in a society a group (including a religious group) is made up of what we might call "consenting adults." In order for the group to work or have substance, there must be a collection of individuals who give over some of their identity and independence explicitly or implicitly to the group. This giving over is a social transaction. Many such transactions provide the basis for social accounting.

Aaron Wildavsky summarizes the key cultural issues. The individual—in his or her own behavior—answers two questions: "Who am I? (free to negotiate or bound by a group?) and What should I do? (follow detailed prescriptions that vary with role or decide for myself?)."[29] By literally counting—or at least estimating on the basis of observation—the number of times individuals choose to engage or not to engage in observable patterns of behavior within a specified period, we can do a social accounting. Through their behavior, individuals collectively make known their answers to the two questions of culture: "Who am I?" and "What should I do?"

Social Accounting

The grid-group model begins with the statement that *the side-effects of culture are visible in the sum total of the social transactions of individual participants*. This means that there is a story behind the way the individual makes choices and enters into the many transactions that constitute his or her life. This story is the key to understanding the reason for certain cultural behavior patterns. As Mary Douglas points out, "It consists of social action, a deposit from myriads of individual decisions made in the past, creating the cost-structure and the distribution of advantages which are the context of present day decisions."[30]

This story of the way an individual makes choices is a history of social action and the result of past decisions. The story of past choices makes itself felt both in the opportunities it makes available to the individual and in the constraints it places upon the individual's available options. The study of these myriad transactions is social accounting. The individual makes real decisions; culture is simply the sum total of these decisions. The side-effects of culture are visible in the social transactions that take place. Culture is not static; it is a dynamic system. Social accounting is a mechanism for studying the myriad transactions that make up lives of individuals. Social accounting is the key for making the grid-group model into an ethnographic method.

Douglas offers helpful contrasts with other ways of understanding human culture. Some anthropologists see culture as an entity in and of itself. For them, culture can be studied apart from the people and processes that bring it into being.[31] Structuralists would fall into this category.[32] Structuralists claim that culture's forms transcend environment. Douglas describes others as "deterministic."[33] They see the development of culture in the adoption of societal rules and explanations, for example, in the early development of the child. For these anthropologists, the development and change of culture is often described in Darwinian terms. The cultures we see are only those that have survived in differing habitats. In this view, the development of culture is the process of a society's adapting to the ecology of the environment in which it finds itself.

In the grid-group model, culture is revealed in the dynamic system of interactions between individuals. The individual is the primary element for describing culture. The individual actively makes real choices and adapts more or less successfully to the social situation as it presents itself. Consequently, understanding the way that individual operates in society is the key to understanding culture. Culture is a tensile structure made up of the myriad of interactions between individuals. In turn, this structure is the web of interactions that help determine future choices available to each individual.

If culture is the total of individual decisions made by the participants in that culture, then the essence of cultural anthropology is an "accounting" of those transactions. Social accounting is that method of study. It seeks to examine the actions of individuals—the results of individual deci-sions—not the explanations or justifications for those actions that the people in a group or society make. When grid-group becomes an ethno-graphic method, observations of social transactions are literally counted up according to categories of evidence hypothesized before formal obser-vations begin.

This theory of culture is neither culturally unbiased nor detached. The power of grid-group analysis comes from the fact that it is strongly at-tached to traditions of British social anthropology. This power is the ability to translate and interpret foreign belief and behavior patterns and bring them into conversation with our own. When E. E. Evans-Pritchard attempted to describe the "practical use" of anthropology, he offered more informed or enlightened colonial government. Cultural critique is the contemporary answer to this question of relevance. At this experi-mental moment in the human sciences, the motivation of biblical scholars is to find new ways to unpack or reveal the meaning of an ancient text *in order to inform our own preference selection.*

The Two-Dimensional Form of the Model

Understanding and interpreting the culture of a society is difficult be-cause culture is invisible. There is a seemingly endless array of variables or forms in which culture may appear and an even wider array of man-ifest statements of cosmology. In order to arrange these variables into a pattern that is useful for interpreting various aspects of culture, we con-struct a model, a paradigm, for measuring social organization.[34] We need a picture of culture that will permit comparison and interpretation. We need a heuristic tool.

One common method of interpreting a social situation in which there is contention or discord is to place the participants along a line relating them to each other. For example, the "proto-gnostic libertines" who are attacked in the paraenetic section of Paul's letter to the Galatians are frequently placed at an opposite point of a line continuing through Paul to the "arch-conservative Judaizers from Jerusalem." Opposing theologi-cal positions become the extreme pole positions, and everyone else exists somewhere along the line between. Paul is described as mediating be-tween these positions.[35] This kind of interpretation lends a visual perspective to the attitudes of the participants and makes them easier to understand and to "place." It is a single-dimensional heuristic classification of theological positions related to specific people within the early Christian movement. Its limitation is its inability to include other forces in the model.

Single-dimensional models for interpretation are quite appropriate in describing two-party conflicts. But as soon as there are three people involved and certainly when there are three distinct positions expressed, there is the logical possibility that the line will become a triangle.[36] Three positions can exist on a line, one the intermediary of the two extremes, but three positions can also be mutually exclusive. Geometrically, three points not on a line describe a plane. The surface of the plane is described with a map.

The two-dimensional model is a logical and ideal form. In theory, it has no gaps. Intuitively, one suspects that any possible position can be mapped in relation to every other. But society is complex and, for most social situations, not all alternatives may be accounted for in only two dimensions. Some have tried to extend the simple two-dimensional model to three and more dimensions using quite complex mathematical formulae to define the interrelationships of the myriad of individual decisions.[37] Quantifiability of more than four variables is a desirable goal. Still, the ability of the two-dimensional grid-group analysis map to assimilate large amounts of conflicting data for the human mind and assist in interpretation is quite appropriate as an end in itself.

The grid-group model—as proposed by Douglas—is a method for interpreting data developed by the social accounting of a cultural unit. It seeks to "map" the sociological position of a society (or a social unit within society) in order to predict the "cosmological"[38] presuppositions of that social unit or society. This map is two dimensional. The base dimension consists of a linear measure of the importance to the individual of participation in group process. The vertical dimension consists of a linear measure of the importance of hierarchical social structure to the individual in his or her interaction with others.

Grid-Group Analysis: A Definition

The model Douglas constructs for describing the social context of the individual in a culture and her or his correlate cosmology she calls "grid-group analysis." With this tool she seeks to describe the social context of the individual based on the behavior displayed by a collection of individuals within the social environment. The social environment of the individual transactions that make up the culture or group under study is graphically displayed on a two-dimensional map. This model is quite like the grid management approach to studying leadership style in business organizations.[39]

Grid-group analysis does *not* assume a cause-and-effect relationship between cosmology and social accounting of individual transactions. Rather, the word "correlation" is to be taken seriously; the two are interlocked. For example, the interlock of conceptions about the human body and social forms is simultaneous.[40]

Grid-group analysis treats the experiencing subject, the individual in society, as a subject choosing, an individual actively making choices every day. "It does not suppose that the choices are pre-determined, though costs may be high and some of the parameters may be fixed."[41] The model allows for the cumulative effect of individual choices on the social situation itself. The individual and the environment can interact, and either can move, because the environment is defined as consisting of all the other interacting individuals and their choices.

> The reason for focusing upon the social context defined in this way is that each pattern of rewards and punishments moulds the individual's behaviour. He will fail to make any sense of his surroundings unless he can find some principles to guide him to behave in the sanctioned ways and be used for judging others and justifying himself to others. This is a social-accounting approach to culture; it selects out of the total cultural field those beliefs and values which are derivable as justifications for action and which I regard as constituting an implicit cosmology.[42]

To summarize Douglas's statement, there is a correlation between an account of the social context of an individual and that individual's way of explaining the world, his or her "implicit cosmology." This correlation is important because it allows a researcher to come to an understanding of the relationship between the cosmology and the social accounting of a culture. Cosmology becomes predictable on the basis of empirical observation of the social context. For example: the concept of adoption found in the letters to the Romans and the Galatians is a part of Paul's way of explaining or justifying his participation in the Pauline church. Therefore, it is important to do a social accounting of the Pauline church to see the context of Paul's adoption language and imagery and to begin to allow a dialogue with our own justifications of behavior.

The social-accounting analogy places the individual at the center of the study of culture. It proposes that culture is a system of relationships built up through countless transactions. This theory sees culture as dynamic.[43] Mary Douglas's word is "plastic."[44] If culture appears static and more enduring than the individual, it is only because the system is temporarily in stasis. Stasis exists only in dynamic tension when all the forces of reward and punishment for specific behavior are in balance as accounted in individual choices. Stasis is fragile. The Pauline church faction exists in a social environment that is changing. New pressures from changes in the political environment of Judea as well as from changes in the make-up of the developing organization mean that the corresponding cosmology— revealed in the way Paul explains or justifies his behavior—is also in a process of change.

Grid-group analysis as an ethnographic method interprets anthropological data—that is, observations of patterns of behavior—so as to be able to predict the bias of the culture's cosmology. More specifically, grid-group analysis is an attempt to plot in two dimensions the social context of the individual in a society and to *predict* on the basis of that mapping the beliefs and principles that "justify" or measure the appropriateness of any action that individual may undertake. There is no systematic reason why any "cosmology" (Douglas's term for the complete system of principles and beliefs) should be stable or be generalizable to more than one individual except that the "tensile structure" (my term for the structure of society) makes it so. The relationship is *not* one of necessity or of cause and effect, but of interactive forces.[45] This means that cultural patterns and belief systems themselves may participate in the dynamic process of social pressures that affect individuals in society at each moment.

The Grid-Group Map

The results of an accounting of the dynamic process of social pressures, the visible patterns of behavior, are described in a two-way grid. The base line describes the individual's investment in the social life of groups.

This line quantifies the importance of membership in a group to the individual and the effect of group participation on decisions. The vertical line describes the extent of individual investment in ascribed status. This line quantifies the impact of differentiation between individuals because of rules, regulations, and taboos that affect the choices an individual makes.

Drawing a picture of, or "mapping," a social context for an individual makes graphic the fact that there is more than one dimension to a social context. Douglas constructs two scales on which the interactions of the individual may be measured. These are drawn at right angles to each other, making an array of positions available for the social context (see Figure 1).

The vertical scale, called the grid scale, reflects the "individuation" of the social context. The horizontal scale, called the group scale, reflects

Figure 1 The Grid-Group Map

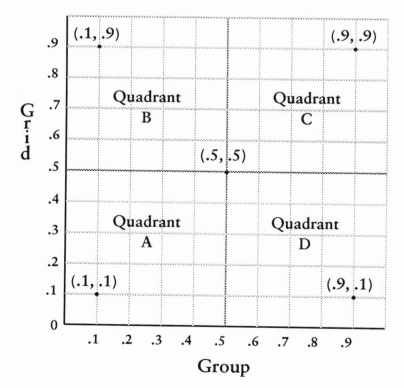

the degree of social incorporation. The grid scale measures the effect of social rules and classifications in the society. The group scale measures the claims that corporate groups make on their constituent members, their boundaries, rights, protections, levies, and constraints.[46] "Douglas holds that just two dimensions are enough to describe important variations of social context: one, the extent to which a person's social life depends on his membership in social groups (group) and two, the extent to which his social life is restricted by rules which pre-ordain his social relationships (grid)."[47]

Each of these scales represents several socially defined variables. These variables are observable in the behavior of individuals. They reveal cultural bias because they are the side-effects of culture. Each scale is made up of at least four "predicates" or measurable categories of social interactions between individuals. Each predicate represents the measurements of the frequency of or presence of at least two observable patterns of behavior. Grid-group analysis uses the word "polythetic" to describe this multivariant approach. For example: the presence of signs of participation in the holy kiss and signs of exclusion in the anathema offers evidence for inclusive and exclusive behavior, indicating the importance of group boundary to the Pauline church faction.

The group scale measures the extent to which people are bounded by the social unit under study.[48] Higher group scores result from longer time and greater frequency of interaction between individual members. It also results from more exclusive interaction between members with patterns of behavior that put boundaries around the group. These may function to keep outsiders out or insiders in.[49] Group is measured in the limited and technical sense of the diagram by the type of pressures that are exerted in face-to-face contact between members.[50] This makes the amount and extent of contact between participants an important measure of group strength.

No one can be invested in a group and not be concerned with its structure. The grid measure reflects not group structure, but rather individuation.[51] Movement on the grid scale measures progressive change in the mode of control exhibited in patterned behavior. Higher grid scores result from greater differentiation of roles for individuals within the social unit. It also results from classification of members according to social, racial, or economic considerations.

At the strong end, there are visible rules about space and time related to social roles; at the other end, near zero, the formal classifications fade, and finally vanish. . . .

Moving slowly down grid, the boundaries begin to be arbitraged. Individuals, deciding to transact across them, weaken the classifications. The mode of control changes its nature. It sinks below the surface. The substantive signs of ascribed status are scrapped, one by one, and supplanted by abstract principles. Of these, one is sacred still, that is the holiness of contract itself. As individuals are supposed to transact more and more freely, the rules governing transactions may even multiply. Society turns into a veritable market, and for every new kind of deal, further external effects transform the social structure.[52]

This grid-group map follows the work of Douglas. She says about this model for interpreting human culture:

It is a method of identifying cultural bias, of finding an array of beliefs locked together into relational patterns. The beliefs must be treated as part of the action, and not separated from it as in so many theories of social action. The action or social context, is placed on a two-dimensional map with moral judgments, excuses, complaints and shifts of interest reckoned as the spoken justifications by individuals of the action they feel required to take. As their subjective perception of the scene and its moral implications emanates from each of them individually, it constitutes a collective moral consciousness about man and his place in the universe. The interaction of individual subjects produces a public cosmology capable of being internalized in the consciousness of individuals, if they decide to accept and to stay with it.[53]

Grid-group analysis is simply a heuristic tool. It helps in understanding and interpreting the relationship between social action and belief system. "So this method of grid-group analysis is a tool for testing. It does not help the researcher to know what are the values and ideas that constitute the local culture, but it does help to be able to locate them in the appropriate part of the population. . . . It never tries to dive into the murky area of what is happening inside the psyche."[54]

The Four Typologies of Cultural Bias

Each quadrant of the grid-group map corresponds to a particular cultural bias. The explanations and justifications that individuals offer for their behavior are conditioned by this bias. According to Gross and Rayner, "the grid/group typology suggests that there are as few as four prototypical patterns of culture. Each consists of a characteristic behavioral pattern and an accompanying justificatory cosmology. Each cosmology extends, for example, to attitudes toward competition and cooperation, to concepts of good and evil in personal or community decision making, and to the organizational structure of families, businesses, and other institutions."[55] The four typologies are defined by the grid-group map: (1) Quadrant A: low grid, low group; (2) Quadrant B: high grid, low group; (3) Quadrant C: high grid, high group; and (4) Quadrant D: low grid, high group.

There is some confusion in New Testament circles as to the description of the typological cultural bias of each of these quadrants.[56] Until a standardization of these is worked out for New Testament research, this confusion will remain an impediment to the use of the grid-group model. The descriptions adopted in this study for the typologies of cultural bias in each quadrant as well as for the definition of grid and group are those used by Jonathan Gross and Steve Rayner.[57]

The Social Environment of Quadrant A. The social environment of Quadrant A is dominated by strongly competitive conditions between individuals.[58] Individuals contract with each other freely. This means that the social scale within the cultural unit is open to anyone to move, up or down. Each person is responsible for him or herself.[59] This is the entrepreneurial culture where rules for making contracts and specialists in each field of human endeavor abound. This is a stable social environment of competition and achievement.

The Social Environment of Quadrant B. The social environment of Quadrant B is dominated by insulation.[60] Social, economic, or social class classifications are rigid. Isolation in one category creates dependency on others. This is a strongly regulated environment in which exploitation by others from outside the social unit is probable.[61] This is the slave culture where control is arbitrary and comes from someone further down grid. We can expect social isolation and passive behavior because all social status is ascribed. This is an unstable social environment. It is stabilized by movement to group control as institutionalized by inclusion into a recognizable social caste system or deconstructed by revolution, with new roles achieved.

The Social Environment of Quadrant C. The social environment of Quadrant C is dominated by the large group.[62] The group justifies both its own existence and the strong classifications of individuals in roles in the group.[63] Mary Douglas describes it thus: "The uses of nature in moral justification are all-pervasive in the C group. Going against nature means a threat of failure, un-natural vice is condemned . . . this is the kind of social environment in which doctrines of atonement flourish and which can make sense of a full once-and-for-all historical incarnational theology."[64]

This is the corporate culture where large and stable organizations persist. Individuals understand their place and purpose in society in terms of the greater good of the society. Transactions with others can be traced both horizontally in symmetric role relationships within social levels and vertically in asymmetric role relationships. Specific tasks are reserved for special classes of participants. These are not achieved roles, but are ascribed to categories of status. The stability for the individual is the security of knowing his or her place within the social system and of having a purpose within the cosmos.

The Social Environment of Quadrant D. The social environment of Quadrant D is dominated by the small group.[65] The population is divided into those outside and those inside the group. There is an antithetical relationship between the two as group boundaries are defined. The leadership in this quadrant tends to be charismatic, with no plan for succession.[66] This is the sectarian culture where small and institutionally unstable groups respond to forms of charismatic leadership.

Distinctions between members of the small group are blended. Leadership classification or authority is an achieved status. Even though internal distinctions are limited, there is a clear boundary defining those who are participants and those who are not. Millennialist groups and cargo cults inhabit Quadrant D.

Ostrander's Interpretive Model

David Ostrander offers a succinct statement of the way a two-dimensional model for the study of culture is effective in discerning the relationship of a social mapping and religious and magical practices.[67] His study is a paradigm for interpreting grid-group analysis and the religious practice of a culture or group. He describes three levels of analysis for inferring the probable religious cosmology of various possible grid-group mappings. These are the dimensional, interactional, and emergent levels.

> The dimensional level indicates what aspects of a symbol system vary according to each dimension independently. The interactional level examines those symbolic elements which vary along a secondary dimension created by the covariance of the primary dimensions (i.e. the stable vs. unstable diagonals). The emergent level analyzes the cosmological configurations which arise from the combination of dimensional and interactional symbolic elements in each quadrant of grid-group space.[68]

Ostrander defines five statements concerning the symbolic order for each quadrant following dimensional and interactional descriptions of each quadrant. These can be distributed according to the pattern of the grid-group map (see Figure 2).[69]

Each combination of statements is reviewed comparatively. The dimensions and interactions of these statements provide a context for discerning the relationship of grid-group mapping and symbolic behavior and the side-effects of cosmology. Each combination is examined independently. This is the pattern we will use in Chapter Seven to interpret the results of our social accounting of Paul's church faction.

Dimensional Level

Notice that the group scale is defined by those with whom one interacts. Thus, the dimensional description matches the degree of identity of the individual with a specific group and proposes that the same degree of identity will exist in the way the individual views the society's relationship to nature. This is statement 1 in Figure 2. Statement 4 indicates the goals of symbolic action as they relate to the individual or to the group. This varies according to the level of identity with the group.[70]

Dimensional Level: Grid Scale

The grid scale is defined by the way one interacts with others in the society. The higher on the scale, the more likely there are to be con-

Figure 2 The Distribution of Beliefs and
Values on the Grid-Group Map

G
r
i
d

1. Society and nature
   separate
2. #1 negatively valued
3. Routinized symbolic
   action
4. Ego-oriented goals
   of action
5. Unelaborated
   symbolic system
 	
                    B
	1. Society part of nature
	2. #1 positively valued
	3. Routinized
	   symbolic action
	4. Group-oriented goals
	   of action
	5. Elaborated
	   symbolic system
	
	C

A
1. Society and nature
   separate
2. #1 positively valued
3. Personalized symbolic
   action
4. Ego-oriented goals
   of action
5. Elaborated
   symbolic system
	D
	1. Society part of nature
	2. #1 negatively valued
	3. Personlized symbolic
	   action
	4. Group-oriented goals
	   of action
	5. Unelaborated
	   symbolic system

Group

straints on individual options and social insulation of individuals. Symbolic action will parallel this pattern of constraint and social insulation in personal life. This is reflected in statement 3 in Figure 2.

Interactional Level

On an interactional level there are contrasts that may be described between complementary quadrants. The diagonals of the chart show these contrasts in statements numbered 2 and 5 (Figure 2). These categories vary conversely with the dimensional categories. The two diagonals are distinguished by their relative stability, by their attitude toward the social order, and by the manner and the degree of elaboration in their symbolic system. The more enduring the social structure, the more elaboration, the more that society or that group is seen as a part of the "natural order." The more integrated into the "natural order" the society or group is, the more stable it will be.

Emergent Level

The emergent level of analysis is more descriptive in style. It integrates the information found in the dimensional and interactional levels in a "cosmological configuration." A different typology of behavior and values exist for each quadrant. This typology is particularized in specific social settings. For example, adoption terminology used by Paul is a specific example of the particularization of the emergent typological cosmology within his historical social setting.

Conclusion

Grid-group analysis is a heuristic tool for the western interpreter. It is useful for revealing the consistent relationship—noticed by Durkheim—between "the structure of social organizations and the patterns of ideas and behavior that they sustain."[71] Grid-group analysis provides a mechanism by which cultural patterns may be compared. It uses only two polythetic or multivariant scales to measure the behavior of individuals to discern and map the way the cosmology of a social unit can be interpreted. The mathematical descriptions of these polythetic scales are the subject of the next chapter. For now, notice that there is not an infinite array of social options, but only four types of cultural possibilities particularized in specific social and historical environments.[72] This model results in an ethnographic method based on a social accounting of the repetitive behavior of individuals.

The concept of the fictive adoption of participants—found in Romans 8 and Galatians 4—is a part of the particular theological or cosmological description of the Pauline church. In order to find a social context for this adoption terminology, we will first do a social accounting of the Pauline church. Social accounting literally means an accounting of the observable behavior of those who participate in the Pauline church. Chapter Four makes grid-group analysis operational for New Testament research. It does this by providing an initial hypothesis from which an accounting of the observable behavior of the Pauline church may be made. Chapters Five and Six do that accounting. Chapter Seven uses the interpretive mechanism offered by David Ostrander to examine the particular historical expression that is the Pauline church faction. Chapter Eight uses this information to help in the interpretation of the concept of adoption and place it in its functional social context within the Pauline church faction and in relationship with our own patterns of preference.

4

A Working Hypothesis for a Social Accounting of the Pauline Church

Grid-group analysis is a tool for understanding the various forms human culture can take as it is observed by the ethnographer. The individual is the centerpiece of this ethnographic methodology. Initial observation of the choices a few individuals actually make—and inference of the aggregate of these for the whole cultural unit being studied—results in hypothetical categories for observing patterns of behavior. Clearly defining this hypothesis is critically important, for from it comes the ability to hear as well as to observe the cultural unit. This chapter describes this method and adapts it for use with the Pauline material.

Some will consider this chapter pretty dry going. Indeed, parts of this chapter are repetitive because accounting—even social accounting—is a repetitive science. Nevertheless, before we can do an ethnographic study of Paul's church faction, we must pay attention to the cultural theory under which we operate. Social accounting is the basis of the grid-group analysis as described in the preceding chapter. Social accounting is the process of observation for ethnography *within this model*.

Only after compiling an accounting of the social interactions of the participants of the Pauline church as they may be observed or inferred is it possible to describe Paul's social context. This social context is described in sociological terms. Theological concepts or symbolic behavior are interpreted within this sociological context after the social accounting is complete. This chapter makes grid-group analysis operational for New Testament study by (1) modifying the method to make it possible for a social historian to work with fragmentary evidence, and (2) providing a working hypothesis for the purpose of doing a social accounting of the Pauline church faction.

In order to interpret theological concepts sociologically, sociological categories must be used. This chapter provides a definition of those categories together with a means for evaluating the data and sorting it into categories of evidence. We cannot emphasize enough the importance of defining the categories of evidence in an initial hypothesis. The questions we bring to the data will determine our results. These questions must be carefully thought out and presented sequentially.

The promise of grid-group analysis is that we can identify an archetypal cosmology intelligible to a western European audience today that is nonetheless correlated to the social environment of the participants of the Pauline church faction. By comparing Paul's manifest theological statements to this archetype, we will be able to both test the model and better interpret his manifest theological statements. This is possible because the model claims that the cosmological presuppositions of a society or social unit are predictable on the basis of a social mapping provided by a grid-group analysis. By juxtaposing Paul's cosmology with our own, we will critique our own presuppositions, justifications, and explanations.

The selection of evidence, its type and form, and the categories into which the evidence is placed (the predicates of grid and group) are determined by the requirements for finding that social mapping. This is in accordance with the common language of ethnography—functionalism. In this chapter we accomplish this goal by providing a well-defined hypothesis. Defining this hypothesis—though it might seem repetitive and pedantic—is required for doing our social accounting in the following two chapters.

The sequence or priority is important. It is axiomatic in doing social history as in archeology that you will always find what you are looking for. If our hypothesis and method are not well and carefully described, then we will find only that which we already know and can readily perceive. In the field of Palestinian archeology, Kathleen Kenyon developed the stratigraphic method in order to provide a systematic means of categorizing evidence. Just so, social accounting is an ethnographic method—it provides a systematic means of categorizing data into evidence. Ethnography requires that we observe the foreign culture according to the canons of functionalism as we make claims about it and bring our own into conversation with it.

Social accounting literally means counting—according to preselected categories—the transactions individuals have with others within a specified time. In order to do this accounting, one must form a hypothesis that provides an initial series of categories for the evidence. The categories for ordering the evidence are defined on the basis of the method, not the appearance of the data to the ethnographer. This is accomplished by preparing a formal hypothesis with a preliminary awareness of the data. This chapter provides that working hypothesis for the Pauline church faction so that we may proceed with our social accounting in Chapters Five and Six.

The Types and Forms of Evidence Appropriate to a Social Accounting

In examining the letters of Paul, we want to observe those things the inhabitants of the Pauline churches actually did. That is, we want to observe their actions, especially their repeated actions. These transactions will reveal the externalities, the side-effects of individual decisions. We want to identify who these people were and how they were interconnected. In line with these concerns, we want to know about their social status. We want to know how the behavior they exhibited was different from other possible behaviors that were available to them but which they chose not to do. This will allow a social accounting of the Pauline church. Only then will we be able to examine the ways Paul explained or justified this behavior.[1] Before attempting theological descriptions, we must first prepare a *sheer description*[2] of the social mechanisms of the Pauline church.

"Sheer description" is a technical term that is used to identify the kind and type of data in which grid-group analysis is interested. It is derived from functional analysis and the work of Robert K. Merton, reviewed in Chapter Two. The term distinguishes Merton's categories from Clifford Geertz's term "thick description."[3] Ethnographic thick description attempts to put the *ideas* and *attitudes* of a subject social unit into sociological perspective. A dialogue is formed between cultures as the whole story of symbolic behavior and meaning is described, much as a novel unfolds. Sheer description, by way of contrast, attempts to put observable *behavior* into sociological perspective by describing repetitive, patterned, behavioral evidence according to a canon of observation. The reason we cannot do an ethnographic thick description of the Pauline church is that dialogue is impossible. The novel is written by the bias of the dominant culture when the interpreter works in the library or the office. Imposing a restrictive pattern of observation on the interpreter forces dialogue in the process of interpretation.

Our first task is to identify the kind of evidence that is appropriate to our study. The data in which we are interested are evidences of repetitive or patterned behavior found in the letters.[4] We must maintain an awareness of each category of evidence.[5] The problem of circularity—arguing from theological category to sociological and back to the theological—is avoidable if we clearly separate the categories of evidence. Theological statements must be distinguished from evidence of repetitive or patterned behavior. This is especially important when patterned behavior of the community must be inferred from manifestly theological statements in the letters.

The repetitive or patterned behaviors to which Paul most often refers in his letters are related to various rituals in the cultic practice of the Pauline church faction.[6] Wayne Meeks lists these: minor rituals, baptism, the Lord's supper, and unknown and controverted rituals.[7] These rituals are the forms in which the cultic expression of the Pauline church faction existed.

Other repetitive behaviors include the support offered to visiting charismatic leaders as well as the hospitality offered to Christians visiting from other places. Patterns of governance or organization are implied in the house church meeting form[8] and in the collection for the saints.[9] Authority in the churches of Paul, as revealed in the letters of Paul, is in a state of change. Conflicts produced by the process of the legitimization of authority are part of the group's patterned behavior.[10] The letters themselves are an "unwitting regularity" we are able to observe independently.[11]

We have evidence of patterns of exclusion from the faction in the anathema (Gal. 1:9; 1 Cor. 12:3, 16:22; Rom. 9:3) and patterns of inclusion in the holy kiss (1 Thess. 5:26, 1 Cor. 16:20, 2 Cor. 13:12, Rom. 16:16). These patterns of inclusion and exclusion are the means of identifying participation in the Pauline church faction.[12] These remains of patterned or repetitive behavior are precisely the type of evidence in which we are interested.

The letters of Paul are literary documents received in edited form. Paul is not concerned with a description of the behavior of the participants in the Pauline church, but rather with his reaction to that behavior. The sheer description required for functional analysis is not available to us from independent observers. However, we can infer some facts about the behavior of the Pauline church from Paul's reactions. That process requires careful separation of theological reflection from inferred behavior. From unwitting or inadvertent information in the letters, especially in greeting and postscript, we can identify with more confidence patterned behaviors of the Pauline church participants.

The EXACT Method

Jonathan L. Gross and Steve Rayner have defined a mathematical model for grid-group analysis of culture they call the EXACT model.[13] This is a mathematical definition of the grid-group model described by Mary Douglas. Grid and group, as they define the terms, require "quantifiable polythetic scales." These scales are "constructed in accordance with procedures commonly used for psychological test construction."[14] "Polythetic" is an adjective that refers to multiple variables within quantifiable or mathematically definable scales. I describe their work in terms suitable for historical and literary investigation in this next section. This description will achieve our first goal of modifying the method for use with New Testament data fields.

The EXACT method is a process for doing a social accounting. Social accounting is made possible by dividing the task into several "predicates" or partial definitions of the grid and group scales. Our modified version of this EXACT method is the process for doing our social accounting of the Pauline church faction that is used in the next two chapters.

The order of the presentation of data determines its usefulness and its impact as evidence. Grid-group analysis, and more explicitly the EXACT model, provides a basis for organizing the data.[15] EXACT is an acronym for the five parts of the mathematical model on which the method is based. E = the set of nonmembers who are eligible for admission to membership. X = the set of members of the unit. A = the set of activities in which members interact. C = the set of publicly recognized roles that members assume in the activities. T = a time span during which a typical distribution of activities occurs. The EXACT model is a mechanism for interpreting social networks.

Estimating the "Tendency"

The EXACT method begins with a definition of the process for gathering the data. Gross and Rayner recommend—as with other ethnographic procedures—that participant observation be the means of gathering the data for true EXACT modeling.[16] The participant observer evaluates and counts up the transactions each participant has with others within the time span alloted. This is obviously not possible when one is studying ancient factional groups. Even questionnaires, their second choice, are impossible. Our alternative is to analyze the *tendency* of the formula or, in statistical terms, to make an estimation of the likelihood[17] for each variable of grid and group as it relates to the EXACT model through inferential observation of literary and archeological remains.

The data on the behavior of the participants of the Pauline church are incomplete. The purpose of estimating the tendency of each variable is to make useful decisions on the basis of incomplete data. We are looking for clues to the mapping of the Pauline church. Although this method is not precise, it yields verifiable results. We are interested in determining the relative strength of each predicate of grid and of group, not an interval measure.[18] Examination of the polythetic formula for each predicate of grid and group will enable a *decision rule* to be determined for each variable. This *decision rule* allows for an "estimation of the parameters corresponding to each set of observed sample values."[19]

In simplest terms, statements or definitions of several aspects of grid and of group are devised. Each of these is called a predicate statement and is cast in mathematical terms. A range of values are then determined for each variable in the formula for each predicate of grid and group. Plugging in the lowest and the highest observed or inferred values results in a likely range for each predicate. These ranges are compared to produce a likely mapping for the Pauline church faction. This mapping is cast in terms of a range, not a specific point.

Because we have only the letters of Paul from which we may glean primary observations of the behavior of the participants of the Pauline church, the sample observations are neither random nor unbiased. We will not find the exact estimator with the greatest likelihood. We are sifting the evidence for the extremes of the range of variability. This process results in a statement of the range or "tendency" of each predicate of grid and group.

The EXACT Graph

The EXACT graph of a social unit or a social network attempts to describe in a two-dimensional picture the interactions of those who are selected for research. Drawing it is a preliminary step to working with the EXACT model. "The set X corresponds to the established sociological concept of an interactive social network, which can be represented as a labeled graph. Two individuals xi and xj are linked by a line if there exists an activity ak in which they interact."[20]

The EXACT graph simply plots one point for each person identified within the social network or social unit under study. The placement of the points on the graph is determined by a "best fit" process. The observed interactions between the individuals are recorded as connecting lines between the graphed points. "Interactions in the social unit are expressed by the EXACT graph. For each member xi of the unit there is a point labeled xi. For every pair of members xj and xk who interact in activity ai, there is a line labeled ai with endpoints xj and xk."[21]

More elaborate versions of the EXACT graph might include sophisticated weighting and hierarchical directional notations. Any graph of the Pauline church, however, is based on incomplete data. The basic notation of "connectedness" between points is all that can be interpolated. The "best fit" for the Pauline church puts Paul in the center, those connected to him in mission to more than one local church around him, and the distribution of the local churches on the perimeter, schematically representing their geographic distribution. In the EXACT graph presented in Chapter Five, the several lines of "connectedness" between local churches and Paul and those around him are reduced to one representative line, for the sake of clarity.

Our Working Hypothesis

The process of forming a working hypothesis is used to adjust grid-group analysis to the limitations we face when considering the Pauline church faction. Each predicate of grid and group is a proxy for measuring one aspect or indicator of the strength of grid or group. We cannot measure culture directly. Therefore, we examine the side-effects of culture in the decisions people make to find the bias of culture revealed in their cumulative decisions.

A working hypothesis cast in mathematical terms for the predicates of group and grid as they apply to the Pauline church is formed first.[22] Not all of the predicates formed by Gross and Rayner are useful for the study of historical situations.[23] The predicates of group they identify are *Proximity, Transitivity, Frequency, Scope,* and *Impermeability.* Each of these measures specific aspects of group involvement; they are proxies for the measurement of the importance of group participation to the individual. Gross and Rayner define predicates of grid as *Specialization, Asymmetry, Entitlement,* and *Accountability.* Each of these are proxies intended to measure the influence of specific aspects of hierarchical social categories. Each of these predicates is premised on participant observation as the basis for ethnography. They must be adapted for use with historical and literary materials. We will take these proposed predicates in sequence and propose an alternative predicate for each.

Working hypotheses for each of the predicates of group and of grid measure are formed according to preliminary observations of the social situation being studied. The social science mechanisms by which Gross and Rayner form their hypotheses are not available to the social historian. In the following pages the group and grid predicates are translated into usable form for New Testament study.

Measures of Investment in Group

Proximity

Proximity is a measure of the degree of contact the participants have with each other, their "closeness."[24] The letters of Paul offer information about specific participants in the Pauline church in the greetings and inadvertent information disclosed in various references to individuals.[25] It is possible to draw an EXACT graph of those about whom we hear and interpolate the kinds of contacts others would have had. In this way, the range of dyadic (two-person) relationships within the whole Pauline church will be inferred.

For example, in a small group that meets and shares meals together regularly, it is likely that within a reasonable time each member has direct contact with every other member of the group. The proximity score would be one. Every member has at least one direct transaction with every other member of the group within the specified time.

The mathematical formula for finding the proximity score for the entire Pauline church is the average of the proximity scores for individual participants:

$$\text{prox}(X) = \frac{Xa1 + Xa2 + Xa3 + Xa4 + Xa5 \ldots + Xan,}{n}$$

where "Xa" equals the average distance proximity score for an individual member.

The average distance proximity score for an individual is calculated by adding the total dyadic links required for that person to interact with any other member of the social unit. This total is then divided by the total number of members of the group less 1. There is no simple way to calculate the dyadic links between individuals; they must be observed. These dyadic links are visible on an EXACT graph.

Calculating the individual average proximity score is impossible for each participant in the Pauline church. But it should be possible to find the tendency based upon an EXACT graph of the Pauline church interpolated from the people mentioned by Paul in his letters, and by inferring the dyadic relationships between the participants in the local church setting. The range of variability is quite high, however, because of the highly inferential nature of the EXACT graph itself. We begin with the experience of the local church factions and examine the effects of the geographic distribution of those churches and their apostolic leadership. An estimate of the tendency of proximity is based on the patterns found.

Transitivity

Transitivity is a measure of the degree to which the contact between members of a social unit is reflected in relationships with other members of the group.[26] An EXACT graph of the relationships found by inter-polating the dyadic and triadic relationships found among those mentioned in Paul's letters is useful in determining this category. But because the people most often mentioned in Paul's letters are those who have contact with more than one local church, the interpolation of the participants in the local church setting is also required.

The mathematical formula as defined by Gross and Rayner for finding the transitivity score for an individual is

$$\text{trans}(Xti) = \frac{\text{the no. of complete threesomes that contain Xi}}{\text{the no. of connected threesomes that contain Xi}}.$$

Transitivity exists when one can infer the existence of a relationship between two individuals because of their common relationship to a third individual in the group. The formula for finding the transitivity score of the entire Pauline church is found by averaging the individual transitivity scores:

$$\text{trans}(X) = \frac{Xt1 + Xt2 + Xt3 + Xt4 + Xt5 \dots + Xtn,}{n}$$

where "Xt" equals the transitivity score for each individual.

Again, as with the individual proximity score, calculation of the individual transitivity score presupposes participant observers. Such observation of each triadic relationship of the participants of the Pauline church is not possible. Still, it should be possible to find the tendency of transitivity based upon an EXACT graph of the Pauline church interpolated from the people mentioned by Paul in his letters and by inferring the triadic relationships among the participants in the local church setting. Again, we would expect the range of transitivity to be quite wide to account for the strongly inferential nature of the evidence. An estimation of the experience of the local church faction is the starting point. The effects of geographic distribution of local churches and the apostolic leadership is used to estimate the tendency of transitivity.

Frequency

Frequency is a measure of the relationship between the allocable time available to each member of the social unit and the proportion that is actually spent in activities associated with the social unit.[27] How does the participant choose to allocate time? This predicate is impossible to determine for the participants of the Pauline church. Even the tendency of frequency cannot be inferred from Paul's letters.

Time, in this case, is used as a proxy for the deferential allocation of limited resources by participants. Another measure of the allocation of limited resources by participants in a group in relationship to other potential allocations is to discern the relative deferential participation or nondeferential participation of identifiable individuals in the Pauline church. This new predicate is also a proxy for the group predicate scope and will be described after a discussion of scope.

Scope

Scope is a measure of the proportion of activities associated with the social unit in which each participant engages in relation to the total number of activities available to them outside the social unit.[28] Scope is another measure of the ways participants allocate the limited resources available to them. Whereas frequency measures this allocation in terms of time, scope measures the choice concerning the allocation of limited resources in terms of the overall activity level of the individual. This is impossible to measure for the same reasons we cannot measure frequency. Participant observation is not available; we simply do not know about the activity level of Pauline Christians outside of the faction. Although some inferences can be made, even an estimate of the tendency of scope is unattainable.

Deferential Involvement

Because of the difficulty of finding the tendency of the group predicates frequency and scope, substitutes for these proxies of group strength are required. These two predicates use the allocation time and relative activity level to measure investment in group. Estimating the commonality of participant experience enables us to measure one side-effect of the allocation of limited resources.

The question is, insofar as we have evidence, did the participants enter the Pauline church faction through their own choice or because of outside pressure or status: for example, kinship, *ordo,* or social role? Also, we want to know if continued participation is supported or not supported by the whole of society. Are there signs of group identification in members' participation in the Pauline church faction?

The difficulty is that in the case of high grid, low group, the appearance of participation and group investment may exist because of strictures on activity coming from elsewhere in the society. In the case of low group, low grid, participation may appear to exist because of the formation of mutually beneficial contracts or cartels between entrepreneurs. Therefore, two measures are required to test for deferential group involvement: one to identify signs of participation, and another to check for a false positive result. The task is to measure the side-effects of the allocation of limited resources by individuals. This group predicate has its own two-part polythetic scale made up of independent tests for deference and for commonality. Deferential involvement is described first, then commonality; then the two are combined in terms of the mathematical model.

The Deferential Involvement Deference Score. The first part of this two-part predicate is called the *deference* score. It is expressed mathematically for the whole social unit as the unweighted average of two ratios. The first is that proportion of members who freely choose to participate relative to the total membership. The second is the number of members who experience some form of persecution from outside the group or onerous cost of membership from inside the group solely because of their group membership, that number proportionally to the total number of group members. Mathematically, this is described:

$$\frac{\text{members who}}{\text{total membership}} + \frac{\text{members who experience}}{\text{total membership}} = 2 \text{ (Deference)}.$$

Some interpolation of the situation of the Pauline church is required to determine values for this predicate, but this is possible because this predicate is measured unit-wide. A different form of decision rule is used in determining deferential involvement than is used with either group proximity or transitivity. The question is the extent to which participants offer evidence of deference to group concerns in their participation in the Pauline church faction. An estimation of the tendency of the choice participants had in initiating their involvement and an estimation of the tendency of the choice in continued participation are averaged to find the deference score.

The Deferential Involvement Commonality of Experience Score. A correlative of this measure of deference as it applies to scope is suggested by Gross and Rayner. They identify "commonality of experience" as a particular subset of special activities perceived as identifying a group.[29] The presence of such activities as would define a commonality of experience for the Pauline church adds weight to the deferential involvement score and tests for a false positive result.

Shared experience of members is a proxy for group investment. The primary points of shared experience in a group are: (1) a common beginning or entrance (similarity of experience or initiation); (2) a common social background (similarity of social or economic class); (3) a distinctive creation or ritual myth (shared primal story); (4) a distinctive group ritual (corporate signs of inclusion); (5) distinctive signs of participation (common language, purpose, goals).

The presence of these five factors acts as a test for commonality of experience. It is impossible to score these five categories of commonality as continuous scales because there is no available participant observer. Each of these points of shared experience can be scored as present, not present, or ambiguous if the evidence is not conclusive. If there is no evidence available, the category must be left out.

The form of this decision rule is based on the question of presence. Evidence for presence scores a 1. If there is evidence for the lack of presence (not simply silence), the category scores a 0. If there is evidence both for and against presence the score is .5. The results of these five tests for commonality are combined and divided by the number of tests applied to find an estimate of the tendency for commonality score for the whole social unit.

$$\text{Commonality} = \frac{C1 + C2 + C3 \ldots + Cn}{n},$$

where "Cn" = the results of the test for commonality in one category.

Measuring Deferential Involvement. Two tests, one for deference and the other for commonality, result in two scores that are combined to find the deferential involvement score. Because both scores require some interpolation of the evidence for the whole of the Pauline church, they can be added together and averaged directly to estimate the tendency of deferential involvement. Although the expected scoring range is wide, the combination of predicates acts as a filter for false positive results in low group environments.

$$\text{Deferential involvement} = \frac{(\text{deference} + \text{commonality})}{2}.$$

Impermeability and the Boundary Score

Impermeability is a measure of the likelihood of any eligible nonmember's attaining membership in the social group under study.[30] This is expressed in a ratio of permeability, the proportion of eligible nonmembers who actually do join. The mathematical complement of this ratio is the impermeability score. We do not have information about the numbers of those eligible to join who may have been, for whatever reason, rejected by local house church clusters.

From Paul's discussion concerning impermeability in the letter to the Galatians, it might be supposed that anyone who expressed an interest in the Pauline church faction would be included. This level of inclusivity is impossible to demonstrate, but, if true, the impermeability score would be 0 because the set of eligible nonmembers would be empty. Without information about individuals who were not baptized, however, an estimate of the tendency of impermeability is not possible. Paul's letters provide no source material in this matter because they were addressed to participants, not nonparticipants.

The intent of the impermeability score is to measure the strength of the boundary of the social unit. Access to participation in each of the Pauline churches is difficult to measure, but other tests for the strength of group boundary are available. The concern for purity expressed in various sanctions for breaking taboos is one example of boundary markers, as are the frequency of "in-house" jargon and the use of we-they metaphors.[31] The presence of boundary markers, entrance rituals, and signs of exclusion and inclusion are signals of boundary. Expressing these possible predicates in measurable mathematical terms is difficult. The most useful method of expressing this predicate is, again, to combine evidences. These will demonstrate the tendency of the Pauline church on a relative scale without interval measure. As with the predicate deferential involvement, this predicate will be made up of its own polythetic scale. It is called the boundary score.

> While the initial problem is posed by the difference between "our" kind of thinking and "theirs," it is a mistake to treat "us" the moderns and "them" the ancients as utterly different. We can only approach primitive mentality through introspection and understanding of our own mentality. . . . To solve the puzzle of sacred contagion we can start with more familiar ideas about secular contagion and defilement. In English-speaking cultures, the key word is the ancient, primitive, and still current "dirt." Lord Chesterfield defined dirt as matter out of place. This implies only two conditions, a set of ordered relations and a contravention of that order. Thus the idea of dirt implies a structure of idea. For us dirt is a kind of compendium category for all events which blur, smudge, contradict, or otherwise confuse accepted classifications. The underlying feeling is that a system of values which is habitually expressing a given arrangement of things has been violated.[32]

The structure of ideas implied in the identity of that which is dirt in a society is made objective in the way we recoil from or clean up the disorder around us. Disorder or dirt is associated with different behaviors on each end of each scale. We shall use the idea of purity in a specific way that identifies various behaviors on the group scale. For our purpose, a concern for the purity is not a concern for a hierarchy among the participants, but a concern about the boundaries of the group. Purity and the perception of danger in taboos are markers for group separation from the rest of the world, which is perceived as impure.[33]

The signs of a concern for this scale related to purity are sanctions against behaviors that do not involve the performance of roles but, rather, participation in the group itself. These can take the form of coercive sanctions: the threat of expulsion, death, or physical abuse, and the like from the group; or noncoercive sanctions: the interpretation of misfortune or sickness in the group as a result of impurity on the part of the participant.[34]

The division of experience into that which precedes and that which follows membership initiation is an indication of this group concern for purity. The baptismal rite is not a ritual washing to return the believer to a preexisting state of purity.[35] "Rites of passage are not purificatory but are prophylactic. They do not redefine and restore a lost former status or purity from the effect of contamination, but they define entrance to a new status. In this way the permanence and value of the classifications embracing all sections of society are emphasized."[36] To measure the importance of initiatory rites, we must look at their side-effects, their "externalities."[37] These include ritual patterns of separation in the rite itself as well as reminders of the separation in controls on interaction with "pollutants" outside the group.

Remaining pure while in the group is the continuing problem. Mary Douglas points out: "It seems that physiological pollutions become important as symbolic expressions of other undesirable contacts which would have repercussions on the structure of social or cosmological ideas."[38] The markers of pollution are controls, expressed as sanctions, on behavior. These are not the same as controls on, or better accountability for, the performance of specific roles related to the group. The violation of these controls related to pollution is a great concern of the group, not just for superiors who are concerned with performance of roles assigned by the group. Consequently, the awareness and use of such sanctions should be an identifiable category or predicate of the group dimension.

We do not have access to independent observations concerning the use of controls in the Pauline churches, but we do have Paul's own recommendations for controls. These recommendations may be used to test for the presence of sanctions related to a concern for purity. A sum of the tests for the presence of these categories will be used to measure the concern for boundary.

The polythetic mathematical description of the boundary score is made up of three concerns: (1) the universality of the entrance ritual; (2) the universality of concern for purity (expressed in sanctions and purification rites); (3) the universality of sanctions against association with outsiders or outside groups.

The boundary score is expressed as an average for these categories for the entire Pauline church as discovered in the letters of Paul. We determine boundary by testing for the presence of five factors: (1) an entrance ritual; (2) sanctions against interaction with outsiders and outside groups; (3) controls on behavior exercised in the name of the group; (4) concern about ritual pollution incurred for the group; (5) members who gain their life support from or through the group.

It is impossible to score these five categories of boundary as continuous scales because we cannot intimately observe the behavior of the Pauline church. They can, however, be scored as present, not present insofar as we know, or as ambiguous if the evidence is contradictory. Each of the five categories functions as a test for boundary. If there is evidence for presence, the category scores a 1. If there is evidence for the lack of presence, the score is 0. If the evidence is ambiguous, with some presence and some nonpresence, the score is .5. If there is no evidence, the category is eliminated from the discussion.

The results of these five tests are combined and divided by the number of tests applied to find the average boundary score (Xt) of the group.

$$\text{Boundary } (Xt) = \frac{T1 + T2 + T3 \ldots + Tn}{n},$$

where "(Tn)" = the result of the test in one category.

Predicates for Measuring Group: Summary

The predicates for measuring group in the Pauline church are (1) proximity, (2) transitivity, (3) deferential involvement, and (4) boundary. These predicates are all positively valued for group scoring. The group score is an unweighted average of these predicates. Together they are the working hypothesis on which a social accounting of the Pauline church will be done in Chapter Five.

Measures of Investment in Grid

The measures of grid are formulated into four predicates by Gross and Rayner.[39] These also require translation into usable categories for the historian. The following sections translate these grid predicates into usable form. Each grid predicate described by Gross and Rayner uses role distribution and measures of symmetry as proxies for measuring the amount of influence that publicly acknowledged categorical distinctions have in the choices an individual makes. The unit of time during which exchanges take place is defined by the social unit under study. For our purpose, time is always the duration of Paul's active ministry.

The measures of grid that are adapted for use in studying the Pauline church are those defined by Gross and Rayner. Role distribution and measures of symmetry in role transactions are translated into tests for the presence of supporting social structures for role specialization and of asymmetry in role transactions. Other measures of grid exist. For example, the grid predicate "information transmission" is described by Mary Douglas and Jonathan Gross in a series of articles.[40] Each predicate of grid, however, needs to be redefined in order to be measurable. To keep definitions clear, I have given the predicates with new definitions new names.

Specialization

Specialization is a grid measure of the distribution (expressed as the mathematical complement of a ratio) of available roles among the members of the social unit.[41] It is the opposite of role diversification.[42] This predicate is intended to measure the "narrowness" or "broadness" of the diversification among the members of the responsibility for accomplishing the tasks demanded by the social unit.

The mathematical model for specialization for a member of a group under study is

$$\text{spec}(Xi) = 1 - \frac{\text{the number of roles (Xi)}}{\text{(C)}},$$

where "(Xi)" is the individual participant and "(C)" is the total number of roles available within the Pauline church. (We subtract the ratio from 1 to find its complement.)

This formula compares the total number of roles available to the number of roles actually taken on by a participant in a specific period of time. It is reasoned that the more insulated the individual is, the fewer the number of roles the participant will choose relative to the total available to all members of the group. The ratio of the number of roles a participant is observed to have undertaken to the total number of roles available within a given time frame is the complement of specialization. Therefore, this ratio is subtracted from 1 to produce the specialization score for an individual. Specialization for the group is defined as the combined average for all members of the Pauline church faction.

$$\text{Spec}(X) = \frac{X1 + X2 + X3 \ldots + Xn}{n}.$$

Again, since we do not have an independent observer available to report to us, it is impossible to quantify this predicate. Paul's reporting of roles does not permit a social accounting based on observations or even interpolations of role diversification among members.

Role Differentiation

An alternative mechanism to measure the diversification of role is to test for the presence of recognized, permanent, authoritative, commissioned, legitimate, paid offices in the Pauline church faction.[43] If these exist and to the extent that they exist, we may assume the presence of role specialization in the faction and a consequent insulation of participants. This new grid predicate is called "role differentiation" to distinguish it from specialization.

The place of individuals in the social network can be identified by the various role functions they fill.[44] The greater the definition of the individual task, the greater is the insulation from insecurity in its accomplishment. Defined role functions are thus indicators of grid in that they both empower the individual with authority and limit the choices available with responsibility. Authority and responsibility are measured in categories of control.[45] Role differentiation is measured in categories of insulation.[46]

The side-effects of insulation are revealed in categories of behavior that support the classifying of individuals in society. One way to determine the concern for identifying place and role for individuals in society is to test for the presence of a network of commonly recognized social functions that are accomplished by commissioned individuals. The presence of a network of these role functions is signaled if (1) there are commonly identified or recognized titles for social functions; (2) these functions have an order, a rank; and (3) there are individuals who are commissioned to fulfill specific roles. "All that is necessary for our measurements is that status differentiation be recognized and practiced within the social unit, in the case of high grid, or be deliberately denied by it as in the case of low-grid sects."[47]

The test for grid role differentiation is made up of five parts that test for the presence of (1) titled offices distinct from social functions; (2) task descriptions; (3) role-based sanctions on behavior; (4) a hierarchy of organization; (5) individuals commissioned to accomplish the tasks described.

These five categories are not scored as continuous scales. They are scored as either present, not present insofar as we know, or contradictory. Each of the five categories functions as a test for role differentiation if it is found that these social functions are present. If there is evidence for the presence of a social function, the predicate test scores a 1. If there is evidence for the lack of the exercise of authority, the score is 0. If the evidence is ambiguous, with some evidence on either side, the score is .5. If there is no evidence, the category is eliminated from the discussion.

The results of these five tests are combined and divided by the number of tests applied to find the role differentiation score. Of course, if there is no evidence for the presence of social functions, the score for role differentiation is 0.

$$\text{Role differentiation} = \frac{T1 + T2 + T3 \ldots + Tn}{n},$$

where "(Tn)" = the result of the test in one category. Role differentiation is positively valued for grid.

Asymmetry

Asymmetry describes the exchange of roles among members by connected pairs of participants.[48] The issue here is not the distribution of roles, but the exchange of roles between specific pairs of members of the social unit who have role-based contact with each other. The more asymmetrical relationships that exist, the more hierarchical is the organization, even if roles are widely distributed among clusters of participants. For the whole social unit this is expressed as an average of all member asymmetry scores.

The mathematical relationship that defines asymmetry for each participant (X) is

$$\frac{\text{the sum of asymmetrical relationships (X) has}}{\text{the total number of relationships (X) has}}.$$

There is a relationship between group proximity and asymmetry. In the case where the group proximity is low, even a few asymmetrical relationships force the asymmetry score up. In the case where the group proximity is high, many asymmetrical relationships are required to drive up asymmetry. The mere presence of asymmetrical relationships does not itself indicate a high asymmetry score.[49]

The interpolation of EXACT graph relationships is useful for estimating the tendency of group proximity. However, this does not tell us about the quality of those relationships nor about their symmetry or asymmetry. In the Pauline churches there are no independent observations of the exchange of roles among members. The intention behind measuring role-exchange asymmetry is to test whether the score for specialization applies to all members. That is, to what extent do categories of role-based social hierarchy affect the choices available to a participant in the social unit under study? This is the question of authority. How much does deference to legitimated or institutionalized authority affect the choices made by the individual?

Authority

High group environments are stabilized by an unequal distribution of power among individuals within the social unit. There is a natural movement of social groups up grid toward a more stable organization or down group with the breakdown of group investment.[50] In a high group environment, movement up grid is the process of institutionalization;

movement down group is the process of denominationalism or factionalism.[51] Highly differentiated low group environments are similarly
unstable. There is a natural movement down grid toward individual autonomy or the development of societal support for authority in increased
investment in group. Although authority itself is an elusive social quality
to trace, its side-effects in these movements should be visible.

In the case of the grid predicate authority, we are interested in observing the extent to which the Pauline church has institutionalized authority.
How much control does the individual exhibit?[52] Control of others in an
environment of high group investment implies responsibility that in turn
limits individual choice. In low group environments it implies a class of
autonomous individuals who successfully limit the choices others, further
up grid, can make. Bengt Holmberg follows Annie Jaubert in using the
term "dialectical authority" to describe asymmetric relationships of
mutual dependence in the Pauline church faction.[53] The asymmetric
relationships implied within the Pauline church create a web of role-
based interactions. Tracking authority in this complex environment requires inferring this web of interactions from what we read in Paul's
letters.

The side-effects of authority are revealed in categories of behavior that
support legitimated authority[54] or the control of others. These are (1) a
hierarchical social mechanism for conflict resolution; (2) a system by
which role expectation is communicated; (3) individuals who exercise
authority in the social system.

Tests of the categories of the grid predicate authority look for evidence
of the presence of: (1) a system to resolve conflicts between individuals;
(2) a system of offices within the faction; (3) ambiguity in the requirements of individual responsibility (revealed in behavior and negatively
valued for grid); (4) conflict over leadership (revealed in behavior and
negatively valued for grid); (5) specific leaders with legal or rational legitimated authority.

As with the group predicate boundary, these five tests cannot be scored
as continuous scales because we cannot closely observe the behavior of
the Pauline church. They may, however, be scored as present, not present
insofar as we know, or ambiguous. Each of the five categories functions
as a test for legitimate authority. If there is evidence for presence, the
category scores a 1. If there is evidence for the lack of presence, the score
is 0. If the evidence is ambiguous, with some presence and some nonpres-

ence, the score is .5. If there is no evidence, the category is eliminated from the discussion. Silence, in and of itself, is not evidence. In the case of negatively valued tests, the score is subtracted from 1 before averaging to find their mathematical complement.

The results of these five tests are combined and divided by the number of tests applied to find the average authority score (At) of the Pauline church. The third and fourth tests, (T3) and (T4), are both negatively valued and must be subtracted from 1 if they are valid (that is, there is evidence one way or another or the evidence is ambiguous).

$$\text{Authority} = \frac{T1 + T2 + (1 - T3) \ldots Tn}{n},$$

where "(Tn)" = the result of the test in one category. Authority is positively valued for grid.

Entitlement

Entitlement quantifies the distinction between achieved roles and ascribed roles.[55] Categories of status within the social unit under study may be internal (years of service or kinship) or external to the group (wealth or social standing). Those roles that are not available to the whole membership on the basis of competititon are ascribed roles. Those roles to which any member of the group can aspire are achieved roles. As the proportion of ascribed roles increases, the entitlement score increases, demonstrating increased classification among the membership.

The mathematical formula for finding the entitlement score for each member (Xi) is

$$\text{entitlement (Xi)} = \frac{\text{the number of ascribed roles (Xi)}}{\text{the number of roles (Xi)}}.$$

Entitlement is the average of the individual entitlement scores for the whole group.

$$\text{Entitlement(X)} = \frac{E1 + E2 + E3 \ldots En}{n},$$

where "En" is the entitlement score for an individual in the faction.

As with the other role-based predicates of grid, an accounting of ascribed roles for individuals in the Pauline church faction is not available. The predicate entitlement measures the ratio of ascribed roles to the total number of roles an individual assumes. The mathematical complement of this ratio is the proportion of achieved roles the individual assumes. The presence of achieved roles signals competition for these roles on the part of individuals. The lack of achieved roles is a side-effect of high entitlement. This is the question of individual initiative. Are there social supports for individual initiative in the form of roles that reward successful competition among participants? Competition is a sign of decreasing grid strength.[56]

Initiative

Competition, along with autonomy and individual control, are signs of decreasing grid strength.[57] One side-effect of competition is a social system of rewards for successful competition among participants. This social support system for competition is signaled by the presence of achieved roles and by the presence of negotiated relationships. It is also signaled by the presence of insecurity.[58] Insecurity in one's status provides the invisible social control that keeps the individual striving for gain. In this way, initiative is the side-effect of competition.

The indicators of the grid predicate initiative are: (1) achieved roles, (2) insecurity, and (3) negotiated relationships.

The test for grid initiative is made up of five parts, evidence of the presence of:[59] (1) conflict over the individual status or rights of participants; (2) negotiated settlements for disputes between participants; (3) ascribed roles (negatively valued for grid initiative); (4) individuals who make a personal sacrifice to work for the group (in the presence of high group investment), themselves (in the presence of low group investment), or both; (5) conflict over negotiated rules for competing individuals.

As with the group predicate boundary, these tests cannot be scored as a continuous scale because we cannot closely observe the behavior of people related to the Pauline church. These tests may, however, be scored as either present, not present insofar as we know, or ambiguous. Each of the five categories functions as a test for initiative. If there is evidence for presence, the category scores a 1. If there is evidence for the lack of presence, the score is 0. If the evidence is ambiguous, with some presence and some nonpresence, the score is .5. The value of these scores is subtracted from 1 in the case of negatively valued tests. If there is no evidence, the category is eliminated from the discussion.

The results of these five tests are combined and divided by the number of tests applied to find the grid initiative score of the Pauline church. The test for ascribed roles (test T3) is negatively valued and must be subtracted from a value of 1 if the test is valid (that is, there is evidence one way or another or the evidence is ambiguous).

$$\text{Initiative} = \frac{T1 + T2 + (1 - T3) \ldots + Tn}{n},$$

where "(Tn)" = the result of the test in one category. Initiative is negatively valued for grid.

Accountability

Accountability presents the ratio of hierarchical role relationships between connected pairs to the total number of role relationships.[60] The hypothesis is that categorical distinctions between members depends upon hierarchical relationships, with either coercive or noncoercive sanctions encouraging performance. These sanctions are based on the performance of roles. They imply a dominant and a subordinate role relationship in the pairings. Note that these sanctions are different from conditions of membership, in that they are role-based sanctions applying to the accomplishment of role tasks. These are to be distinguished from sanctions related to group membership, boundary, or purity.

The accountability score for each individual (Xi) is

$$\text{Acc}(Xi) = \frac{\text{the sum of the number of acc/roles } (Xi) \text{ assumes}}{\text{the total no. of roles } (Xi) \text{ assumes}},$$

where the accountability interactions "(acc/roles)" are those roles assumed by an individual in which the individual takes either a dominant or a subordinate position.

This involves the imposition of both coercive and noncoercive sanctions based on performance in the role relationship. The point to the accountability score is that each member "is likely to have his sensitivity to categorical distinctions strengthened either when he accounts to someone else or when someone else is accountable to him."[61] In other words, are there role-based sanctions present that reinforce hierarchical role relationships? Again, an accounting of hierarchical role relationships is not available, nor can an accounting be inferred from Paul's letters. But the side-effects of sensitivity to categorical distinctions should be observable. If grid is high, we would expect there to be social mechanisms that would reinforce role specialization. If grid is low, the social mechanisms should reinforce individual freedom. This is the question of autonomy. How much freedom does the individual have? The less freedom of choice an individual has, the higher the value of grid in the society.

Autonomy

Autonomy, along with individual control and competition, is one of three signs of movement down grid.[62] A series of tests measure the side-effects of autonomy. These are listed by Douglas:

> A person who is not in a strongly classifying, insulating environment, will be moving down towards zero if he can enjoy a good degree of independence in his decisions. So autonomy contributes a component in measuring the downward shift toward an individualist environment. To estimate it, one could ask how freely a person disposes of his own time, of his own goods, chooses his collaborators, chooses his clothes and food.[63]

The score for autonomy is negatively applied to grid. It is the complement of grid value. It consists of a series of tests[64] for the presence of the (1) freedom to dispose of time; (2) freedom to dispose of private property; (3) freedom to choose collaborators; (4) freedom to choose clothing; (5) freedom to choose food.

As with the other grid predicates, these tests cannot be scored as a continuous scale because we cannot directly observe the behavior of the Pauline church. They may, however, be scored as either present, not present insofar as we know, or ambiguous. Each of the five categories functions as a test for autonomy. If there is evidence for presence, the category scores a 1. If there is evidence for the lack of presence, the score is 0. If the evidence is ambiguous, with some presence and some nonpresence, the score is .5. If there is no evidence, the category is not a valid test and is eliminated from the discussion.

The results of these five tests are combined and divided by the number of tests applied to find the grid autonomy score of the Pauline church:

$$\text{autonomy} = \frac{T1 + T2 + T3 + \ldots + Tn,}{n}$$

where "(Tn)" = the result of the test in one category. Autonomy is scored negatively for grid.

Predicates for Measuring Grid: Summary

The four predicates of grid in this study are (1) Role differentiation, (2) authority, (3) initiative, and (4) autonomy. Autonomy and initiative are negatively valued in relation to grid strength. Role differentiation and authority are positively valued. In each of these four predicates of grid the determining factor for discerning the tendency is Paul's instructions for the interaction of Pauline church faction participants. Along with this observation of tendency are inferences based on Paul's own behavior, information on the behavior of participants gleaned from the letters, and information inferred from the house church meeting form. Together the four predicates form a working hypothesis on which a social accounting of grid value will be done in Chapter Six.

The Grid-Group Working Hypothesis

Four group predicates and four grid predicates for doing a social accounting of the Pauline church faction are described in this working hypothesis. The group predicates are all positively valued. They are proximity, transitivity, deferential involvement, and boundary. The grid predicates are role differentiation, authority, initiative, and autonomy. The first two are positively valued; the second two are negatively valued for grid. Each predicate has its own definition and standards for evaluation of data. The scoring of each predicate is the process of a social accounting of the Pauline church faction. Finding the tendency on the basis of observation and inference results in the determination of a region with greatest likelihood on the grid-group map.

Chapter Three describes the grid-group model from which we have derived a social accounting approach to ethnography. This chapter fully and carefully describes the adaptation of this social accounting method for our use with the Pauline literary materials. The working hypothesis for the predicates of grid and group provides us with the categories for a social accounting of the Pauline church faction using the data we have available to us. Once this social accounting is done (Chapters Five and Six), I describe the context of Paul's theological language using David Ostrander's paradigm for the distribution of values and beliefs on the grid-group map (Chapter Seven).

The first step in doing a grid-group analysis according to the method of Gross and Rayner is to draw an EXACT graph of the social unit under study.[65] This task is taken up in the next chapter.

5

A Social Accounting of the Pauline Church
Group Scale

Doing a social accounting of the Pauline church on the group scale[1] requires that we infer the social transactions of its participants from their literary remains found in Paul's letters. We use the predicates of group outlined in the preceding chapter to categorize and evaluate the data, and we find that Paul's churches and Paul himself are highly invested in group concerns.

The evidence that is available to us is fragmentary; much of it must be inferred from literary texts that have purposes other than communicating sociological data. As social historians, we must look at the consequences, the "externalities," the "side-effects"[2] of the individual transactions that make up investment in group values. In these we find the social controls and the patterns of individual contracts in the Pauline church faction. The period for measuring the transactions appropriate to each predicate of grid and group is the active ministry of Paul, the period in which he wrote his letters.

Grid-group analysis requires a process of estimation even when one is attempting to define contemporary cultural patterns by survey or through participant observation. Attempting to apply this method to the Pauline church faction requires an extra step of estimation, that of "estimating the tendency" of each variable in the formula for each predicate of grid and of group. When evaluating the Pauline church faction, we seek the extremes of the range of variability, in the belief that the actual score for the Pauline church faction—were we to have available independent observations—would fall somewhere between the extremes. The "decision rule" that enables this estimation of extremes for each predicate is described in Chapter Four.

Only the information available in the relatively uncontested letters of Paul will be considered reliable in this study: Romans, the Corinthian correspondence, Galatians, Philippians, 1 Thessalonians, Philemon. We are interested in observing the behavior of Paul and those around him insofar as we can observe that behavior. In this chapter we will estimate a range for the score of each predicate of group.

The EXACT Graph of the Pauline Church

A schematic form of an EXACT graph of the Pauline churches is based on the collection of references to people listed by Paul in greetings or mentioned in his letters. The organizational chart of titles and interactions between Paul and his coworkers offered by E. Earle Ellis,[3] as well as Bengt Holmberg's description of Paul's coworkers,[4] has been consulted in constructing this graph (see Figure 3).

The relative scale and interactions of the house church unit have been inferred from studies of the form of the house church meeting.[5] The number of connecting lines from Paul and his coworkers to each local house church cluster has been reduced to one for the purpose of schematic clarity. In fact, the number of connecting rods between Paul and individuals in the house churches would have been substantial.

This graph bears some resemblance to the low proximity, high transitivity model graph offered by Gross and Rayner (see Figure 4). This resemblance appears if one imagines each cluster on the model graph as a schematic representation of a house church. Each participant in the house church has transactions with every other participant in the house church cluster. For each house church the proximity score and the transitivity score would be 1. The relatively few number of participants who have interactions with other house church clusters is signified schematically by the few connecting rods between clusters. If the Pauline church as a whole reflects this pattern, it would score low on the proximity scale (the average participant is more than two removes from others in other church clusters) and high on the transitivity scale (the diadic links that do occur are likely to be also triadic because most occur within house church clusters).

Figure 3 The EXACT Graph of the Pauline Church Faction

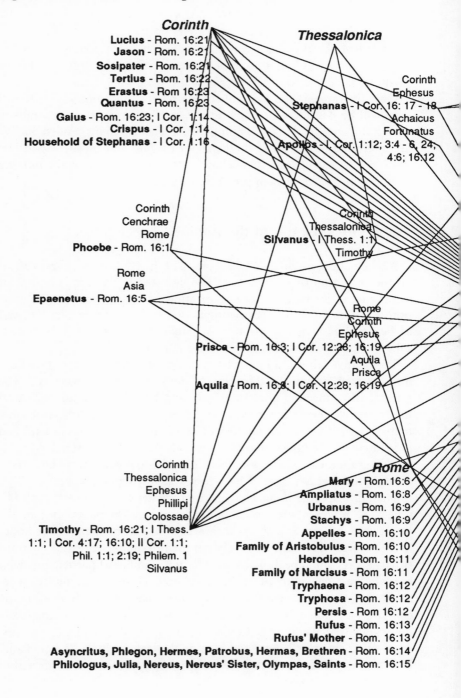

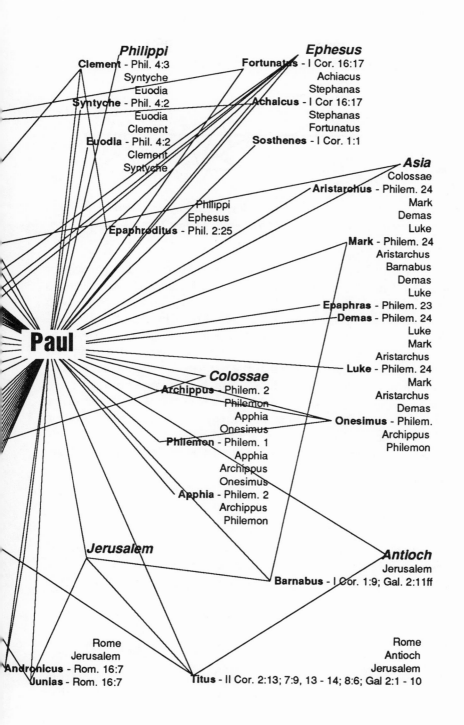

Philippi
Clement - Phil. 4:3
Syntyche
Euodia
Syntyche - Phil. 4:2
Euodia
Clement
Euodia - Phil. 4:2
Clement
Syntyche

Epaphroditus - Phil. 2:25
Philippi
Ephesus

Ephesus
Fortunatus - I Cor. 16:17
Achiacus
Stephanas
Achaicus - I Cor 16:17
Stephanas
Fortunatus
Sosthenes - I Cor. 1:1

Asia
Colossae
Aristarchus - Philem. 24
Mark
Demas
Luke
Mark - Philem. 24
Aristarchus
Barnabus
Demas
Luke
Epaphras - Philem. 23
Demas - Philem. 24
Luke
Mark
Aristarchus
Luke - Philem. 24
Mark
Aristarchus
Demas
Onesimus - Philem.
Archippus
Philemon

Paul

Colossae
Archippus - Philem. 2
Philemon
Apphia
Onesimus
Philemon - Philem. 1
Apphia
Archippus
Onesimus
Apphia - Philem. 2
Archippus
Philemon

Jerusalem

Antioch
Jerusalem
Barnabus - I Cor. 1:9; Gal. 2:11ff

Rome
Jerusalem
Andronicus - Rom. 16:7
Junias - Rom. 16:7

Rome
Antioch
Jerusalem
Titus - II Cor. 2:13; 7:9, 13 - 14; 8:6; Gal 2:1 - 10

Figure 4 Low Proximity, High Transitivity

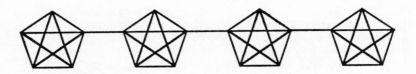

Source: Jonathan L. Gross and Steve Rayner, *Measuring Culture: A Paradigm for the Analysis of Social Organization* (New York: Columbia University Press, 1985), p. 85.

In the EXACT graph of the Pauline church (Figure 3) each participant named by Paul is listed in boldface type with references. Connections with local churches are listed above each participant; connections with other individuals on the chart are listed below. Clusters of highly connected participants, marked with place names in italic, represent the house churches. Since the membership of each of these is small and they met frequently, we can assume that the participants had regular contact with each other.[6] Within each house church, therefore, both the proximity and transitivity scores would tend toward 1 as predicted in the schematic representation (Figure 4). The effect of the larger organization of the Pauline church is more difficult to determine. These issues are discussed in the next sections under the headings Proximity and Transitivity.

Group Predicates

The predicates of group for the Pauline church are: (1) proximity, (2) transitivity, (3) deferential involvement, and (4) boundary. The range of scores is determined for each, and the tendency of each category is determined in sequence.

Proximity

As we examine the connections among house church clusters in terms of proximity, we find that the situation described by the EXACT graph of the Pauline church is somewhat more complex than initially suspected. The central point to which many participants in the house churches are connected is Paul. Because of Paul's central location, his proximity score would be high, not near 1 as in the local clusters, but still quite high. This is because no participants in the Pauline church faction are more than two removes—two connecting rods—from Paul.

The points related to Paul are coworkers who we know are related to one or more local clusters. Again, their proximity scores would be high, but because they are not related to all Pauline church clusters directly— but only through Paul—their proximity score is lower than is Paul's. None of these coworkers is more than three removes from any other— connected through Paul—and most are at no more than two removes.

Finally, there is a lack of connecting rods between some local clusters. This would tend to reduce the proximity score for individuals with connections to Paul or his coworkers toward .5. We infer that the average individual is no more than two removes from any other in the Pauline church faction and is usually connected through Paul himself, and that no participant is more than four removes from any other participant.

The tendency of individual proximity scores in the Pauline churches remains well above .5 because of the relative density of pairings within each house church cluster. Since the total proximity score is an unweighted average of the participant scores, the total score tends to remain well above .5, with a lower limit above .5 and an upper limit below .8. The larger the Pauline church becomes—that is, the more members it has in disparate places—the closer to .5 the proximity score moves. The greater the number of coworkers and traveling local church apostles who interact with local church clusters, the higher the proximity score even as the number of local church clusters increases. By contrast, imagine what happens to the proximity score when Paul disappears from the map.

Transitivity

Transitivity is similarly affected by the central location of Paul. Though his central and multifaceted connections with participants in each house church tend to keep his transitivity score with each church near 1, the lack of connections between house churches radically reduces his transitivity score as well as the scores of those who are connected with him. Physical geography limits the completion of connected threesomes through Paul. On the other hand, Paul's coworkers act on the graph to increase the transitivity score. They provide paths for threesomes that can be connected either through Paul or through the house church clusters.[7] The supposition that Christians visited in house churches as they traveled would increase the transitivity score.[8] Finally, the collection for the saints, an activity in which all of Paul's local church clusters participate, would serve to provide connected threesome links between local church clusters as church-appointed apostles move between clusters.[9]

Within each house church cluster, the odds that any connected pair (each dyad counted in the measure of proximity) is connected to a third member is 100 percent and the transitivity score is 1. But because the strength of transitivity within each cluster is diminished by the central placement of Paul on the EXACT graph, the tendency of the transitivity score between two local clusters of equal size will be to move toward .5. The two factors, central interaction with Paul and his coworkers and the tight clustering of the local churches, balance each other around this score. As more local churches are added, the average transitivity score diminishes because of Paul's central location. This process of a geographically induced reduction in the transitivity score through Paul is countered by the collection for the saints and by an increased number of coworkers. Note also that as the number of participants in each local cluster increases, the number of connected threesomes increases geometrically while the number of unconnected threesomes through Paul increases arithmetically. The range of tendency in transitivity covers the middle third of the scale. This wide range takes into account our limited knowledge of the numbers of participants at the local level but it excludes the extremes of the scale.

Summary of Group Proximity and Transitivity

The EXACT graph has been used to estimate a range for group proximity and transitivity. The estimated range for these scores is quite wide, but both tend to have their greatest likelihood somewhere near the middle of the scale, with proximity above .5 (.55–.80) and transitivity approximately .5 (.35–.65). These identified ranges represent the extremes of estimated likelihood, and the actual scores, could they be found, would occur within the defined range for each predicate.

Deferential Involvement

In order to find the deferential involvement score, we must look for behavioral evidences of the decisions of individuals related to group participation.[10] Do the people who show up in the letters of Paul have a choice whether to be a participant or not, and do they show signs of a commonality of experience in their participation? What is the cost of membership either overtly or covertly, in shared resources or in societal pressures against participation? The more choice the membership has in contracting for inclusion and the greater the relative cost of membership, the higher the deferential score. The more evidence there is for common experience in the Pauline church faction, the higher the score for commonality of experience. These two scores are combined to find the deferential involvement score.

The deference score—like other grid-group scores that average participant scores—cannot be accurately calculated without facts about each individual. But the tendency of each of these relationships can be inferred for the whole group.

Choice in Joining. What percentage of the participants in the Pauline church faction had little or no choice about their participation? Paul's use of the term *kat' oikon* for "house church" implies more than the location of the meeting.[11] Whole extended households were apparently brought into the Pauline church faction when only the head of the household had choice. Luke, in Acts, refers to the baptism of whole households following the actions of only one member: 16:15, 16:31–34, 18:8. Paul's letters confirm the existence of this practice. In 1 Cor. 1:16 and 16:15 Stephanas and his household are commended to the Corinthians. Several people are greeted as part of households (Rom. 16:10–11, 1 Cor. 1:11, Phil. 4:22).

The case of Philemon and Onesimus depicts a conflict between individual participants in the Pauline church who also participate in one household. It demonstrates that, at least in this instance, Onesimus, a slave, became a Christian *after* his master, Philemon, who had already acted as a host for the church in Colossae (Philem. 1–2, 10). Norman R. Petersen's study of the situation of Onesimus, Philemon, and Paul's letter is a new attempt to find meaning by coupling literary and sociological methods.[12] He moves from the letter to a sociologically informed narrative of the events and back to the letter to interpret the text. His differentiation of evidence is important to observe. He concludes that Paul "polarizes the options open to Philemon and his church."[13] In doing so, Paul takes the risk that Philemon would choose not to participate, and from this we conclude that Philemon had some choice.

Wayne Meeks summarizes the situation in the Pauline church:

> If the existing household was the basic cell of the mission, then it follows that the motivational bases for becoming part of the *ekklesia* would likely vary from one member to another. If a household became Christian more or less *en bloc*, not everyone who went along with the new practices would do so with understanding or inner participation. Social solidarity might be more important in persuading some members to be baptized than would understanding or conviction about specific beliefs. Differential qualities and degrees of engagement with the group from the beginning would not be surprising.[14]

The evidence for the first ratio, the proportion of those who freely join to all those who join, is decidedly mixed. From Wayne Meeks's description of the prosopographic evidence and from indirect evidence of the participants in the Pauline church at Corinth as described by Gerd Theissen,[15] we learn that the house churches are made up of people from many levels of society. What these churches have in common is not their social standing, but inconsistency in their social role and rank.[16] Diversity is a part of the Pauline church, and this diversity is reflected in the degrees of choice participants exercise in joining the faction. What evidence we have indicates that the tendency of the first ratio is to range around .5, but we must extend the range of variability: .2 to .8.

Choice in Participation. The evidence for the second ratio, the proportion of members who experience some cost of membership to the total membership, is less mixed. In one of Paul's earliest letters he refers to persecution in overt forms as the expected condition (1 Thess. 1:6, 2:14–15, 3:1–4). In the passage 1 Thess. 3:4 ("For when we were with you, we told you beforehand that we were to suffer affliction; just as it has come to pass, and as you know") Paul reminds the Thessalonians that he forewarned them about suffering in his teaching. Paul mentions his own sufferings as a missionary in the context of arguments about authority (2 Cor. 11:23–27). The disassociation of new Christians from their former religious practices[17] brings both new relationships and an end to old relationships. These transitions are part of the real and the continuing cost of membership. We could conclude from statements within Paul's teachings that carry unintended information about group life that there is a commonality of experience among members in social and physical suffering because of group membership.[18]

On the other hand, Paul nowhere mentions the sharing of possessions that Luke tells us occurred in Palestinian Christianity (Acts 4:32–5:11). The cost of membership does not include the abolition or communality of private property.[19] The collection for the saints in Jerusalem held multiple layers of significance for the Pauline church and for Paul. We have already noticed that the collection provides the context for increased proximity and transitivity among members of geographically disparate house church clusters. The collection also increases the cost of membership. Paul's motivational discussion of giving in 2 Cor. 8–9 bears this out. His pride in the Corinthians supports their group identity.[20]

Within the Pauline church faction the cost of continued membership was continued purity, as differentiated from the social practice of the rest of society. The threat of expulsion from the faction hung on sexual taboos (1 Cor. 5:1–6). These concerns added to the cost of group membership but are considered more fully under the area of group boundary.[21]

The tendency of the averaging of these ratios is to place the deferential score above .5. The evidence for the first ratio is mixed and varies widely around .5: .2–.8. The tendency of the second ratio is to score higher, with evidence of the participants in the Pauline church faction experiencing some cost of membership: .4–.8. The average of these two tends not to be less than .3 and ranges upward to .8. There is some reason to believe that the participants in the Pauline church faction are significantly affected by their participation in this group, and therefore the estimation of greatest likelihood would be above .5. We need confirmation in a commonality of group experience to rule out a false positive result due to social constraints or interest in individual contract.

Commonality of Experience. The primary points of shared experience are (1) a common beginning or entrance (similarity of experience or initiation); (2) a common social background (similarity of social or economic level); (3) a distinctive creation or ritual myth (shared primal story); (4) a distinctive group ritual (corporate signs of inclusion); (5) distinctive signs of participation (common language, purpose, goals).

The decision rule tests for the presence or nonpresence of each of these signs of shared experience. This form of decision rule functions on a participant-wide basis, testing for signs of commonality.

Common Beginning. Wayne Meeks points us to the "soteriological contrast pattern" that Paul uses on more than one occasion in his letters.[22] This pattern of motivational argument relies upon the similarity of shared experience of the participants in the Pauline churches. Its force lies in the fact that Paul could contrast the pagan background of most of the participants of his churches to their present status as "pure Christians." This sense of having "crossed the boundary" is common to all members.

Each one of the Pauline Christians experienced, either directly or secondarily, the Pauline mission. That is, they experienced visits and letters from Paul or his coworkers. On this evidence, common beginning should score 1. The dissimilarity of the religious and cultural background of those recruited into the Pauline church faction, however, gives us pause in scoring common beginning. Obvious differences in the way diaspora Jews and Gentiles may have received Paul's message cause us to score common beginnings in a way that reflects this ambiguity. Common beginning scores .5, with some tendency to expect the score to be higher.

Common Social Background. We do not have access to data concerning the allocation of time made by each Pauline church participant in relation to the outside social world. The controversy Paul has with the Corinthian church concerning the proper form for the celebration of the Lord's supper (1 Cor. 11:17–34) indicates that the social divisions that occupied the participants outside the Pauline church faction were carried over into behavior within the faction.[23] The Pauline congregations "reflected a fair cross-section of urban society."[24] Common social background scores 0.

A Distinctive Creation or Ritual Myth. The division between the former life and the present is marked for each participant by the rite of initiation into the Pauline church faction. The baptism of the convert is an emotionally powerful event, which attracted to itself cultic myth and story. We have little evidence about the precise form of the event, but conjecture and inference from Paul's statements have led to interesting descriptions.[25] We can be sure that every participant in the new faction experienced initiation.[26] The elements of this initiation included water and teachings about the history of the cultic practice. These became part of the background of every member. The stories of Jesus' preexistence (Phil. 2:5–11) and his death (Rom. 6:3–11) quickly became part of the Pauline church faction experience. Creation myth scores 1.

Distinctive Cultic Ritual. Other signs of shared experience in the Pauline churches include a shared ritual with prayers and ecstatic utterances, a common meal, a claim to special status or teachings separate from the rest of the population, letters, and the greeting with a holy kiss. These signs of participation in the Pauline church faction provided the participant with a pattern of shared experience. Such patterned behavior as ecstatic utterances and "gifts of the Spirit," of which speaking in tongues was one phenomenon, were part of the Pauline church experience. So much so that, in Corinth, Paul had a problem containing it to allow other levels of group participation and shared experience to develop.

This wealth of common experience was offset by the different levels of social status enjoyed by the Pauline Christians. Their experience outside of the faction, though marked by a common differentiation from their past *religious* experience, was separate and distinct from their common, communal, cultic ritual. The controversy at Corinth over sharing in the common meal—which brings these distinct concerns into the faction—contrasts with patterns of behavior that support group unity. Glossolalia is at least one distinctive cultic ritual, causing us to score this sign of commonality as 1.

Distinctive Signs of Participation. There are distinctive signs of fellowship in the group.[27] Common language for terms of belonging identify the participants.[28] Common language for terms of separation to distinguish those who do not belong also identifies the group by locating its boundaries.[29] Patterns of behavior that distinguish group participants in the Pauline church include speaking in tongues, common meals, and reading letters.

One of these patterned behaviors in cultic practice was the holy kiss. Stephen Benko's study of the function of the holy kiss in the early church concludes that it is indeed a sign of unity in the faction even in the face of social difficulties (it is a sign of the cost of membership).[30] He concludes his study with the understanding that "the holy kiss through the Holy Spirit established unity."[31] He suggests that imagery from marriage relations used to explain theological concepts came "naturally" in this context. The holy kiss also indicates a pattern of inclusion in group behavior, causing us to score 1 for signs of participation.

Scoring Commonality. The five scores for commonality—common beginning .5, common social background 0, distinctive creation or ritual myth 1, distinctive group ritual 1, and distinctive signs of participation

1—produce an average score of .7. This indicates that the score for the commonality of experience is not absolutely 1, but the tendency of the Pauline churches would be to score high, around .7. This estimate of greatest likelihood confirms the deference score and discounts the possibility of a false positive result for group investment.

Scoring Deferential Involvement. Deferential involvement combines the scores for deference and for commonality:

$$\text{Lower limit: } \frac{.3 + .7}{2} = .5.$$

$$\text{Upper limit: } \frac{.8 + .7}{2} = .75.$$

Those about whom we hear in the letters of Paul, those who participate in the Pauline church faction, differentially choose to be involved in the group. This result is not likely to be a false positive in a low group environment.

Boundary

The boundary score, described in the preceding chapter, is made up of its own polythetic scale. There are five factors to be tested, each a sign of the presence of group boundary: (1) the presence of an entrance ritual; (2) the presence of sanctions on interaction with outsiders; (3) the presence of group controls on behavior; (4) the presence of concern about ritual pollution; (5) the presence of members who gain their life support through the group.

These five factors are considered separately and scored independently for presence, ambiguity, or absence. Again, the decision rule is based on a participant-wide approach. The scores for these signs of group boundary are averaged to find the boundary score.

Entrance Ritual. The rite of passage that marks the separation of a profane preexistence and the pure current existence in the Pauline church faction is baptism. Although there is the possibility that some other sign of conversion marked this transition,[32] signs that demarcate this transition are sufficient to demonstrate the presence of an entrance ritual.

We cannot accurately describe the ritual act. Baptism is not a ritual bath to be repeated before each participation, but is rather a delimiter of existence (1 Cor. 6:11).[33] Its side-effects or externalities are apparent in the marking of this division (pre- and postbaptism), not in signs of—or concerns for—ritual cleanliness. Paul uses baptism both as a common starting point in arguments with local congregations, Rom. 6, 8:12–17; Gal. 3:26–4:6; 1 Cor. 1–4, 12,[34] and to remind the believers about their former impure state.[35] The universality of baptism as an entrance ritual results in a score of 1 for entrance ritual.

Sanctions on Interaction with Outsiders. Wayne Meeks finds "ambiguity" in the "Christian group's boundaries" when Paul approves of eating meat offered to idols and disapproves of any active participation in another religious faction.[36] But both of these can fit the model of the definition of group boundary. The issue at hand is the identity of the individual with the group. Only participation with another group threatens that identity.

Paul's intent in making this distinction is not to open the way for evangelism. Indeed, he never calls on new Christians to be responsible for bringing their friends and acquaintances into the faction. Rather, he is making a practical—and to him obvious—distinction between various categories of activity as they relate to faction boundaries. We will examine separately signs of sanctions on participation in outside religious factions and participation in other areas of society.

The sanctions Paul places on participants in the Pauline church against involvement in outside religious factions are coercive and not open for compromise. The basis of Paul's rather sophisticated distinction between the freedom in Christ to eat meat purchased in the market (1 Cor. 10:25) and the sanction against "drinking the cup of demons" (1 Cor. 10:21) lies in signs of an individual's participation in cultic practices. The issue of 1 Cor. 8 and again in 10:23ff., that is, the practice of eating meat that has been offered to idols, is decided on the basis of group commonality, not purity or boundary. The "strong" are to be sensitive to the concerns of the "weak." The issue of participation in the worship of idols is not at question.

Hans Conzelmann describes the contrast between these two concepts when comparing 1 Cor. 8 and 1 Cor. 10:

> But what is the problem involved here [1 Cor. 10:14–15]? Is the topic the same as in chap. 8, that is *eidōlothuta,* "meat sacrificed to idols"? A connection does exist, but we have also to notice a shift. In the former passage

it was a question of eating, here it is a question of the food. There the rule was freedom (together with the limitation of it by our brother). For the matter of eating was to begin with an open question. Where the worship of idols is concerned, on the other hand, there is no question at all. Here the rule is the apodictic *pheugete*, "shun!" There the criterion was the conscience, which has to decide. Here the emphasis is on the sacrament, which creates exclusiveness.[37]

The "exclusiveness" of participation in the sacrament is not limited to Gentile religious factions but is also applied to Judaism itself. Just as there can be no active participation in sacrifices to idols by believers (1 Cor. 10:14), there can be no active participation in works related to the Jewish law: "Now I, Paul, say to you that if you receive circumcision, Christ will be of no advantage to you. I testify again to every man who receives circumcision that he is bound to keep the whole law; you have fallen away from grace" (Gal. 5:2–4).

Betz summarizes the situation for Gentile believers:

> But Gentiles who have become Christians and who wish to become Jews in addition demonstrate that for them "grace" and "Christ" (i.e., the salvation through Christ outside of the Torah) are not sufficient and that to come under Torah is necessary for their salvation. By implication, then, "Christ" is no longer a savior and "grace" is no longer grace. As a result, such people do not merely change "denominations," but become real converts to non-Christian Judaism. This conversion then, also sets in motion the curse of excommunication issued in [Gal.] 1:8–9.[38]

In both cases, participation in Gentile religious factions and Jewish law, Paul identifies the signs of participation in lists of excluded and included behavior. In both cases Paul rejects the possibility of participation with outside cultic practices and simultaneous participation in Christian cultic practice. Sanctions on participation in outside religious factions scores 1.

But there remains this distinction between (*a*) sanctions against participation in another religious faction and (*b*) individual freedom to participate in society. Both of these characterize Pauline Christianity. The Pauline Christian can and should remain "in the world" (1 Cor. 5:9–13). Meeks identifies the "missionary motive" and "self-defense" as the motives for encouraging "openness to the world."[39] He finds that these motives result in "tension" between the need to promote inner group cohesion (commonality) and the need to be open to the larger society. He identifies the "missionary motive" as the driving force behind this tension.

This tension, visible in the experience of community organizers like Barnabas and Paul as they went out from Antioch to spread the word, is apparent in the Jerusalem conference.[40] Paul reflects this experience at several points in his argument (1 Cor. 9:19–23, 10:31–11:1). Whether or not a missionary drive is the motivation for limited sanctions on interactions with outsiders, we have evidence that participants in the Pauline church faction carried on with normal economic and social transactions with outsiders.

Although there are coercive sanctions against participation in outside religious factions, there is tension between (a) identifying a clear separation between group participants and the world and (b) participating in society. The tests for sanctions on interaction with outsiders results in .5, with evidence on both sides of the scale.

Group Controls on Behavior. The same tension that reduces the score for sanctions on interaction with outsiders increases the universality of group controls. The previously identified missionary and self-defense motives for encouraging openness to the world result in tension or social conflict.[41] The self-defense motive is described by Paul in the 1 Thess. 4:10b–12: "But we exhort you, brethren, to do so more and more, to aspire to live quietly, to mind your own affairs, and to work with your hands, as we charged you; so that you may command the respect of outsiders, and be dependent on nobody."

The signs of participation in the Pauline church faction (signs of commonality described above) are distinguished from signs of nonparticipation in several lists that contrast types of behavior (Gal. 5:16–26; 1 Cor. 5:9, 6:9, 18, 10:8; 2 Cor. 12:20). In this regard, 1 Thess. 5:8–9 is interpreted by the later Rom. 13:12b–14: "Let us then cast off the works of darkness and put on the armor of light; let us conduct ourselves becomingly as in the day, not in reveling and drunkenness, not in debauchery and licentiousness, not in quarreling and jealousy." Since the contrast pattern reflected in these lists represents a concern for purity, the universality of these concerns causes the group control on behavior to score 1.

Ritual Pollution. Group controls center on a concern for ritual purity. The most obvious of these concerns that Paul conveys is his concern about sexual purity. Abstinence is highly recommended (and is observed by Paul), that the believer may remain pure (1 Cor. 7:1–9). He shows this concern in instructions from the earliest of his letters: "For this is the will of God, your sanctification: that you abstain from immorality" (1 Thess. 4:3).[42] The depth of this concern for sexual purity is evidenced by the surprise at sexual immorality found among the Corinthian churches (1 Cor. 5:1–13).[43] "The more surprising that anomaly is taken to be, the clearer the evidence that the categories which it contradicts are deeply valued."[44]

Paul's surprise at the report of incest is followed by a demand for the expulsion of the sinner. Purity is appropriately the concern of the group and—in this case—coercive sanctions are to be applied. Paul carefully disassociates this concern for purity within the group from impurity outside the group (1 Cor. 5:9–13 and the possibly related text 2 Cor. 6:14–7:1).

The concern for ritual purity is also demonstrated in other controversies with the Corinthian churches. The threat of magical sanctions is used to reinforce cultic taboos (1 Cor. 11:27–30).[45] The whole community is at risk because of the inappropriate behavior of some in relation to the cultic meal. The sanction is stated in terms of misfortune that occurs without human intervention.[46]

The universality of the concern for ritual purity scores this category as 1. This concern for purity is uniformly expressed as a group concern: "Brethren, if a man is overtaken in any trespass, you who are spiritual should restore him in a spirit of gentleness" (Gal. 6:1). This concern for purity also supports the scoring of group controls on behavior.

Members Who Gain Life Support through the Group. The controversy at Corinth also involves questions about Paul's authority.[47] One aspect of Paul's response to the Corinthians concerns his "tentmaking ministry" and support received from other churches (2 Thess. 3:7–9; 1 Cor. 9:3–7; 2 Cor. 11:7–11, 12:13–18; Phil. 4:10–20).[48] Those who receive their life support from church factional groups to whom they preach also gain authority over the group.[49] In the 2 Corinthians passages Paul responds to this concern.

This conflict between competing types of missionary endeavors is described in detail by Theissen.[50] He concludes that Paul and Barnabas represent a type of community organizer who goes out to found new religious factions in urban areas of the empire. Meanwhile, Paul's competitors represent a type of itinerant charismatic missionary who "arose in the social circumstances of the Palestinian region."[51] The contrast between these two types or patterns of missionary endeavor is brought to light in the Corinthian correspondence.

Paul defends the right to receive remuneration for work in the Pauline church faction, at the same time justifying his own renunciation of support. This is more than simply a tactical decision in the missionary environment. It seems right and logical to Paul in his explanation of his behavior that "You shall not muzzle an ox when it is treading out the grain" (1 Cor. 10:9). But his behavior, as well as that of those around him, is contrary. Paul, even though he does accept some support from some churches (Phil. 4:14ff, 2 Cor. 11:9) and asks to be received and supported by others (Rom. 15:28, 32), does not receive his life support from or through the group.

The case of the "superlative apostles" (2 Cor. 11:5ff.), however, who come to the church in Corinth, is different. A portion of their authority comes from their acceptance of support from the Corinthian church. Paul himself instructs the congregation at Galatia, "Let him who is taught the word share all good things with him who teaches" (Gal. 6:6).[52] Because Paul is forced to argue against others who do receive their life support from Pauline churches, there must have been some who received such support. But because Paul himself and those around him did *not* receive such support; the evidence is ambiguous so the score is .5.

Scoring Group Boundary. Paul exhibits a great concern about the boundary between participants in the Pauline church and the rest of the world. The distinction is never more clear than when Paul uses "in-group" language, which places a marker on this distinction. For example, at 1 Thess. 5:4–8: "But you are not in darkness, brethren, for that day to surprise you like a thief. For you are all sons of light and sons of the day; we are not of the night or of darkness. So then let us not sleep, as others do, but let us keep awake and be sober. For those who sleep sleep at night, and those who get drunk are drunk at night. But since we belong to the day, let us be sober, and put on the breastplate of faith and love, and, for a helmet the hope of salvation." Paul uses mixed metaphors to mark the two opposing sides. The purity of the factional group is his first concern.

Averaging the various categories of the measure of boundary—the presence of an entrance ritual 1, of sanctions on interaction with outsiders .5, of group controls on behavior 1, of concern about ritual pollution 1, and of members who gain life support through the group .5—we discover a high level of concern for this proxy of group investment: the tendency for the boundary score is to range around .8, the estimate with greatest likelihood. This score is quite high and confirms the range of the deference score.

Summary of Group Score

The components of the group score range as follows:

	Low	High
Proximity	.55	.80
Transitivity	.35	.65
Deferential involvement	.50	.75
Boundary	.80	.80

The average score for the lower range is .55; the average for the higher is .75. Group scores thus fall into a range that demonstrates a high level of investment in group on the part of individual participants in the Pauline church. The interpretation of Paul's theology must take this fact of social mapping into account.

6

A Social Accounting of the Pauline Church
Grid Scale

Continuing the social accounting of the Pauline church faction, this chapter locates Paul and the church faction associated with him on the grid scale. The predicates of grid are outlined in Chapter Four. We find that Paul's churches and Paul himself are highly competitive. Status in the faction is individually achieved rather than ascribed to a legitimated office or because of social status.

Grid Predicates

The predicates of grid we use for the Pauline church have been defined in Chapter Four: (1) role differentiation, (2) authority, (3) initiative, and (4) autonomy. A range of possible scores is determined for each of these predicates. Role differentiation and authority are positively valued for grid measure; initiative and autonomy are negatively valued. Negatively valued scores are subtracted from 1 before being averaged to find the grid score range of greatest likelihood.

The first three predicates use various measures of the distribution of roles as a proxy for grid investment. Paul is very clear about what he thinks the distribution of roles in cultic practice should be.[1] Both in controversy in the Corinthian church and elsewhere in paraenesis, Paul calls for a radical equalization of the level of membership and of roles.[2] The controversy about the importance of speaking in tongues is one example. In the passage 1 Cor. 12–14 Paul explicitly denies that there is a hierarchy of roles—roles he terms gifts of the Spirit.[3] This theme is repeated in paraenetic instruction: "Do not think more highly than you ought" (Rom. 12:3–8, 1 Cor. 4:6–7, Gal. 6:3–5). The result of this teaching concerning behavior in the faction is that cultic roles are available to all members. But this teaching has paraenetic purpose and may not, therefore, reflect the behavioral situation.

There are indications that specific functions were undertaken by specific individuals. 1 Cor. 12:28: "God has appointed in the church first apostles, second prophets, third teachers, then workers of miracles, then healers, helpers, administrators, speakers in various kinds of tongues." And again, the salutation of Phil. 1:1b: "To all the saints in Christ Jesus who are at Philippi, with the bishops and deacons." These suggest that some individuals have roles that are different from and not exchanged with others.[4] Certainly Paul understood himself to have a special role—apostle to the Gentiles—that was not like other roles. It is apparent that this role is not exchangeable, although others in the Pauline church faction could be called apostles. Paul is jealous of maintaining the role of founding apostle. There is, therefore, at least one titled office and an accompanying asymmetric role differentiation.

The interplay of prophecy and teaching in the Pauline church may be an example of the development of church order taken over from the Palestinian experience. If Heinrich Greeven is correct—that by the time of 1 Corinthians prophecy, teaching, and administration in the church are practiced by closed sets of individuals—then specific social functions are located with specific sets of individuals.[5] Role-based sanctions for prophecy would include the test of prophecy by the church, which Paul instructs the church to practice (1 Thess. 5:19–21).

To quote again the point of scoring accountability for role interactions in a grid predicate, each member "is likely to have his sensitivity to categorical distinctions strengthened either when he accounts to someone else or when someone else is accountable to him."[6]

Role Differentiation

The letters of Paul are confusing evidence for role differentiation because they contain contradictory messages. Bengt Holmberg's study of

Paul and the distribution of power within the local Pauline churches summarizes the secondary literature and offers a concise presentation of the data for each category.[7] We refer to his work extensively. The predicate grid role differentiation consists of five tests, for the presence of (1) titled offices distinct from social functions; (2) task descriptions for the offices; (3) role-based sanctions on behavior; (4) a hierarchy of organization among offices; (5) individuals commissioned to fulfill the duties of offices.

The results of these tests are determined and are averaged to find the role differentiation score. The range of the role differentiation score is expected to be wide because of contradictory indicators found in the initial examination of the evidence. Each test for presence is taken up separately; then the results are averaged together.

Titled Offices Distinct from Social Functions. Holmberg begins at the "natural starting-point" to review roles in the Pauline church: the list of spiritual gifts or *charismata* in 1 Cor. 12:28.[8] He reviews the titles Paul uses and analyzes the social functions they represent. Then he asks, "Can these functions be termed 'offices'?"[9]

> We have now seen which elements of office characteristics already existed in Paul's days: permanent acknowledged functions in local churches filled by stable groups of persons who lead and serve and take responsibility for their congregations in different ways, in some cases even having a designation or title and some form of material support. The conclusion must be that we can rightly speak of offices in Paul's churches, even if they are not yet fully developed or legally authorized.[10]

This affirmative conclusion is questioned on the same page, however, in Holmberg's review of the extent to which the authority of these offices had developed. "Must we not conclude that the local church leaders had no authority of their own, or in other words that their function of leading was so rudimentary as to be almost non-existent?"[11]

At a minimum we must say that the evidence for the existence of titled offices separate from social functions is mixed. The tendency remains that we should answer affirmatively. The minimal score for titled offices is .5, with a high end of the range at 1.

Task Descriptions for the Offices. As he reviews each of the *charismata* listed by Paul in 1 Cor. 12:28, Holmberg describes these positions in the context of the local Pauline church.[12] Neither in the context of Paul's listing of local church functions, ministries, or *charismata* nor in the context of controversy does Paul offer a job description for any of these positions except, perhaps, for that of an apostle. This lack of task description is not surprising if one considers that the people to whom the letters are addressed are already participants in the church. Those addressed are familiar with the content of the office job description. On the other hand, it is also possible that the very rudimentary development of the office meant that any description of task was situational, in which case Paul would not have a concrete description to which he could refer.

At those places in the letters where we might expect Paul to refer to a job description for support in establishing leadership, he does not (1 Thess. 5:12, 1 Cor. 16:15). He does not refer to any offices that he instituted himself.[13] These arguments from silence suggest that task descriptions are developed ad hoc as the church develops in each location. There would be, therefore, no clear, identifiable task description even for that of the founding apostle, Paul himself.

In his defense of himself as an apostle in the Corinthian correspondence, as well as in Galatians and Philippians, Paul offers partial descriptions of his activities. His relationship with the pillars of the church has been negotiated at some expense. He has achieved his status and rank as apostle; there are none better or greater than he. He is a "master craftsman." A task description as understood by Paul may be inferred from defensive statements when Paul is in controversy.[14]

Although it is possible that there existed clear task descriptions for offices in the Pauline church, the evidence is at least mixed. The maximum score for task description remains 1 (Paul may simply have not mentioned job descriptions), but the minimum score is at least .5 and may be lower.

Role-Based Sanctions on Behavior. The key to this test for grid role differentiation is identifying sanctions related to *role* within the faction. Robert Banks describes the situation:

> In several places in his letters, and notably in I Corinthians, Paul talks about specific aspects of the church's meetings, clarifies the principles upon which decisions in the area should be based and gives concrete advice on the sorts of arrangements that follow from them. But *nowhere* does he address his remarks to a group of persons (or any one person) who alone have responsibility for dealing with these affairs. . . . He constantly re-

minds the *whole* community of its obligations in these matters and calls upon *every* member to deal with them in a proper fashion.[15]

Following Banks's argument, it may be supposed that there are no sanctions related to role in the Pauline church faction. A lack of sanctions would score role-based sanctions on behavior as 0. Paul's claim to a unique status as "father" of each church (1 Cor. 4:15), however, implies an asymmetric relationship within the church between founding apostle and the local church.[16] Such as asymmetric relationship would encourage analogies to implied sanctions related to the socialization processes within the Pauline church faction: "Shall I come to you with a rod, or with love in a spirit of gentleness?" (1 Cor. 4:21b). But even if it is the case that Paul has this dominant role relationship through the process of founding, local church leaders have not achieved a comparable status related to role.

Paul does recommend that the hearers of his letters be "subject to such men" as Stephanas and his household (1 Cor. 16:16) and that they "respect" those who are over them in the Lord (1 Thess. 5:12). Yet there are no sanctions related to role or to hierarchy in these examples. Paul's continuing concern is purity, and purity is a function of group boundaries, not of individual insulation. Even in the case cited above, 1 Cor. 4:21b, Paul's concern is not role accountability, but purity and moral behavior.

The range of scores for role-based sanctions on behavior is between 0 and .5. Although there is the possibility that no sanctions related to role exist, controversy related to the role and status of Paul himself result in a mixed score.

A Hierarchy of Organization among Offices. Holmberg takes up this question in the form "Was there any difference of rank between the offices (functions)?"[17] He goes to Rom. 12 and 1 Cor. 12–14 to look for evidence of order and sequence in Paul's lists of *charismata.* Two points are made about the lists: apostle is first and glossolalia is last. This ordering may have paraenetic importance which the fact of church order— such as it was in the Corinthian church—did not support. Paul argues for a special world of equal rank for task accomplishment. Holmberg theorizes that the criterion of rank for Pauline theology is *oikodomae,* that is, "the value or objective benefit a gift has in building up the church."[18] But this possible objective ranking had more to do with Paul's crusade against enthusiastic elements in the Corinthian church than with dispassionate observation of the situation as it existed.[19]

> In reality there hardly existed any *hierarchical* differentiation between the various functions or, in other words, no function at the time of Paul's letter-writing was legally subordinated to any other ("I as a prophet order you, a mere *episkopos*, to do so and so"). We know for certain that Paul's purpose in I Cor. 12 is explicitly anti-hierarchical (cf. especially 12:21–26), even if we can read between the lines that all functions do not have the same value.[20]

The office of apostle is listed and numbered first on Paul's list in 1 Corinthians, but it is left out of Paul's list in Romans. Perhaps there the office of apostle is assumed. Holmberg discusses Paul's coworkers and finds a pattern of rank among their citings in the letters. For example: "From the prescripts to the two letters to Thessalonica and from 2 Cor. 1:19 it appears that the later highly trusted Timothy stands below Silvanus in rank—a piece of information which agrees with the report in Acts about the second Missionary Journey (Acts 16–18)."[21]

Yet Paul argues for equality both among the leaders of the church and among the participants. The evidence is at best mixed. The minimum score for hierarchy among the offices is 0 showing the lack of development of the offices. The maximum range is .5, showing the mixed evidence.

Individuals Commissioned to Fulfill the Duties of Offices. The issue here is straightforward, but the evidence is again contradictory. Did Paul pick and ordain individuals to accomplish specific tasks, or did individuals rise up or volunteer to fulfill required functions? Are individuals only later recognized by Paul for their efforts? Holmberg quotes Grelot's conclusion: "The real access to ministerial functions seems to be situated at the point where the upsurge of individual charisma . . . meets the actions of the apostle, who has recognized the authenticity of these charisms and joined their incumbents to himself as co-workers in the preaching of the Gospel and the building up of the Church."[22]

In other words, it is likely that Paul simply sanctioned those who had already accomplished the task and rewarded those who achieved a demonstration of the *charisma* required. This rather opportunistic strategy is successful because it rewards those already motivated to accomplish the social functions of the group. It also leads to confusion when one is considering whether individuals are commissioned for offices. In a strict interpretation of the term "commissioning," the answer would be no: individuals are not commissioned for office. Commissioning after achievement is recognition of achievement. Such an interpretation would mean a score of 0 for this category. But, in a looser interpretation, this evidence is mixed and so this test would score .5. The likely range of commissioning scores 0 to .5.

Scoring Grid Role Differentiation. The scores for the five tests of grid role differentiation have resulted in a low and high tendency for each. As predicted, the range of these scores is wide. Role differentiation scores positively for grid. The components range as follows:

	Low	High
Titled offices	0.5	1.0
Task descriptions	0.5	1.0
Role-based sanctions	0.0	0.5
Organizational hierarchy	0.0	0.5
Commissioned individuals	0.0	0.5

Averaged, the scores for grid role differentiation are .2 (low) and .7 (high).

Authority

Given our finding of a high group investment, any process of legitimization of authority within the Pauline church would be a part of the process of the institutionalization of the group.[23] That is, if the Pauline church is engaged in a process of moving up grid in a high group environment, it is also engaged in the process of institutionalization and stabilization. Alternatively, the controversy at Corinth—which implies that small factions are aligning themselves with the various leaders described by Paul in 1 Corinthians—could be a part of a process of factionalism. That is, it is equally possible that the Pauline church is engaged in a process of moving down the group scale away from group controls toward greater stability in a low grid, low group social environment. Grid-group analysis, however, is not intended to trace or measure the move-

ment of power.[24] We are interested in understanding the externality of
power revealed in categories of authority at one moment of time.

Paul, and those around him in the mission to the Gentiles, produces a
number of proximity role relationships on the EXACT graph that appear
to be asymmetrical. Though Paul attempts to share his experience of the
house churches in letters, he does not give up his status as founding apostle. John Schütz's important study of asymmetrical role relationships and
authority in the Pauline church faction concludes:

> The apostle is distinguished from all others within the community, and *yet*
> *they are equated charismatically with him.* The apostle is not a member of
> any local community which he addresses, yet with all such members he
> belongs to one body. If he did not share with all others the experience of
> being "called" he could not be called to his specific task which dis-
> tinguished his status from that of others. To be over the community one
> must first be part of it; to be its paradigm one must be its member. In order
> to be an authority Paul must constantly stress what he shares with others.[25]

According to Schütz, the exercise of authority for Paul requires equality of status. This social dialectic is noticed both in the study of Bengt
Holmberg on authority in the Pauline church and the study of Gerd
Theissen on the development of community organizers within the leadership of the Pauline church.[26] In order for charismatic authority to operate, the one with authority that has not been legitimated must be the
equal of the other participants. In the context of the present category,
Paul must identify himself as exchanging some roles with others although
at the same time he does not exchange one role to which he has aspired:
that of apostle.

This social dialectic produces a confusing and contradictory pattern of
behavior in which to evaluate grid authority. Again, we can expect that
the range of grid authority will be wide. Categories of the test for grid
authority are evidence for the presence of (1) an adjudicatory system to
resolve conflicts; (2) a system of offices; (3) ambiguity in role requirements (negatively valued for grid authority); (4) leadership conflicts
(negatively valued for grid authority); (5) leaders who exhibit legitimate
authority.

These five tests are considered separately and the results are averaged
to find the score for grid authority. Notice that some tests for the side-
effects of role interactions gain importance in the total grid score by their

repetition in more than one predicate. This statistical fact, which functions to increase importance or effect, is a result of the translation of grid categories into available categories of observations of the Pauline church faction concerned with role-based interactions among individuals.

An Adjudicatory System to Resolve Conflicts. In 1 Cor. 6:1–8 Paul offers instruction concerning the resolution of legal conflicts between members.[27] They should stay out of the court system dominated by pagans. We cannot tell for certain from Paul's language in this passage that the church at Corinth has experienced Christian versus Christian lawsuits in pagan courts.[28] Still, it is at least possible to conclude that such lawsuits might have happened, because no one in the Corinthian church has the authority to settle disputes between members (v. 5).

This analysis indicates that at Corinth there may have been no operative system for deciding conflicts between individual participants.[29] Even then, the Corinthian situation may not be exemplary of the rest of the Pauline church in matters of church leadership.[30] The situation of Onesimus and Philemon offers concrete insights into the process of conflict resolution between members. In the preceding chapter, in the analysis of group deferential involvement–deference score, the negotiated settlement of this conflict between Christian slaveowner and new Christian slave is discussed. This situation is resolved (insofar as we know) by negotiation, not by referral to higher authority.[31] Where Paul could have referred the resolution of conflicts to appeals to authority, he did not. Indeed, he did not even resolve them himself by direct reference to his own authority to decide conflicts ("Philemon, as apostle, I order you to receive Onesimus . . .").

Norman Petersen points us to the rhetorical form of the letter to Philemon when considering the reality of Paul's use of the language of appeal rather than that of command. Paul's appeals are also an expression of his role as apostle. Petersen claims Paul's appeal in the letter to Philemon "only very thinly masks a command."[32] By distinguishing Paul's social relations—ambassadorial appeal—from his social role—command from the apostle—Petersen is able to illustrate the paradox of Paul's social reality. Philemon may have apprehended the power of Paul's role through the form in which it was expressed, but—in keeping with Paul's paradoxical appeal to weakness for authority—the literary evidence does not affirm such an appeal to authority.

When clear issues of group boundary come up—that is, the acceptability of uncircumcised Gentile Christians—the church in Antioch defers to defers to the leaders of the church in Jerusalem for a decision. Paul says: "I went up by revelation; and I laid before them (but privately before those who were of repute) the gospel which I preach among the Gentiles, lest somehow I should be running or had run in vain" (Gal. 2:2). This statement pictures a Christian tribunal of sorts made up of specific individuals who have the authority to make decisions about the whole enterprise of the mission to the Gentiles.[33]

Paul's description of these negotiations concerning group boundary between Jerusalem and Antioch does not tell us about the hierarchical structure of the Pauline church, nor about the way individuals within the Pauline church related to each other. Wayne Meeks points out this distinction between inter- and intra-church faction relations. "None of this [the Antioch incident] tells us much about the specific organization of Pauline Christianity. Indeed, there is reason to take Paul's defeat in Antioch as the starting point for his formation of a more clearly distinct and self-conscious missionary organization of his own."[34]

We conclude that no regularized system of conflict resolution existed for the Pauline church faction. The score for a judicatory system of conflict resolution is 0.

A System of Offices. The question of the existence, description, and organization of offices in the Pauline church faction has been taken up under the grid category of role differentiation. The question of the system of offices as it existed in the Pauline church is complex. Holmberg concludes that the presence of the apostle Paul himself limits the development of legitimate offices (that is, the presence of Paul himself limits movement up grid to stability and institutionalization).[35] As above under the test for "titled offices distinct from social functions," the conclusion is a range, minimum .5 (mixed evidence), maximum 1 (evidence for the existence of at least one office, that of founding apostle).

Ambiguity in Role Requirements (Negatively Valued). Ambiguity in role requirements is the correlated test for the clarity of task descriptions above under "task descriptions for the offices." It was determined that the range of score for the existence of task descriptions was minimum .5 (indicating mixed evidence) to maximum 1 (indicating evidence for existence). But no constitution or clear pattern of organization is found, and it is possible that there are no effective task descriptions for roles in the Pauline church. The range is wide but tends to the middle of the scale. On the other hand, signs of ambiguity in the Pauline church related to role interactions are readily available. Consequently, the use of a correlated test may provide a useful means of assessing concern for role-based social hierarchy in the Pauline church faction.

Although the list of *charismata* in 1 Corinthians is the logical place to begin a description of the tasks of the various roles in the Pauline church, evidence of ambiguity is found at points of controversy. Evidence of controversy about role task and role relationship is a side-effect of ambiguity.[36] Since the letters of Paul were occasional, it is likely that answering controversy would play a greater part in them than in the encyclical letter form. Two controversies related to role stand out.

The conflict between the "strong" and the "weak" of 1 Corinthians demonstrates the existence of ambiguity in role requirements. This conflict is resolved by Paul in the case of meat offered to idols, not on the basis of a clearly laid out pattern for behavior, but on the basis of decisions of "conscience."[37] Theissen's studies on the social stratification of the Corinthian church[38] are used by Holmberg to conclude that the bulk of 1 Corinthians is addressed to the rich and educated members of the church who dominate its life.[39] The picture we have of the role of the strong is made more complex by the issue of glossolalia. After a review of the Corinthian situation related to this controversy, Meeks concludes:

> We are left then with more suspicions than positive evidence for the interactions among the authority of apostles and their loyal adherents, the authority of wealth and position, and the authority of the spirit-possessed in Corinth. Probably there were conflicts not only between persons but also between different kinds of authority. Undoubtedly the real alignments were more complex than any picture we might construct.[40]

Authority and role requirements for leadership in Corinth are confused. This is evidence for great ambiguity. Holmberg agrees with Greeven in concluding that in Corinth "*nobody* exercised the functions of leadership."[41] Although it is possible that the chaos of leadership in the Corinthian church is not representative of all the Pauline churches, the Corinthian evidence of ambiguity in role requirements is strong.

Several times in the Corinthian correspondence Paul defends himself in the context of controversy about his role as apostle. In 1 Cor. 9 he tells us that he has chosen not to exercise "his right" as an apostle to receive financial support or his right to travel with a wife. His behavior causes conflict because of the contrast with the behavior of other apostles, especially the wandering charismatics in the Palestinian tradition.[42] Some Corinthians question his authority on this ground and display ambiguity in the role requirements for the one office clearly identified in the Pauline church faction.[43] The letter that is most clearly a response to a specific crisis of role ambiguity in the office of apostle is that to the church of Galatia.[44]

In the letter to the Galatians, Paul defends himself and his identity as an apostle in the context of a role-related controversy. The apologetic letter form itself—as noted by H. D. Betz—"presupposes the real or fictitious situation of the court of law."[45] Within his defense, Paul's invocation of the curse (Gal. 1:8–9) and the blessing (Gal. 6:16) makes Galatians a "magic letter," carrying the power of his initial mission work among the Galatian people.[46]

As Betz has shown in a carefully worked out summary of Paul's rhetorical argument, what is on trial is not Paul, nor even primarily his apostolic office, but his gospel to the Gentiles.[47] In this context of controversy about the status of the Gentile converts as uncircumcised, Paul's apostolic authority rests on the acceptance of uncircumcised Christians within the faction. His achieved status as apostle is a consequence of their status. Paul has earned his identity as an apostle to the uncircumcised. His defense is based upon the process by which he earned his status among the Galatians.[48] They have heard the same gospel still preached by Paul among the uncircumcised.

Universalizing the Corinthian experience results in a high score for ambiguity in the Pauline church: 1. The corroborating situation at Galatia, where Paul's own authority in the context of conflict over role ambiguity is called into question, affirms this score.

Leadership Conflicts (Negatively Valued). Just as ambiguity over role relationships scores high, so too does conflict over leadership. The Corinthian correspondence reveals conflict over leadership, both in identifying who the righteous apostles are and in determining how the "strong" should interact with the "weak."[49] The Galatian letter refers to several who "trouble" the Galatian Christians and lead them astray.[50] The Philippian letter warns the Christians, "Look out for the dogs" (Phil. 3:2).

The conflict we see in Paul's response to local situations in his letters makes it clear that there was consistent controversy over leadership in the Pauline church. This test scores a 1.

Leaders Who Exhibit Legitimate Authority. "Legitimacy" as a term in reference to authority is a quality of the social system. The term refers to the development of "a pattern of roles, status and deference."[51] Among the participants of the Pauline church, identifying those who exhibit legitimate authority is difficult because we have only Paul's description of the social situation.[52] We can assume that his purpose in writing and his paraenetic concerns influence his description of the "rightness"[53] of patterns of subordination in the Pauline church faction. The actual pattern of behavior *may* be masked in his letters.

The letters do offer a witness to the relationship of Paul himself with those in the Pauline churches. Holmberg concludes that Paul exercises a depersonalized, routinized charismatic authority in his churches.[54] His charismatic authority is legitimate insofar as the participants of the local churches share the belief that it is appropriate for him to impose his will upon them.[55] Controversies resulting in the letters to Galatia (Gal. 3:1–5) and especially to the church at Corinth (2 Cor. 11:4–21) demonstrate that this belief in the appropriateness of Paul's imposition of will is not universally shared in all the churches at all times.

Paul in his letters exhibits a concern for the existence of at least one leader, Paul himself, who has legitimate authority. Others outside the faction are to recognize the appropriateness of his leadership within the Pauline church faction in negotiations. But the evidence is also contradictory when controversies in specific churches are considered. Local church leaders do not seem to have the same recognized authority among the participants.[56] The score for legitimated authority ranges from .5 (mixed evidence) to 1, in recognition of the vitality of evidence from the fact that Paul's letters were preserved.

Scoring Grid Authority. The scores for the five tests of grid authority have resulted in a high and a low tendency for each:

	Value	Low	High
Judicatory system	+	0.0	0.0
System of offices	+	0.5	1.0
Ambiguity in role	−	1.0	1.0
Leadership conflict	−	1.0	1.0
Legitimated authority	+	0.5	1.0

The average scores for authority are .2 (low) and .4 (high).

Initiative (Negatively Valued)

Restrictive categories of membership can be internal or external to the group. The patron of the individual house church enjoys an ascribed role based on restrictive categories of membership from outside the faction: wealth and honor.[57] The economic status of patrons makes it possible for those particular persons to host the church in their homes. These are also the people who tend to show up most frequently in a Pauline prosopography because the house churches are listed by the name of the patron in greetings in Paul's letters. They enjoy special recognition as a class of members.

Three people listed from the Corinthian churches—Gaius, Crisipus, and Stephanas—all have an economic status that allows them to host the whole Corinthian church (Rom. 16:23), to have formerly been the head of the synagogue (*archisunagogos,* Acts 18:8), and to go with special delegations to meet with Paul (1 Cor. 16:17). These enjoy a social status that admits them to roles in the faction not available to others.[58] These are ascribed roles.

Contrary to this pattern of ascribed roles in the church, Paul preaches the equality of all in the Pauline church faction. More to the point, he voices his appreciation for the personal sacrifice or achievements of the patrons in the name of the faction. The predicate grid initiative is made up of five tests for the presence of (1) conflict over individual status; (2) negotiated settlements for disputes; (3) ascribed roles (negatively valued for initiative); (4) individuals who make a personal sacrifice for the group; (5) conflict over negotiated rules for competition.

Conflict over Individual Status. The Galatian controversy is an example of conflict over the status of the individual within the faction. Insecurity about the status of individual membership develops among the Galatian Christians. Insecurity is a side-effect of controversy or ambiguity over status. The Galatians are looking for a mechanism to achieve greater security in the faction. Paul argues that one behavior, one he identifies with faith, is more appropriate than another behavior, which he identifies with works of the law.

The conflict over status in the Pauline church faction includes the status of Paul himself. In the Corinthian correspondence he defends himself with reference to his achievements. 2 Cor. 11:23: "Are they servants of Christ? I am a better one—I am talking like a madman—with far greater labors, far more imprisonments, with countless beatings, and often near death."

William Baird has examined the experiences of revelation Paul cites to support his apostolic ministry: 2 Cor. 12:1–5 and Gal. 1:11–17.[59] He concludes that "Paul refrains from boasting in visions, so that 'no one may credit me with more than one sees or hears from me' (2 Cor. 12:6). In other words, Paul's ministry is accredited by the public credentials of his suffering service."[60]

Paul refrains from using an ascribed status, even a spiritually conferred ascribed status, to defend his apostolic calling. This pattern of Paul's behavior sets up conflicts over status in the new church faction.[61] But we have little evidence about most of Paul's direct contact with local churches—only his letters with their rhetorical form. Paul's paraenetic instruction is that leaders who serve the church are to be followed (1 Cor. 16:16). We conclude that this situation seems to have applied generally among the local church meetings. Conflict over individual status scores at least .5 (mixed evidence, little indication of conflict in many church situations) to 1 (evidence from the letter to the Galatians).

Negotiated Settlements for Disputes. The letter form itself, which Paul uses, is evidence for negotiated settlements in the Pauline church. The one reasonably well-defined case of conflict and its proposed resolution between Christians is the situation of Onesimus and Philemon. Whatever the possibility for requiring Philemon to receive Onesimus, the fact is that Paul negotiates with him on behalf of Onesimus. As Petersen points out, Philemon could have chosen not to participate.[62] The evidence for negotiated settlements in the Pauline church is strong, scoring a 1.

Ascribed Roles (Negatively Valued). Competition is a side-effect of the predominance of achieved roles. Insecurity is the invisible force behind competition, the force that keeps people striving to achieve.[63] Ascribed roles, to the extent they exist, create security and inhibit achievement.

To the extent that roles and places in the Pauline church faction are ascribed because of status, insecurity is limited. Paul's strategy of baptizing individuals capable of being patrons of the church in a given location[64] results in individuals who appear to have ascribed roles. These are the same people who are most often noticed in Paul's letters. But Paul's notice recognizes their accomplishments and encourages their initiative.[65] This encouragement is a sign of achievement, and, therefore, of achieved roles. We simply do not hear of those who fail to achieve in Paul's letters.

The situation of women in the Pauline church faction is addressed by 1 Cor. 11:2–16. Competition for roles in the faction is ruled out for this class of participants. Certain roles are proscribed. The role of women in the faction is, to this extent, ascribed—even though we have some evidence that women took up various roles within the faction in the earliest period (see, for example, the patronage of Prisca, Rom. 16:3). The score for ascribed role ranges from .5 (mixed evidence) to 1 (in consideration of the instruction that the role of women be limited).

Individuals Who Make a Personal Sacrifice for the Group. The presence of individuals who make sacrifices for the group does not measure the effect of persecution on the Pauline church. Persecution affects the measure of the cost of group membership and impacts group boundary. This test measures the personal sacrifice of people who are the "leaders" of the local church, those who travel from place to place in the empire, those who make themselves important to the work of the church, those who "labor," in Paul's words (1 Thess. 5:12). The words of encouragement Paul offers those who have sacrificed are a sign of achieved role in the faction.[66] He reinforces the benefit of the sacrifice that participants make by singling them out for praise and recognition. For example, these from the letter to the Philippians: Timothy (Phil. 2:20–22), Epaphroditus (Phil. 2:29–30), Syntyche (Phil. 4:2), and these from Corinthians: Stephanas, Fortunatus, and Achaicus (1 Cor. 16:15–18).

Evidence for the personal sacrifice of participants outside of the class of patrons in the Pauline church faction is fragmentary because we have only the letters of Paul. The score for personal sacrifice among members of the Pauline church ranges from .5 (mixed evidence on the basis of silence) to 1 (evidence of the personal sacrifice of those mentioned by Paul).

Conflict over Negotiated Rules for Competition. Conflict and its negotiated resolution at the Jerusalem conference—you to the Gentiles, we will go to the Jews—is an example of conflict and negotiated rules among the leaders of the church outside of the Pauline sphere. Again, there is the appearance of the signs of power and control: competition among autonomous individuals who each in turn controls others further up grid.[67]

Paul may fall into this pattern—moving down the group scale—when he relates to the Jerusalem church leaders.

Paul reports the results of the Antioch conflict in his letter to the Galatians. His report, however, is in response to the Galatian situation, not a historical or objective reminiscence. The Galatian situation reveals insecurity over achieved status in the Pauline church faction among the participants—a sign of competition. Paul is engaged in a conflict over rules for competition in the faction. Who is in a better position to achieve status in the faction, a circumcised Gentile or an uncircumcised Gentile?

Within the local church, the Corinthian correspondence offers evidence of a series of conflicts among participants over rules concerning interaction and leadership. The conflict between those Paul identifies as the strong and the weak is acted out in various situations in the Pauline church faction at Corinth.[68] The score for conflict over rules in the church is 1.

Scoring Grid Initiative. The scores for the five tests of grid initiative have resulted in a high and a low tendency for each:

	Value	Low	High
Conflict over individual status	+	0.5	1.0
Negotiated settlements	+	1.0	1.0
Ascribed roles	−	1.0	0.5
Personal sacrifice	+	0.5	1.0
Conflict over rules	+	1.0	1.0

The average scores for initiative are .6 (low) to .9 (high).

Autonomy (Negatively Valued)

The score for autonomy consists of a series of tests for the presence of the (1) freedom to dispose of time; (2) freedom to dispose of private property; (3) freedom to choose collaborators; (4) freedom to choose clothing; (5) freedom to choose food. The results of these tests are averaged and scored negatively for grid.

The Freedom to Dispose of Time. We have little evidence and no observation of the way participants spend their time. We believe the Pauline church meets frequently, yet Paul insists from the earliest letter that the new Christians behave quietly and work for a living (1 Thess. 4:9–12). They do not remove themselves from the world. Therefore, we assume that they need to have the time to ply their trade. The freedom to dispose of time scores 1.

The Freedom to Dispose of Private Property. Here, too, we have little evidence and no independent observations of the way participants dispose of their private property. In contrast with the Palestinian Christian experience, however, we can assume that—except for the collection for the saints, which functions to reinforce group investment—private property is not shared or controlled by the Pauline church.[69] Again, the requirement to continue to work and not change one's station in life would mean that private property continues to be controlled by the individual. The "communism" of the Jerusalem church does not carry over to the Gentile church of Paul.

Paul extends the possibility of choice even to giving to the collection for the saints, 2 Cor. 8:8–10.[70] The freedom to dispose of private property in the Pauline church scores 1.

The Freedom to Choose Collaborators. It is important to Paul that participants in the church be afforded the opportunity to interact with others. Paul and those in his church associate with anyone. Only group considerations of purity and boundary limit this access. In two situations Paul argues against patterns of behavior that limit access to specific classes of people.

In Galatians he reviews the argument he had with Peter over the accessibility of Gentile Christians. Although we cannot be sure that his arguments carried the day in Antioch, it would seem likely that the Pauline mission was founded with this inclusive pattern of behavior. Jews and Gentiles eat together.

In the Corinthian correspondence Paul argues that the weaker Christians, identified with lower social classes, are not inferior and should be included in church group functions with some sensitivity by the stronger Christians, identified with higher, more educated social classes.[71] In this case, because Paul's letter has been preserved, we can assume that new rules for the interaction of Christians in Corinth were accepted.

The freedom to choose collaborators scores 1 for the Pauline church. Where there are existing patterns that exclude individuals from interaction, new rules are enacted that open the way. The ambiguity that functions to reduce group boundary score functions to increase grid autonomy.

The Freedom to Choose Clothing. The issue of clothing has two parts. There is freedom to be a participant in the culture. Paul himself claims the freedom to be a participant in the culture in each place he goes. This behavior implies that there is no stricture on clothing, a natural correlative to the freedom of time and personal property. But the strictures Paul places on women in worship must be considered as a limitation on these freedoms.

In the passage 1 Cor. 11:2–16 Paul limits the level of participation of female participants in the Pauline church faction and places a stricture, the veiling of the hair of women.[72] He sets up a classification of participants who are not allowed to carry out certain group functions. They are named as participants in his greeting and singled out for their achievements in the faction, but their choice of apparel is limited.

This category scores lower than the rest of the tests for autonomy, though the scoring is somewhat tentative because of historical cultural considerations. Is Paul in fact more liberal than his contemporaries in allowing more choice for women? Does he give women less freedom than is available to them in the larger society?[73] That Paul has found the need to write to the Corinthian church on this theme implies that their cultic practice is ignorant of this limitation of choice for women. Paul's comment that "the churches of God" have no such custom may imply that no other local church allows this freedom of clothing. It also may imply that Paul is uncomfortable with such freedom and that he is referring to Palestinian customs.[74] The best that can be scored for freedom of clothing is .5, with 0 as a probability. We have no independent observation of the role and dress of women like Prisca, Apphia, and Phoebe within the Pauline church faction.

The Freedom to Choose Food. Clearly, the choice of food is one area in which Paul and the Pauline church have opinions. Only group solidarity concerns limit the choices of the individual. "All things are God's."

1 Cor. 8:8–10, 10:25–28, and Rom. 14:2–3, 13–23 make pronouncements on the appropriateness of eating meat that has been offered to idols and that may, therefore, have acquired the wrong ritual purity. Theologically, Paul claims that "the earth is the Lord's, and everything in it" (1 Cor. 10:26). This theological principle is made practical in his summary in Romans: "I know and am persuaded in the Lord Jesus that

nothing is unclean in itself; but it is unclean for any one who thinks it unclean" (Rom. 14:14). The only limitation on what is to be eaten is situational and is based on the concern for group solidarity.

Though we have no independent observation of the meal patterns of Christians in the Pauline church, these pronouncements of Paul may be assumed to have been effective in the church. Paul has a concern for group solidarity in his missionary environment, especially as regards the common meal between Jewish and Gentile Christians (Gal. 2:11–21). The Christian has the freedom to eat anything sold in the market without concern for ritual purity (1 Cor. 10:25). This test for autonomy should score 1 on this evidence. The letter to the Galatians, however, responds directly to the behavior of at least some in the Galatian church faction. The separation of some from the common meal that Paul discusses in Chapter Two happens in Antioch, not Galatia. Still, the behavior that is the object of Paul's concern in his letter is the observing of "days, and months, and seasons, and years," and the circumcision of Gentiles. There is the possibility in this matrix of concern that the Galatians are declaring some foods unclean. Freedom to choose food scores in the range .5 (ambiguous evidence from Galatians) to a more likely 1 (Paul's instructions).

Scoring Grid Autonomy. Autonomy is negatively scored for grid value. The scores for the five tests of grid autonomy have resulted in a high and a low tendency for each:

	Low	High
Time	1.0	1.0
Private property	1.0	1.0
Associations	1.0	1.0
Clothing	0.0	0.5
Food	0.5	1.0

The average scores for autonomy are .7 (low) to .9 (high).

Conclusions about Mapping

The tendency for the group score is the sum of the tendencies of the group predicates found in Chapter Five.

Group Predicates	Value	Tendency	
		Lower	Upper
Proximity	+	.55	.80
Transitivity	+	.35	.65
Deferential involvement	+	.50	.75
Boundary	+	.80	.80
Totals		2.20	3.00
Group averages		.55	.75

The tendency for the grid score is the sum of the tendencies of the grid predicates found in this chapter.

Grid Predicates	Value	Tendency	
		Low	High
Role differentiation	+	.20	.70
Authority	+	.20	.40
Initiative	−	.90	.60
Autonomy	−	.90	.70
Totals		.60	1.80
Grid averages		.15	.45

The field of likely grid-group mappings for the Pauline church (shaded box) is the field of the high group, low grid, D Quadrant (see Figure 5). We explore the meaning of this mapping in the next chapter. Variation of the predicates gives a wide range to the plotting of Paul's culture on the grid-group map. This wide range could have presented a problem for drawing conclusions about the typology of the belief structure of the Pauline church, except that the entire range of possible mapping points is contained in one quadrant. This field represents the limits of the estimated range of variability. We expect that Paul and the Pauline church faction would score somewhere within this range could we use other ethnographic tools to identify the score exactly.

The mapping of Paul and the Pauline church in the D Quadrant[75] fits those who are heavily invested in a group. They invest in a group that is a voluntary association of individuals who freely contract together. The rules for behavior in the group are individualized or personalized for the members because there are few hierarchical social controls to keep them active in the group. The participants find the group important enough to

Figure 5 The Pauline Church on the Grid-Group Map

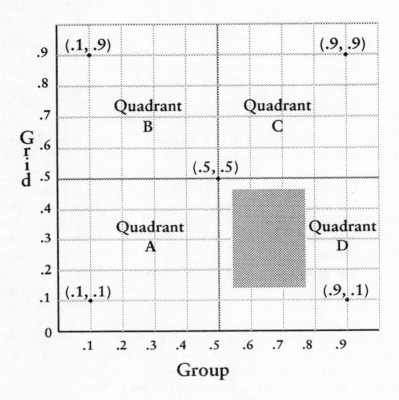

make room for it in their lives. This is visible in descriptions of the ways in which they interact and in rules associated with membership. On the other hand, there are few overt, visible social controls that determine their decisions regarding their participation. This is apparent in the lack of controls related to social hierarchy.

7

Conclusions Concerning Quadrant D Mapping

The preceding chapters have presented a picture of Paul and of the Pauline church faction that is based upon a social accounting. The available evidence demonstrates that Paul and those whom we hear about in his letters should be mapped in Quadrant D of the grid-group map, the field of small egalitarian sects that tend to charismatic leadership and organizational instability.

The Pauline Church Faction and the Big-Man Type

This mapping may come as a surprise. On the basis of resemblance to typology, the cultural script that most closely parallels Paul would be the Papuan Big-Man type.[1] Such a type would map in Quadrant A. The term "Big Man" comes from the description offered by anthropologists who have studied New Guinea.[2] The Big Man typifies those who exhibit a high level of individuation and *little* interest in group investment.

He who seeks it [status] needs to engage a team of supporters, each contracting with him separately for what their allegiance is worth. Anthony Forge describes how a Big Man in Abelam gains control of his own villagers, files a secret dossier of magic on them, one by one, and then uses their work in exponentially prestigious exchanges with an opposite number

in another district. Each leader is out for himself. Their respective follow-
ings gain by each success. But no Big Man is secure. His rival and sup-
planter lurks, who will one day oust him and take his place.[3]

The typological argument for mapping Paul in the entrepreneurial
Quadrant A appears to be quite strong. For example: Paul could be looking for supporters to be faithful to him in Phil. 1:15–18. By their
faithfulness he would gain prestige. He goes on to speak of the "opposition" in v. 28, but, we notice, in this case the opposition results in persecution and therefore is not opposition within the Pauline church
faction itself.

Is Paul asking the Philippians to remain loyal to him as a Big Man
against others, or is he simply an example of faith, wearing the badge of
membership? There is the language of unity in the group: be of one mind
(v. 27). But this could be a request for the Philippians to remain loyal so
that he may "not have run in vain" (Phil. 2:16). Other references in Phil.
2:19ff. could be to new Big Men, no longer fellow workers, who have set
out on their own. In Phil. 4:15–19 some gifts to Paul are mentioned. Is
this support for him as a Big Man received from others further up grid?
2 Cor. 11:8–9, a related text, describes the result of their first gift: "I
robbed other churches by accepting support from them in order to serve
you."

Paul contends that there is power in weakness. In context (2 Cor.
11:21–12:13) Paul may be arguing against other Big Men who participate in the faction. Gerd Theissen demonstrates that Paul and Barnabas
were a type of community organizer in conflict with charismatic missionaries from Palestine.[4] This conflict of leadership in the faction involves
more than a question of leadership style. Paul's authority is questioned
on the grounds of differing "rules" for the social structure of the faction
during an argument over "rules" for contracts. The charismatic missionary leadership types appear to be both competitive and entrepreneurial,
at cross-purposes with the small-group community organizers.

Paul appears to fit the description of the Big-Man typology because of
an exaggeration of the competition between Paul and other Big-Man
types in the social network, James, Peter, Apollos. *If* Paul is a Big-Man
type, the motivation for the Pauline mission to the Gentiles could be
understood as a concern for the expansion of his own following and for
prestige. The negotiation and territorial specialization that Paul reports
out of the Jerusalem conference (Gal. 2:9)[5] would be a type of contract

between Big Men for efficiency and mutual benefit. This parallel to the typology of Quadrant A is appealing, but such a mapping does not fit the behavioral evidence as measured in a social accounting of the Pauline church faction. It is demonstrated—see Chapter Five—using observations of the behavior of Paul and those who participate in the Pauline churches, as inferred from the letters, that Paul and the Pauline church faction are highly invested in group controls.[6] "Proximity to prototype is not alone sufficient to constitute a classificatory model."[7]

Leaping to a conclusion on the basis of the resemblance a social unit may have with a typological description of a cultural pattern without doing a reasonably careful social accounting is dangerous. It is especially dangerous when one seeks to describe a specific historical community. There is no possibility of falsification and therefore no verifiability because the resemblance is in the eye of the beholder. It may be helpful to make such statements when the purpose is to explore variations in the typological descriptions themselves. These explorations of the manner in which various social science models for interpreting culture interact offer new paradigms for study.[8] But they are no substitute for working out those paradigms in a more detailed and falsifiable fashion.

Ultimately, the behavioral evidence of a high level of concern for the group in the Pauline church faction outweighs the typological argument for a Big-Man status for Paul. The typological argument for low group, low grid may exist because Paul, a community organizer, is arguing against others in his social network—especially itinerant charismatic leaders who have adopted the Big-Man mode—but this speculation awaits a social accounting of the Palestinian and Antiochian church factions from the earliest period. Paul and Pauline Christianity, as they exist during the ministry of Paul, are characterized by the small-group Quadrant D environment.

High Group, Low Grid, Quadrant D Behaviors

A high investment in group is indicated by the following patterns of behaviors:

Boundaries	control of interaction with outside
	control of response to persecution
	control of sex and marriage
	the repeated claim "Jesus Christ is Lord"

Rights	access to the voluntary association
	regular meetings, holy kiss, meals
Penalties	expulsion
	magical sanctions, misfortunes

The lack of grid involvement is indicated by these behaviors:

Negative insulation	social equality in faction
Autonomy	independence
	commerce with the world
	no higher authorities
	proliferation of gifts of the spirit
Little control	renunciation of support
Competition	"I worked harder"

Paul and those around him in the Pauline church clearly map into Quadrant D, typified sociologically by the egalitarian small group. A social accounting of the Pauline church based on the behavior of the participants in the faction inferred from the letters of Paul has resulted in this mapping. The cluster of values, beliefs, and symbolic behavior in rituals common to the churches associated with this mapping provides a context for Paul's theological concepts. Paul's theological terminology functions to integrate the perceived ambiguity and conflict found in the presence of unbalanced strengths of grid and group.

Correlating Symbolic Behavior and Belief with Grid-Group Mapping

Having mapped Paul's church in Quadrant D, we now need to correlate his cosmology to this mapping by using language available from Paul's own terminology. Grid-group analysis uses four prototypical descriptions of cultural bias to predict the ideology or cosmology of an observed social unit. Descriptions of these are widely disseminated by those who use the grid-group model, not as an ethnographic methodology, but as a model for interpreting cultural patterns. The function of Paul's theological terminology finds its context in the cluster of values and beliefs associated with Quadrant D mapping. This mapping, however, is first accomplished by observing behavior, not manifest statements of ideology.

The method for describing the correlation between the theological statements found in Paul's letters and the cosmology of the small group Quadrant D is provided by David Ostrander's study of the distribution of beliefs and values on the grid-group map.[9] His three-part method results in a typological description of the symbolic system of Quadrant D participants. By following his pattern of correlating belief pattern and symbolic behavior with the social mapping of Quadrant D, we achieve a specific description of the Pauline church faction.

The general typology for Quadrant D is described by David Ostrander thus:

> We find people's views of society and of nature linked in disequilibrium. They are both fragmented into mutually antagonistic groups and both suffer constant danger from predators, human, natural and supernatural. Existence depends upon membership in a group, and therefore the goal of symbolic action is the protection of the group from outside threats. Sometimes these threats are physical assaults; more often they are the result of witchcraft or magic of some kind, and reveal their presence by sickness, death, a bad harvest or other misfortune. Personalized symbolic action in this square takes the form of divining the malefactor, expelling him, should he be a member of the group, canceling his spell, and responding with one's own magic. The square D symbolic practitioner has a private pipeline to the supernatural with which he outwits his enemies and protects his friends, kin, and clients. Elaboration is at a low level because specialists are not organized and no enduring social structure exists which would support such organization.[10]

This typological description of belief pattern and symbolic behavior emerges through Ostrander's analysis of the cultural bias of Quadrant D. There are three stages in Ostrander's description: the dimensional, the interactional, and the emergent. Each of these is used herein to examine the Pauline letters and thereby form a description of the context of theological terminology within the Pauline church faction.

Dimensional Descriptions of Beliefs and Values

Remembering the map of the grid-group relationships helps one to picture the ways the dimensional descriptive categories are associated (see Figure 6).

Group categories reflect the varying importance of participation in group activities to the participating or choosing individual. The weight of the choices related to group concerns varies horizontally across the map. This variance has been described in Chapter Three. Grid categories reflect the varying emphasis on or the power of strictures on the choices an individual makes. These strictures represent hierarchical social concerns that order the choices related to group investment. These vary vertically on the map and have also been described in Chapter Three. Group and grid dimensions are considered separately.

Group Dimension

Our examination of the dimensional level begins with the results of Chapter Five. Those associated with Paul and Paul himself are highly invested in the social group we call the Pauline church. The concerns that come with a high investment in group include (1) a unity of society and nature, (2) an ongoing concern for the preservation of the group, and (3) a salvation conceived in the context of the Pauline church faction.[11]

Unity of the Church and Nature. Paul explicitly states, in theological terms, the unity of the Christian community with nature. The Christian community and all of creation are linked because both await the end time (Rom. 8:18–25). The social unit, as represented by the faction, and nature, represented by creation, are seen as parts of one integrated system. There is symbolic unity of the faction and nature because both must endure the present difficulties awaiting the time of their redemption.

Concern for the Church. A concern for the preservation and continuation of the group is also associated with a high level of group investment.[12] This concern for preservation is expressed in terms of the symbolic actions of the members of the group in their preparations for the end time (instructions concerning baptism, Rom. 6:1–13, 1 Cor. 15:29ff., and the eucharist 1 Cor. 11:17ff.). Paul identifies the boundaries of the group and makes efforts to maintain its purity (1 Cor.

Figure 6 The Grid-Group Dimensional Map

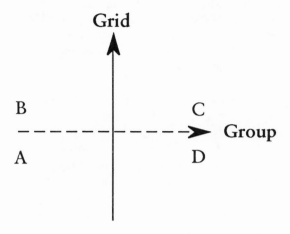

5:9–13, Gal. 2:11–21). He is personally concerned that each local church group continue to be prepared and not backslide as the new age begins (1 Cor. 5:1–8 and 1 Thess. 3).

After a study of Pauline paraenesis in the context of conflict within the Pauline church faction, Wayne Meeks concludes: "Paul uses the mediating symbol of Jesus crucified, not to achieve a theoretical synthesis of these opposing positions, but to signify a way in which the persons who occupied the positions could understand their engagement with one another. The grammar of this moral process is the logic of the interaction that Paul undertakes to bring about."[13]

Salvation in Terms of the Group. Salvation itself is not individualistic, but is conceived in the context of the history of God's people. The individual is saved by faith, but that faith or that salvation is made visible in the community of the faithful, the body of Christ. Nils Dahl accurately describes the context for Pauline soteriology:

> Justification does not simply involve the individual and his salvation. Paul's perspective includes history and eschatology: Adam, mankind and Christ, the promise to Abraham and the Law given to Moses on Sinai, the gospel preached to Jews and to Gentiles, God's work in the past and in the future, the Apostle's own work in the present, the first fruits among the Gentiles

and the remnant of Israel, the unity of Jews and Gentiles in the local congregation and in the worldwide church, Christ's dominion over principalities and powers, and the all-encompassing doctrine of justification is not primarily social; it is theological and soteriological. But the framework which Paul uses to locate the doctrine is social and historical rather than psychological and individualistic.[14]

This statement—with reference to the whole of Paul's letter to the Romans—correctly places Paul's idea of justification in the context of the continuation of the "saved" group, those in a special relationship with God. They are part of a socially and historically identifiable group. They have in common an inheritance that is the promise of God.

Conclusion for Group Dimension. Paul's theological statements relating to group investment are particular examples of the type of responses expected by grid-group analysis of the Pauline church. These theological concerns convey Paul's cosmology. The unity of the church and creation, the concern for the preservation of the church in the new age, and salvation conceived in the context of the church are symbolic images that reflect his high group investment.

Excursus: Stendahl and Käsemann. Some years ago Krister Stendahl and Ernst Käsemann described conflicting understandings of essential elements of Paul's theology. Stendahl saw clearly the importance of the incorporation of the new Gentile Christians into the history of salvation by God.[15] Käsemann focused on the doctrine of justification.[16] He found Paul asking the question, "How can I find a gracious God?"[17] Stendahl, on the other hand, found Paul asking about the possibility of the inclusion of the new Gentile Christians into the messianic community.[18]

The group dimension of Paul's cosmology demonstrates the importance of the incorporation of the new Christians into the "saved group." The context of salvation is inclusion in the group. Stendahl's description defines this relationship after the time in which the law served as custodian:

Once the Messiah had come, and once the faith in him—not "faith" as a general religious attitude—was available as the decisive ground for salvation, the Law had done its duty as a custodian for the Jews, or as a waiting room with strong locks (Gal. 3:22ff.). Hence it is clear that Paul's problem is how to explain why there is no reason to impose the Law on the Gentiles, who now, in God's good Messianic time, have become partakers in the fulfillment of the promises to Abraham (v. 29).[19]

Words like "participation" and concepts of social boundary like faith as the "decisive ground" are group category concepts. Stendahl is correct in recognizing the importance of membership in the Pauline church faction that we find in Paul's cosmology.

Grid Dimension

The description of the dimensional level uses the results, found in Chapter Six, of the low grid investment in Paul's church. Low grid structure is affirmed in "personalized means of symbolic action."[20] Low grid indicates a minimal degree of behavioral restriction that is based on categories of social hierarchy. There are few, if any, constraints on the interaction between individuals within the group. Therefore, resources like time and space are not compartmentalized with formal or ideological separations except as group boundaries constrain or set limits to their use.

Excursus: Käsemann and Stendahl. In the debate between Stendahl and Käsemann the low grid condition is the aspect of Paul's cosmology that is key to Käsemann's reading of Paul. The crisis is individual salvation. Käsemann is correct in understanding the radical individuality in Paul's gospel of salvation and in denying that salvation history opens the way for "an immanent evolutionary process whose meaning can be grasped on earth."[21] Paul presses against any movement up-grid to institutionalize role relationships: "Rom. 5.12ff. makes it clear that the apostle does not understand history as a continuous evolutionary process but as the contrast of the two realms of Adam and Christ. Pauline theology unfolds this contrast extensively as the struggle between death and life, sin and salvation, law and gospel."[22]

This radical individuality is central to low grid dimensional statements of Paul's cosmology. Individual Christians participate in this struggle between opposing forces. Every day, Christians choose life through obedience in faith. It is possible to translate Käsemann's descriptions of Paul's concerns directly into grid categories: "Our task is to ask: what does the Jewish nomism against which Paul fought really represent? And our answer must be: it represents the community of 'good' people which turns God's promises into their own privileges and God's commandments into the instruments of self-sanctification."[23] Translating "privileges" as "ascribed status" and "instruments of self-sanctification" into "a social hierarchy of status" helps describe the low grid cosmology Käsemann sees in Paul's writings. It says: "The object of Paul's ideological concern within the church is ascribed status and social hierarchy."

Personalized Means of Symbolic Action. Although Paul's definition of salvation is stated in terms of participation in the promises of God,[24] the individual who is saved—that is, the one who participates in the Pauline church faction—is saved by his or her own faith.[25] The tension between the two parts of this statement indicates the tension in the social mapping in Quadrant D. Strong group commitment without corresponding strength in ego-centered social or hierarchical categories of control leaves group participation as the only status available to the participant.[26] Hierarchical status and ascribed divisions among members of the group are very weak. Because the boundaries of the group are carefully described but internal divisions are not, there is an inherent tension in the cosmology associated with Quadrant D. This tension is visible both in Paul's thought and in modern understandings of Paul's thought.

Permitting the eating of meat that has been offered to idols is a good example of Paul's apparent flexibility (1 Cor. 10:23–30).[27] While the group boundary is set at the prohibition of the worship of idols, Paul claims that the liberty to eat meat sold in the market is not defined by the behavior or belief of anyone outside the faction. He is concerned, however, with the scruples of another inside the Pauline church faction.[28] This reflects his concern about group solidarity. There is no limitation on the participants' behavior that resembles the limitation or circumscription relating to the group boundaries. Paul is not so "flexible" as he is capable of distinguishing limitations on a participant's behavior from taboos related to group boundaries.

"For freedom, Christ has set us free." This theme is stated in Gal. 5:1 and Rom. 8:2, but the most particular statement of that freedom is in the framing letter of the Corinthian correspondence, the so-called letter C.[29] 1 Cor. 8, 9:19–23, and 10:23–11:1 discuss freedom as it relates to Paul and to the interaction of members of the Pauline church faction. Though purity and restrictions on participation in another religious faction are real concerns, they have to do with the boundary of the Pauline church faction. These concerns answer the question "Who is a participant in the faction?" Specific behavioral restrictions on the activities of members of the faction are based solely on the concern for the preservation of the group. The individual turns from participation in other religious factions to participation as a follower of Christ and the "living and true God" (1 Thess. 1:9, Gal. 4:8–9, 1 Cor. 12:2).[30] After crossing inside the boundary of the Pauline church faction with baptism, each participant is restricted only by the concern for group solidarity.

Wayne Meeks terms those of the Pauline church who signal their presence in the letters of Paul "people of high status inconsistency (low status crystallization)."[31] Theirs is a world that has lost much of the social constraint that a stratified society placed on their lives. The new faction into which they enter places emphasis upon the equality of its participants. Paul explains this equality by deferring to the priority of Christ for every participant. The argument of the letter to the Romans is founded on this explanation (Rom. 3:21–31).[32] Equality in the faction becomes a very important theme for Paul. Paul's answers to the struggles of the Corinthian churches are examples.[33] We can observe the equality Paul assumes concerning Philemon and his relationship with Onesimus, the slave, who now is to be considered a brother, a member of the family (Philem. 16). This assumption is also clear in the polarization of the choices Paul makes available to Philemon.[34]

Conclusion for Grid Dimension. The lack of grid strictures in Paul's church that we see in grid-group analysis leads to an expected lack of constraint on individual behavior expressed by Paul in his letters. The cosmology—that is, the way Paul explains or justifies the related behavior—conforms to that expected by grid-group analysis of the Pauline church. Salvation is expressed in individual terms, that is, by faith alone. High group investment with correspondingly little investment in individual hierarchy results in an unstable social situation and in theological tension, evident in the Käsemann-Stendahl debate.

Interactional Descriptions of Beliefs and Values

The relative strength of grid and group investment are compared in interactional descriptions of the ideology of the social unit. A map of the grid-group relationships shows the interactional descriptive categories (see Figure 7).

Figure 7   The Grid-Group Diagonals Map

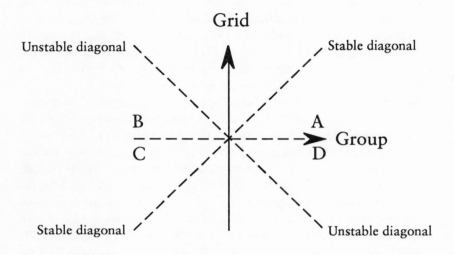

Interactive categories compare the cosmologies of diagonally opposed quadrants. Such a comparison may be obvious when pictured on the diagram, but the opposition of the dimensional variables makes such comparison less obvious in narrative description. Differing relative strengths of grid and group are termed unstable. Low grid, low group A and high grid, high group C mark the stable diagonal. High grid, low group B and low grid, high group D mark the unstable diagonal.

The Stable Diagonal

A short description of the social units that inhabit the stable diagonal offers a contrast to the Pauline situation. Quadrants A and C are the home of successful elites. Because of their matched priority of grid and group strength, they place a positive value on their cosmological order. Things are "right" with the world. There is a high degree of elaboration in the symbolic system and correspondingly long traditions of doctrine and practice. Specialization, either within the group or by individuals, is the mechanism for authority. We would expect to find specialized practitioners for symbolic or religious actions because the complexity of the symbolic system requires a specialist, someone highly skilled or empowered with authority.[35]

The Unstable Diagonal

The results are quite different in the case of the unstable diagonal. Again, as with the dimensional level, the interactional level of Paul's cosmology correlates with the prediction of the grid-group analysis of the Pauline community. The unstable diagonal is described by Ostrander:[36] (1) there is an inherent tendency toward fragmentation; (2) the social order itself is considered a source of danger; (3) the relationship of nature and society is viewed as complex and negative; (4) there is little elaboration of the symbolic system; (5) the specialist practitioners of the symbolic system are part time and unorganized.

The Inherent Tendancy toward Fragmentation. The instability of the church is indicated by the leadership problems Paul encounters. There is a tendency toward fragmentation or factionalism in the very early church, a tendency Paul betrays in his letters. He is concerned about the new Christians' being led astray (1 Thess. 3:5, Gal. 1:7, Phil. 1:15–18, 1 Cor. 1:10–17, 2 Cor. 11:1–6, Rom. 16:17–20). But instability in the new faction is more than just a crisis of leadership.

Paul's concern for unity in the development of the Corinthian church is occasioned by the tendency of low grid, small groups to divide. Paul expects the group to develop cohesively because of a historical transference. Though his ideological position may be based on the concept of the unity of God,[37] the historical situation is the development of the mission to the Gentiles. Christians are to support each other, that is, they are to become a social unit. Paul's conclusion to the discussion of dissension and party strife in Corinth, 1 Cor. 3:1–17,[38] argues that the signs of division—jealousy and envy—have no place within the boundaries of the Pauline church faction. These are signs of those who live outside the boundary.[39]

The purpose that overrides the inherent tendency of small-group Quadrant D to divide is the reason Paul expresses such a level of concern about group solidarity. This overriding purpose comes from Paul's understanding of the faction and its participation in the history of God's people. Paul transfers his concern for the inclusion of Gentiles into his ideological concern for group preservation in the context of individual freedom. Commenting on the letter to the Romans, Robert Jewett hypothesizes that "Romans [is] an ambassadorial letter that preserves common ground by citing and emending materials being used by the competitive wings of the early church. It is the synthesis that constitutes Paul's distinctive perspective, the serious effort to unite the Gentile and the Jewish Christian confessions, hymns, and interpretive traditions."[40]

The Social Order Itself as a Source of Danger. Affliction is a part of Paul's thinking from his earliest letters. Though there may have been historical occasion—including a remembrance of Paul's own persecution of the followers of Jesus—for his teaching on suffering, the remembrance of suffering functions within low grid, small group D cosmology to reinforce distrust of the social order. The social order is not inhospitable to the Pauline church faction; Roman cities offer the opportunity for the Pauline missionary endeavor. Yet Paul has a concern for persecution from outside the faction and promises troubles for the community already in the early Thessalonian correspondence.

He observes that he taught that affliction was normal for followers and that it has already happened, 1 Thess. 3:3–4. He rejoices that the Thessalonians have not been moved from their belief by affliction, 1 Thess. 3:6–10. He contrasts the attitude and behavior of those outside the Pauline church faction with those inside, 1 Thess. 4:1–8. Finally, he demands that those in the faction live independently *of* or at least without undue interaction *with* outsiders *(ekso)*, 1 Thess. 4:9–12.

Ernest Best, in his commentary on this passage in Thessalonians, also makes this distinction between unfortunate but passing incidents and affliction from the outside as it affects the faction. Persecution is not simply a fact of the historical moment for the faction; it functions to reinforce group identity. "Paul is not thinking of a period of persecution which will pass and the church will return to normality; normality is persecution (Acts 14:22). This sense of 'destiny' makes the idea much stronger than the belief that it is a tragic fact of Christian existence that suffering accompanies goodness or that the imitation of Jesus will lead to persecution."[41]

The Negative Relationship between Nature and Society. The complex relationship between society and nature is negatively viewed, as Ostrander's model predicts.[42] It has already been noted that there is a unity of society, represented by the Pauline church faction, and nature, represented by creation. The context of this relationship described in Romans is fellow suffering (Rom. 8:18–25). This suffering is associated with the ending of the present age and order. The unity of the Pauline church faction and creation exists, then, in a complex relationship of future expectation, anticipation, struggles, and present signs and preparation.

Little Elaboration of the Symbolic System. Ostrander concludes that individual participants are able to understand the whole of the symbolic system because it is not complex. Folk traditions may exist, but they will be simple enough to be "inculcated" by individuals.[43]

The relationship of the Pauline church faction and creation is complex. Yet, Paul's reduction of the emerging contemporary Pharisaic codes for social behavior and cultic identity (food laws, circumcision, and the like in Galatians) is not an evangelistically expedient gesture for the purpose of including Gentiles in this complex situation.[44] This reduction is, rather, a natural correlative of Paul's cosmology. When Paul picks up his opponent's language in throwing out the complex law of the Torah and replacing it with a simplified "law of Christ" (Gal. 6:2),[45] he reflects his own restatement of the whole of the Torah: "For the whole law is fulfilled in one word, 'You shall love your neighbor as yourself'" (Gal. 5:12). Simplification of the rules of behavior is an end to itself.

Part-time and Unorganized Specialists. Paul, himself, puts no one to trouble, by earning his own living. As he renounces support from Corinth, he becomes only a part-time missionary (1 Cor. 9:15–18; 2 Cor. 11:7–11).[46] This lowers his status in the wider social community and causes conflict, yet it is logical and appropriate within his own understanding of the world. Paul declares that his ministry does not depend upon another (Gal. 1:11–12 and 2). He is not simply applying an expedient means to missionary work in uncharted territory; he is justifying his behavior in accordance with the cosmology of small-group Quadrant D. Pressure for ascribed status, routinized authority, and remuneration for leadership positions in the faction comes from the perceived need for stabilization and movement up grid, and Paul reacts to these pressures.

Conclusion: The Interactional-Level Description of Paul's Cosmology

High investment in group controls with correspondingly little investment in hierarchical organization results in an unstable social situation. The only status that is available is group participation, but the definition of that group is fragile. There is a tendency for the group to dissolve or break up. There is also a competing tendency for the group to institutionalize its social controls. Paul's response to these conflicting currents is predictable, according to David Ostrander's description of the interactional level of Quadrant D.[47] Paul's justification of his behavior is consistent with Quadrant D typology.

Emergent Descriptions of Beliefs and Values

The emergent description is most simply expressed as the combination and integration of the dimensional and interactional descriptions. Expressed in general terms, it is a typological description of the ideology of social organizations that are mapped in one quadrant. When Paul's terms are used, however, it becomes an historical expression of that general typology.

Paul's Emergent Cosmology

The general description of the cosmology of those who are mapped in Quadrant D is worked out by combining the dimensional and interactional descriptions. Using Ostrander's model, we can make five statements about Paul's churches.[48] These statements describe the combined dimensional and interactional levels of Paul's cosmology; combined, they narrate the emergent level of his cosmology. The typological expressions of these statements are: (1) the society is a part of nature, but (2) the relation between the group and nature is negatively valued. (3) Religious or symbolic action is highly personalized, but (4) the goals of symbolic action are group oriented. Finally, (5) the symbolic system is not elaborated.

Society as Part of Nature

In the Pauline church the fate of the whole of creation and the fate of the Christian are linked in a millennialist view of the world. Only the characteristics of the cultural bias of Quadrant D provide an environment suitable for the development of millennialist groups. Steve Rayner has identified three predicates for the definition of millennialism within the context of grid-group analysis. These are the temporal, spacial, and ethical predicates: (1) the world is ending shortly (2) by powerful outside influence, and (3) in the end everyone will be recognized as moral equals.[49] He concludes that only Quadrant D provides the social environment where the bias of the cosmology can support millennialism.

> It is only possible collectively to maintain millenarian beliefs in a social environment in which it is possible collectively to foreshorten historical time and compress geographical space. (These are seen as the logical conditions of millenarianism.) In terms of grid and group, these conditions can only exist within a strong group boundary and increase in likelihood as the grid weakens and provides fewer points of historical and spatial differentiation.[50]

The various theories of both relative deprivation[51] and cognitive dissonance,[52] which seek to explain the rise of millennialism, focus on the third predicate, the ethical predicate, to the exclusion of the other two. Neither of these theories is able to predict the rise of millenarian movements.[53] Stress in the social environment, in the symbolic environment, or both is thought to produce the social situation in which millennialism—identified within the ethical response to stress—is an appropriate response, but not the only available response.

Theories of social or symbolic conflict focus on one aspect of the social environment, which is the historical context of the millennial movement. This perceived conflict is integrated into the cosmology of the group participants by reversing or by renewing the social order in the millennial expectation myth. Other variables must be at work, however, because there is no necessary cause-and-effect relationship between social or symbolic conflict and millennialism. Stress does not necessarily result in millennialism. By focusing attention on two other aspects of the perceived social environment—the perception of space and time—Steve Rayner provides a more complete description of the millennial environment.[54]

Millennialist Ideology. The expectation that there will be a sudden end to the present age, the expectation that this ending of the present way of things will come from outside intervention, and the equalizing or reversal of values and worth in this age are marks of millenarianism. Millennialist cults, also known as cargo cults from descriptions of their Melanesian examples, expect the complete transformation of this world to occur within a specific and short time. This ending of the age is expected to be both catastrophic to the present order and near at hand. The coming expected crisis requires participants in the society or faction to make preparations for this ending time.[55] Robert Jewett has demonstrated that the ideology and practices of the Thessalonian church reflect this pattern of millennialist belief.[56]

The historical expression of time in the small-group Quadrant D "literally collapses into the present."[57] Past and future are compressed so that "knowledge of the future in low-grid sects is likely to be as certain and as immediate as knowledge of the past."[58] Operational time, an allocable resource for accomplishing the tasks required of the individual, is not structured or constrained by "classificatory insulations" or "compartmentalization" in the small-group D Quadrant.[59] Similarly, operational space, the places within which people live, is neither ordered nor limited except by the boundary of the small group. Geographic space, the area outside the boundaries of the group, is isolated from operational space by divisions that identify and discriminate between various threats from the outside.[60] Nonthreatening geographic space is—like historical time—compressed into a "single benign category which encompasses the whole system."[61]

Historic Time and Geographic Space in the Pauline Church. Time—that is, historical time—is compressed in the ideology of Paul's letters. This compression results in the confusion of expectant and realized eschatology, both in modern interpretation and ancient hearing.[62] For example, as Meeks has noted, 1 Thess. 1:10 sounds very much like Gal. 1:4 except for the reference to historical time: "Jesus Christ gave himself for our sins, in order to rescue us from the present evil age" (Galatians); "who saves us from the *coming* wrath" (1 Thessalonians).[63] The difference is in the status of the fulfillment of eschatological hopes. Are they present or future? The apparent reversal in evidence here and in the Corinthian correspondence is explained in the functional model by reference to the integration of conflict in the social unit. Wayne Meeks:

> On the face of it, then, Paul's employment of apocalyptic categories here [in Corinthians] seems to be the reverse of that in Galatians. There he used the present experience of factors traditionally associated with the messianic

age to warrant a radical innovation, abandoning the use of the Mosaic law so as to set boundaries between Jew and gentile. Here he uses eschatological language in the future tense to restrain innovation and to counsel stability and order.[64]

The consistent factor, the function that integrates both uses of apocalyptic language, is Paul's concern for "the solidarity and stability of the congregations."[65] This consistent factor is also a historical expression of the typological ideology of Quadrant D.

The compression of geographic space is expressed in the division of geographic space into just two realms. This compression results in the unification of the rest of the (benign) outside world. In the letter to the Galatians, Paul identifies and isolates one threat as coming from the people of James (Gal. 2:12). The rest of the world is unified ideologically under the rubric Jew and Greek; there is no difference (for example, Rom. 3:9).

From the mapping of Paul and the Pauline church in small-group Quadrant D we see a cosmology that will support millennialist cult ideology. There is a contradiction between the first statement—society is a part of nature—and the second general statement of typical small-group ideology—the relation of society and nature is negatively valued. This contradiction parallels the dualism of the millennialist vision.

The Negative Relationship of Society and Nature

The unbalanced strengths of grid and group produce a difficulty for the participant in the small group where the relationship between the small group and the natural world are concerned. The group itself is positively viewed. Participation in the group is perceived to be necessary by the individual. Yet there is little constraint on the actions of the participants in the group, except for the concerns of group solidarity and purity. Members are all of one status, that is, they are all members of the group. The boundary of the group is identified with powerful taboos. Paul allows for no hint of allegiance to other gods and at the same time denies their power (1 Cor. 10:19–22). But the participant, once inside the group, encounters few social barriers to achieved status.

Meeks makes note of the way this conflict works itself out in the

Pauline church by identifying it with terms like "ambivalence" and "ambiguity."[66] In the controversy between the "strong" and the "weak" at Corinth:

> "The strong" adopt a weak-boundary position: they need no taboos against idolatry in order to protect their Christian faith, because they know that the idols are not real; they are proud both of their knowledge *(gnosis)* and of the power *(exousia)* and freedom *(eleutheria)* which this knowledge, the grace they have received as believers in Christ, gives them. "The weak," on the other hand, are accustomed to associate the eating of meat with participation in the cult of pagan gods; for them, "idolatry" is real and dangerous.[67]

Paul strongly resists classifying Christians and giving each category different rights and privileges. Internal divisions are discouraged within the boundary of the church. This boundary is marked for the believer with the transition from the former to the present state in conversion and baptism. Meeks offers a summary of the various clusters of metaphors used by Paul to describe this opposition of good and evil.[68] He concludes that the context of Paul's language about good and evil is entirely theological: "The evil of the world is thus ultimately defined by God's judgment, and it is at the judgment that wrong will be righted. The letters urge the congregations to manifest a paradoxical confidence, endurance, joy, and hope in the face of present experiences of evil and assure them that they can do so because by means of the Spirit they already share the eschatological divine power."[69]

Personalized Symbolic Action

There is also a contradiction between the third and fourth typical statements of the emergent ideology of Quadrant D. Symbolic action is personalized, but its goal is group oriented. In summarizing the debate between Krister Stendahl and Ernst Käsemann, I have already noted the difference in understanding fostered by a focus on low grid or on high group strength by itself.

The means of symbolic activity are more personal, more spontaneous, more flexible in small-group D Quadrant ideology than in higher grid social environments.[70] Ascribed status—that is, superior rank in the group because of restrictive categories of membership or status inferred from rank in the society outside the small group—is less meaningful than is achieved status in the small-group Quadrant D. The means by which symbolic behavior supports group continuation or preservation and enforces the boundaries of the group are personalized, as they reflect achieved status rather than support ascribed status.

Jouette Bassler's study of the theological motif of divine impartiality concludes that Paul used the motif in ways that differed from those of his contemporaries: "In his letter to the Romans, the opening argument on the theme of divine judgment pivots, according to our analysis, on the assertion of divine impartiality. *God recompenses all according to an impartial standard of merit* (1:12–2:11) and thus, in spite of the apparent inequality introduced by the Mosaic Law, both Jews and Gentiles fare alike before his judgment seat (2:11–2:29)."[71]

Faith is the ground of inclusion into the group, the Pauline church. In the controversy reported in Galatians, Paul makes reference to divine impartiality as he considers his relationship to the pillars of the church in Jerusalem (Gal. 2:6).[72] The test of the boundary of the church, that is, faith in Christ, admits both Jew and Greek. This faith is an achieved status.

For example, a concern for the health of the community is found in the admonitions that reinforce "the sense of uniqueness and solidarity of the community."[73] The member who does not participate in the group is asked to leave (1 Cor. 5:9–13). "Is it not those inside the church whom you are to judge?" Those who do not participate are judged by the Lord. Some of the Corinthians are sick and have died because they did not partake of the eucharist appropriately (1 Cor. 11:30). John G. Gager puts it succinctly: "If there is conflict between individual freedom with respect to previous taboos (in this case, reluctance about eating meat sacrificed before pagan idols and later sold in the market) and potentially divisive consequences of exercising this freedom, Paul subordinates the freedom of the individual to the unity of the congregation."[74]

The freedom to achieve together with the constriction of group boundary provides the context for contradictory yet accurate descriptions of Paul's theology: individual and personalized means—yet group-oriented goals—of symbolic action.

Group-Oriented Goals of Symbolic Action

In Mary Douglas's words, in Quadrant C and D

> the powers that control the universe are modelled on human figures. Either they are the spirits of dead fathers and grandfathers, or cultural heroes like big brothers, or a creator god, the most ancestral figure of them all. . . . On this side, where group is strong, social control is built into the cosmos. These humans and human-like powers are activated by moral situations. Ancestors punish and reward; curses avenge moral wrong. . . . The idea of the self is surrounded with prickly moral contexts in which it has to operate.[75]

The sense of exclusionary boundary is strongest in the writings judged to be earlier; the Christian community is described as separate from the larger community: children of light versus children of darkness (1 Thess. 5:5, 8). But it is present in later writings: The definition of appropriate behavior in the light of the predicted salvation is again couched in the alternation of light and dark (Rom. 13:11–13).

Paul's use of the theological concept of divine impartiality does not obliterate the distinction between those who are within the group and those outside. Jouette Bassler:

> Even Paul's vision of impartiality, which dissolves the barrier between Jew and Greek, ultimately without relying on a potentially divisive standard of virtue (Rom. 4:5), is not an unqualified one. It is clearly linked to Paul's missionary activity, and it is actually effective, not for all people everywhere, but for those within the church. God accepts both Jew and Gentile without distinction on the common basis of faith. *There exists, however, a firm distinction between those who accept the way of faith and those who remain outside the church.* Yet even for those outside there remains a measure of impartiality, since Jew and Gentile, without distinction, are judged according to the same standard of merit and all fall short of the glory of God.[76]

The boundaries of the church group were clear to those involved in the Pauline church. These boundaries disassociated them from the surrounding culture, be it Gentile or Jewish, and they were the object of symbolic activity. Paul, in paraenetic sections of his letters, exhibits his concern that those involved with the Pauline church faction be different from those who are not involved. These instructions about behavior distinguish believers and makes more visible the boundary between them and nonbelievers:

> But we exhort you, brethren, to do so more and more, to aspire to live quietly, to mind your own affairs, and to work with your hands, as we charged you; so that you may command the respect of outsiders, and be dependent on nobody. (1 Thess. 4:10b–12)

> Look out for the dogs, look out for the evil-workers, look out for those who mutilate the flesh. For we are the true circumcision, who worship God in spirit, and glory in Christ Jesus, and put no confidence in the flesh. (Phil. 3:2–3)

> Now the works of the flesh are plain: fornication, impurity, licentiousness, idolatry, sorcery, enmity, strife, jealousy, anger, selfishness, dissension, party spirit, envy, drunkenness, carousing, and the like. I warn you, as I warned you before, that those who do such things shall not inherit the kingdom of God. (Gal. 5:19–21)

> For the unbelieving husband is consecrated through his wife, and the unbelieving wife is consecrated through her husband. Otherwise, your children would be unclean, but as it is they are holy. (1 Cor. 7:14)

> I fear that when I come again my God may humble me before you, and I may have to mourn over many of those who sinned before and have not repented of the impurity, immorality, and licentiousness which they have practiced. (2 Cor. 12:21)

Each of these text segments describes different aspects of Paul's concern about the boundary of the group, the group's purity, and his concern that the group not backslide.

An Unelaborated Symbolic System

Paul operates within a web of personal social contacts. There is no single organizational principle nor controlling structure to which he defers. The theological images by which he communicates his understanding of the meaning of following Christ are straightforward. They are the gospel he defends. Wayne Meeks points out: "Some interpreters posit an elaborate system of myth to which the words of Paul are supposed to allude; others resort to ill-defined categories of mysticism. What Theissen says about the image of union between Christ and the believer, however, applies to the whole complex: 'One can call this mysticism, but it is a mysticism of social relations, in which many participate.'"[77]

Conclusion to Emergent Description

Paul's concern for the differentiation of the group from society, his concern for purity in the group, his concern about persecution, his special mission to go as apostle to the Gentiles, his constant squabbles with others in authority in the synagogue, in various governmental bodies, and in the Pauline church faction, his demand for equality among the believers—all these features are correlated with the social setting, providing Paul with his emergent cosmology. This cosmology reflects the social mapping of the Pauline church.

The theological and paraenetic constructs of Paul's letters are the cognitive containers in which social interests of the Pauline churches are fought out.[78] We see these discussions only from Paul's point of view—dimly, as in a mirror—but we see them. The importance or weight Paul places on specific arguments and difficulties is determined by his perception of the local situation. The cosmology with which he explains his world influences his perception of his world as much as does the historical "reality" of the local situation. Not only is Paul's view of the world colored by his social mapping, so is that of his interpreters.

As we interpret Paul's theology and his reaction to specific situations, we must take into account low grid, high group cosmology. This small-group cosmology—with its concern about persecution, its factionalism, its charismatic leadership, its concentration on group salvation accessed by individual achievement—is different from the social environment in which most people of the early Roman empire lived, as well as the social environment in which most Americans live. Attempting to interpret the statements Paul makes in his letters without an awareness of these differences results in confusion. The concluding chapter offers a concrete example of appropriate interpretation in a study of Paul's selection and use of the term *huiothesia*, "adoption."

8

Paul's Use of the Term *Huiothesia*

With rare exception, there are no new finds for the New Testament scholar to examine. Instead of finding new data, we apply new methods of study to the old data. We ask old questions in a new way. Seen in a new light, the observations we have available to us become significant evidence for a new understanding.

It may be that our clearest vision comes when the observations that result from the use of a new method confirm and elucidate prior conclusions. Affirmation and clarification are useful, for they enhance our understanding of the material.

The problem is that new methods of study do not come prepackaged, ready to use. New methods require the development and testing of new tools for research, new terminologies to understand. This study has adapted research tools developed by Mary Douglas and others in the field of cultural anthropology so that we may use them with New Testament material. This exercise requires that we be open to using new methods with new presuppositions, new perspectives, and new language.

In this chapter we seek to understand a unique word that Paul uses, the word *huiothesia*, "adoption." This word is a particularly appropriate example of the way Paul integrates theologically the concept of inclusion without an associated concept of social hierarchy—a summary of the results of our grid-group study. The data are familiar: we have philological and ideological background material concerning the use of the term *huiothesia*. However, the data we have do not make the meaning and significance of "adoption" in Paul's use *self*-evident.

Although the data are familiar, the methodology is not. In applying the cultural anthropologist's tool of grid-group analysis, we have described the correlation of social experience and ideology in the church of Paul's time. The result is a new view of the church that sheds light on the concept of adoption as it functioned for Paul and the Pauline church. John G. Gager summarizes this point: "the positive value of a comparative and theoretical method is precisely that it offers a source of 'external controls and supplementary information by means of a more morphological analysis and more or less systematic comparison with similar movements elsewhere.' In other words, new 'data' may come in the form of new models."[1]

Adoption, as used by Paul, is a theological concept that integrates his experience and the experience of the Pauline church faction. This ideological concept performs the function of explaining experience and justifying Paul's behavior in the Pauline church. *Huiothesia* performs this function by incorporating both the concepts of equality and interactive participation among participants in the new fellowship. This integrating function is not discernible by observing the term *huiothesia* itself, nor is it obvious in either the philological or the ideological background of its use. Indeed, the concept of equality may be misread if one refers to a lexical study of "adoption" in the Roman world.

This question of function is sociological when we seek to discern the purposes of an observable, repetitive behavior or of a manifest ideology among the participants in a society or socially bounded group. These purposes may be apparent to the participants, or the purposes may be latent within the behavior, or both. Cosmology is the means by which participants explain their experience or justify their actions—their world view. Since theology is a subset of cosmology, Paul's way of integrating experience includes his theology.

There are problems with applying a comparative or sociological method. Again, John G. Gager:

> One major obstacle in applying it [a comparative method] to a movement such as early Christianity is that the historical evidence is so diffuse and fragmentary. Obviously the data are insufficient to serve as the basis, by themselves, for generating major theories. In addition, that lack of satisfac-

tory controls means that our conclusions regarding the degree of conformity between a given model and the Christian data must remain tentative and open to reformulation.[2]

This problem of providing satisfactory control may be met only by carefully separating various categories of evidence. These categories of evidence must be derived from the comparative model, not from the material itself. The range of data is determined, therefore, by the method, not the subject. In this chapter we use grid-group analysis and the results of the preceding chapters to analyze the term *huiothesia* as used by Paul. We place Paul's use of the term in language we can understand from our cultural perspective. This makes it possible to both observe Paul's use and to hear his critique of our own cultural patterns.

A relatively recent, innovative study of Paul's letters provides a test of the results of our grid-group analysis. Norman Petersen works from a literary-sociological perspective to interpret Paul's message. Though his method, data set, and language are quite different from grid-group analysis, his conclusions are not. The final section of this chapter reviews and compares Petersen's conclusions with those of the present study.

We begin, however, with a review of the term *huiothesia* as used by Paul in Romans and Galatians. This review relies upon the work of Brendan Byrne and Matthew Vellanickal,[3] who have described the wider semantic field of terms related to *huiothesia* and have considered the theological implications.

Huiothesia in the Letters of Paul

The term *huiothesia* is found five times in the New Testament: Rom. 8:15, Rom. 8:23, Rom. 9:4, Gal. 4:5 and Eph. 1:5. The first four occurrences of the term are discussed in the sections that follow. The possibility that Ephesians is deutero-Pauline removes it from this discussion, but there remains nothing in the use of *huiothesia* in Ephesians that is contrary to Paul's use elsewhere.[4] The four remaining citations occur at high points in theological arguments in Romans and Galatians. The marked transition between Romans 8 and 9 places the occurrences of *huiothesia* in Romans both at the culmination of Paul's argument in chapter 8 and at the beginning of the ramifications for Paul's people in chapter 9.[5] The occurrences of the term in Romans are clustered around this transition.

According to Betz's analysis of the rhetorical form of the letter to the Galatians, 4:1–7 constitutes proofs within the fourth argument of the *probatio* of the letter.[6] The relationship of this passage to earlier references with the example of Abraham (the second and third arguments of the *probatio*, according to Betz[7]) emphasizes the importance of "inheritance" and determining the identity of the "seed of Abraham"—those who will inherit the promise of God.[8] This usage of *huiothesia* in Galatians (4:5) is parallel in context and language to the first usage in Romans (8:23).

These four occurrences of the term *huiothesia* are either clustered or are in a closely parallel context. The use of the term is related both to an inheritance and a future promise as well as to a definition of a new, fictive kinship relationship with the divine.

Huiothesia in Romans

Huiothesia occurs twice in chapter 8 and once in chapter 9 in Romans. These occurrences are related theologically by the expectation of the fulfillment of God's promise—an inheritance—made to those who have a fictive kinship with Abraham, with Christ, and/or with those who are the children of God.[9]

Already by the time of the second Chester Beatty biblical papyrus (p[46])—ca. 200, concern about the apparent contradiction of the already and the not yet of 8:15 and 23 causes the second *huiothesia* to be deleted from the text.[10] Its inclusion in 8:23 is preferred partly because of the difficulty of the reading and partly because of the theological parallelism implied.[11]

The pattern of opposition and reversal found in 8:15, "you did not receive . . . but you have received . . . ," is common elsewhere in Paul's letters.[12] The fact of "having received" (aorist *elabete*) suggests a linkage to baptism.[13] This is in contrast to the use of *huiothesia* in 8:23. Here the term is defined as "the redemption of our bodies"—something believers await. There is a parallelism between the groaning of creation (vv. 19–22) and that of the believer (vv. 23–25).[14]

The problem of the already and the not yet has been variously smoothed or emphasized. With reference to the word "Spirit" and the use of the genitive, C. K. Barrett translates v. 15, "the Spirit which anticipates our adoption as sons."[15] Käsemann, on the other hand, is not interested in smoothing this paradox.[16] C. B. E. Cranfield prefers to distinguish between the fact of adoption, already a fact in v. 15, and the announcement of that adoption, yet to be revealed in v. 19.[17] Byrne, following Michel, prefers to take the genitive qualitatively, thus emphasizing that it is the Spirit which is received. This Spirit "points to" or demonstrates the actual status of "sonship" in the cry "Abba," v. 16.[18]

In contrast, referring to Romans 9:4, Byrne concludes that the use of *huiothesia* comes within a formal list of the privileges of Israel.[19] He uses this concept of a formal list of privileges to inform his interpretation of *huiothesia* in chapter 8.[20] He again cites Michel and analyzes the formal construction and parallelism of the six terms of 9:4 to claim that this list is traditional in form and therefore preexists (in "Hellenistic Judaism") Paul's use.[21] Yet neither of the passages he offers—2 Macc. 2:17 and 4 Ezra 5:23ff., comparable lists of the privileges of Israel—shares the same terms, especially *huiothesia*.

Käsemann focuses on the advantages of Israel within the history of salvation for understanding this list as introductory material to Paul's essential argument in 9–11. He finds that this introduction with its reference to salvation history has its counterpart in 11:33–36. The doxologies of 9:5b and 11:30 frame these chapters of concern for Israel. "On the basis of OT texts like Exod. 4:22 their [*huiothesia*] is recognized, which as an eschatological gift applies elsewhere only to Christians."[22]

In summary, then, the three occurrences of the term *hiouthesia* in Romans are linked. The two occurrences in chapter 8 are linked by theological parallelism in both an existing and future fictive kinship relationship with God. These are marked with baptism and with gifts of the Spirit. The use of *huiothesia* in chapter 9 is linked theologically to the other two by reference to the promises made to those fictively related as the people of God.

Huiothesia in Galatians

The context of the term *huiothesia* in Gal. 4:5–6 is remarkably similar to that of Rom. 8:15. Paul moves from "sonship"—a status—to a demonstration of that "sonship" by gifts of the Spirit, to "inheritance"—a future promise.[23] Byrne points out the common background of Jews and Gentiles in relation to the inheritance: "It is best, then, to see in vv. 1–3 an expression of that situation of slavery, common to both Jew and Gentiles, which was a feature of the religious past of all Christians. . . . Paul's whole point is that 'we' were all in a common situation of helplessness, the background to our equally 'common' situation of salvation in Christ."[24]

This commonality in the background of Jew and Greek removes any status ascribed to one group because of birth. Betz similarly finds that section 4:1–7 discusses that which Paul "had set forth in 3:26–28 (29)."[25] The whole is understood together. Because of the formal relationship of 4:1–7 with 3:26ff., the reception of "sonship" is linked to the ritual of baptism. It is also linked to the "gift of the Spirit," even if the gift of the Spirit and baptism are kept separate.[26] In commenting on 3:26, he says:

> it is exceptional and extraordinary that Paul attributes this status ["sons of God"] to Gentiles now. The question is how this designation can be explained. The explanation is contained in the formulae of the statement, which must be understood in the general context of Paul's theology. One must also recall the argument following the "thesis" in 3:7. It is Christ as the "Son of God" who makes adoption as "sons" available through the gift of the Spirit. *Two formulae state the conditions for the adoption: "through [the] faith" . . . and through incorporation in the "body of Christ," i.e., "in Christ Jesus."* This definition is clearly polemical and must be seen in contradiction to the doctrine of Paul's opponents.[27]

The commonality of Jew and Greek is present only after the adoption as children of God but extends also to the time before. The two aspects of the adoption, stated in two formulae identified by Betz, give definition to adoption—through faith and through incorporation. Symbolic action in baptism is personalized—by faith—but the goal of the symbolic action is group oriented—incorporation into the body.

In our review of Paul's use of the term *huiothesia* in Romans and Galatians we have gathered several impressions:

    (a) The occurrences of *huiothesia* are clustered together or have a related theological context.

(b) *Huiothesia* is related to future inheritance and to present status.

(c) *Huiothesia* refers to a fictive kinship relationship offering the advantages of these privileges of future inheritance and present status.

(d) There is a commonality in the background of those who enter this fictive kinship.

(e) *Huiothesia* is linked to baptism and to "gifts of the Spirit."

(f) *Huiothesia* combines incorporation and faith as signs of participation.

We will return to these impressions at the end of the chapter.

Huiothesia Outside Paul's Letters

The literary and epigraphic background of the term *huiothesia* outside the Bible is not large. The work of Byrne and of Vellanickal has been used to outline the options, presented here in summary form.

The term is not used anywhere in the received text of the Septuagint, including Fourth Maccabees. It is not found in Philo nor in Josephus nor in the later translations of the Hebrew scriptures into Greek. The term does not exist in the corpus of classical Greek authors.

The first citings are inscriptions from the early second century B.C.E.[28] Forms of the word *huiothesia* are found in funerary inscriptions at Delphi and Crete dating from this period. These are the earliest record of the use of the word. They contrast the idea "by birth" with "by adoption" *(phusei* with *kath' huiothesian)*. This fact alone would explain the lack of the term in the Septuagint at those places one might expect its use; the term was not available to the translators. Literary use of the term is documented in two Hellenistic historians of the late first century B.C.E.: Diodorus Siculus and Nicolaus Damascenus.

While largely quoting or paraphrasing Polybius on the story of Aemilius and Scipio (Plb. XXXI, xxii–xxx), Diodorus Siculus uses the term *huiothesia:* Diod. Sic. XXXI xxvi 1 and Diod. Sic. XXXI xxvii 5. In this section generally, Diodorus is reducing the bulk of Polybius' account. Yet in the first citing he adds the term to his close paraphrase of Polybius in order to clarify a relationship (as also at XXX xxvi 4). The second citing reflects, however, the replacement of Polybius' phrase, which carries the idea of adoption, with the term *huiothesia.* Here, Diodorus Siculus appears to prefer the term *huiothesia,* a term that Polybius does not use.

Closer to Palestine is Nicolaus Damascenus who, in his "Life of the Young Caesar," uses the term *huiothesia*.[29] Nicolaus is an advisor in the court of Herod. He uses the term as he recounts Octavian's response to Julius Caesar's death. Two parallels in Greek exist for this account from Roman historians;[30] neither of these, Appian nor Cassius Dio, uses the term.

The term *huiothesia* was in use in Macedonia and Crete by the end of the second century. The term *may*, therefore, have been available to Polybius, who did not use it. Diodorus Siculus, in the next century, chose to use the word, especially when clarifying Polybius' account. He does not prefer the term over others, however, using the term *huiopoiaesasthai* in his recounting of the story of the adoption of Heracles by Zeus and Hera (IV xxxix 2).

The technical status of the term *huiothesia*, therefore, is not well defined. Polybius, like the Septuagint, may not use the term simply because it does not exist in the common vocabulary of classical Greek. Still, the term had been used in inscriptions by the *time* of Polybius. The use by Diodorus Siculus shows a decided preference for the term. He chose it to replace Polybius' phrase. This preference is also demonstrated by Paul (and the writer of Ephesians). Nicolaus Damascenus gives us the earliest literary citing of the term. By the second century C.E. the term *huiothesia* is not used in parallel passages by two Roman historians. There does not seem to be a technical or universally preferred use of this term.

The Concept of Adoption

The concept of adoption, however, if not the term *huiothesia*, is important, especially at higher levels of society, in the early Roman empire.[31] The hypothesis that Paul's use of the concept is derived from Roman law has been variously proposed. Several analogies within Roman law for Paul's use are available. These analogies hinge on the contractual patterns of the various legal transactions, patterns that involve exchanges of power in client-patron relationships.

In the Roman form of adoption (*adoptio*) one comes under the authority, the *patria potestas*, of the adopting father through a purchase. This exchange is basic to the client-patron relationship. The Vulgate translates *huiothesia* with *adoptio*. Indeed, this seems to be the most obvious translation for Paul's term.[32]

For example, witnesses are required for the act of Roman adoption to be valid. Rom. 8:16 has the Spirit bearing witness with the Christian's ecstatic witness that the adoption has taken place. Yet, although two witnesses may have been sufficient to Jewish tradition, the Roman law pertaining to *adoptio* requires five witnesses.[33] The comparable Greek form of adoption has the adopted son retain both natural *(phusei)* and adopted *(kath' huiothesian)* paternal names.[34] The focus of the Greek custom seems to be inheritance for the adoptee and future care in old age for the adopter. Thus the adoption is often associated with a will and testament.[35] This schema corresponds to the passage cited from Nicolaus Damascenus *(bios kaisaros 55)* and to the funerary inscription evidence from Delphi and Crete.

Adrogatio refers, in Roman law, to a similar situation, where one takes an independent man *(homo sui juris)* into full adoption. Again, there is the exchange in which the one adopted comes under the *patria potestas* of the new father. But since this act could be done only at Rome before the *comitia curiata* (later, by the time of Cicero, before thirty lictors and, still later, for provincials, the emperor), this possibility does not seem a likely background for *huiothesia*.

Patria potestas is an important social and legal concept that orders Roman life.[36] By it, the transactions that make up the legal process of adoption are defined. A complex social hierarchy defines differing rights in private and in public life. This complex set of relationships requires careful management and consultation. The head of the family, the *paterfamilias*, has broad discretion to make decisions for everyone in his *familia*.[37] He is in a position of power moderated only by the opinion of his peers: "it was *patria potestas* which was the fundamental institution underlying Roman institutions, . . . public life followed the assumptions of private life, and not vice versa."[38]

The heart of the legal concept *patria potestas* is the patron-client relationship. This relationship defines the experience of Roman society. It involves a social and legal transaction concerning power, privilege, and authority. Even the citizens of Rome are not equals.[39] This hierarchical arrangement of individuals in relation to others in their society gives each person a sense of place and purpose, but it also creates conflicts in respect to property and inheritance.[40]

The concept of *patria potestas* provides the analogy that allows Francis Lyall to conclude that the use of *huiothesia* is a "deliberate, considered and appropriate reference to Roman law."[41] His argument hinges upon

Paul's knowledge of the Roman law involved and its suitability to the passage. Yet the only evidence for the availability of the Roman legal concept to Paul is that Paul is a Jewish lawyer [Pharisee??] and "traveling lawyers tend to pick up knowledge of systems other than their training."

The question of suitability is more complex. *Patria potestas* is, as Lyall describes it, a reciprocal relationship of support and control. By analogy, the Christian is "made part of God's family forever, with reciprocal duties and rights."[42] He concludes that this hierarchical relationship— clearly a parallel of the Roman concept of *patria potestas*—is developed in the "Christian doctrines of election, justification and sanctification." The suitability of the concept of adoption in Roman law as an analogy for use by Paul is premised upon a basic hierarchical relationship implied in the Roman social and legal transaction described in the tradition of *patria potestas*.

To summarize: the Roman and Greek legal conceptions of adoption reflect the contractual attitudes of bargain and transaction. In Roman law and social practice, this transaction is based on the patron-client relationship and the principle of *patria potestas*. The evidence for Hellenistic practice maintains the use of both the natural and adoptive identity. These are the dominant social patterns that define the legal transactions related to adoption.

Adoption in Religious Usage

Hans Dieter Betz, in his commentary on Galatians, compares the Roman legal practice of guardianship to Paul's illustration in Gal. 4:1–2. When he comes to the term *huiothesia*, he notes a legal sense for the term but finds that in the New Testament it is "always used in the religious sense describing adoption as sons of God."[43]

Betz suggests that mystery cult usage is the origin of the "religious sense" of the term "adoption." He finds that sonship must be a link between baptism and the gift of the Spirit, which are kept separate. Paul is arguing from the "objective" experience of the Galatian Christians in their ecstatic cry to a "subjective" self-understanding. Paul claims that the Gentile Galatians understand themselves now as children of God and that even Jews will receive this status only at the last judgment.[44]

In the context of mystery cult usage, Wayne Meeks notes the use of the concept of adoption in inscriptions in the Bosporan kingdom from the early empire.[45] He describes these as Jewish syncretists who referred to each other as "adoptive brothers" while worshiping the "highest god." Their pattern of reference to others in the cult as adoptive brothers reflects the same kind of new fictive kinship relationship that Paul claims.[46]

Adoption is not known as a social or legal institution within either oral or written Torah. Theologically, the parent-child relationship is defined by an act of divinely influenced creation. It is not, therefore, a legal partnership. There is no sense of the transactional outline for adoption common in Roman and Greek law. A threat to the continuation of a family line is not a crisis that is to be solved by adoption, nor is adoption a protection provided for an old age; it is not the definition of a patron-client relationship. Slavery is a much more common solution to these social concerns in the ancient Near East. But there are proposals for finding a Jewish background for adoption terminology.[47]

William H. Rossell concludes that the background of New Testament adoption is "Semitic" on the basis of legal texts from the Nuzi archives. He finds the account of the adoption of Eliezer the slave by Abraham (Gen. 15:2–4) behind Paul's use.[48] He makes the inference that Paul knew Mesopotamian law of the second millennium B.C.E. The parallel that combines slavery, adoption, and inheritance is within the Nuzi legal system and not strictly in the account in Gen. 15. The ancient inscriptions from Nuzi may shed light upon the situation of Abraham and Eliezer of Damascus,[49] but not upon the Pauline construct.

With Paul's identification of adoption with Israel (Rom. 9:4) we find a metaphor built not from legal texts or practices, but rather from an understanding of the relationship of God to Israel. Somehow, through the action of Christ in redeeming and the Spirit in witnessing or sealing, Christians are now enabled to participate in a fictive kinship relationship through adoption. As Adolph von Harnack pointed out in 1918,[50] adoption terminology in the New Testament may be an application to every individual Christian of an older, Jewish understanding of God's relationship with God's people. In this manner, a theological understanding with Jewish roots may have been used by Paul to describe the relationship of Christians to God.

The promise of inheritance figures in both of the covenants that constitute the self-identification of Israel. Adoption may be seen as a metaphor for the situation of the sons of Israel under both the Mosaic and

Davidic covenant models. The Mosaic-Abrahamic covenant results in the inheritance of nationhood and law (Gen. 17, Ex. 19). The Davidic covenant results in dynasty and empire (2 Sam. 7). A relationship defined by a granted covenant "completely rules out," as von Rad puts it, "any idea of a national relationship with the deity of the kind expressed in myths."[51]

Both the patriarchal (Abrahamic) and Sinai (Mosaic) traditions maintain the priority of Yahweh in the relationship. Further, by the time of the Deuteronomist, the divine covenant and the relationship of law and Israel's rendering of obedience have become intertwined. Even the word for covenant becomes one of a series of synonyms for law, commandment, and obedience. Adoption may be an appropriate metaphor for this relationship. Although the use of this metaphor is not common in Palestinian literature, it is used by Philo.

Philo uses the metaphor of adoption with reference to sonship and the true Israel.[52] In *De Specialibus Legibus* I 51 and I 317–318 he identifies the true Israel as made up of both proselytes and those Jews who are true to their birth. Those not seeking the honor of God are to be cast aside even if they are blood related. In *De Sobrietate* 56, Philo again uses adoption as a metaphor for sonship to God. He uses the term *eispoiaetos* to describe the joy of the relationship of the true believer to God.

Both Philo and the mystery cults offer parallels to Paul's use of the term *huiothesia*. Although neither of these are literary and/or historical precursors of Paul's use, they offer insight into the cultural context of the use of the term. This cultural context involves the question of the function of adoption terminology within the Pauline church.

The Concept of Adoption as Used by Paul

In order to understand the use Paul makes of the term *huiothesia*, we have looked at the use of the term in Romans and in Galatians. We have looked at contemporary literary and inscriptive uses of the word and its cognates. We have summarized the concept of adoption in relation to the social and legal transactions based on the principle of *patria potestas* in Roman culture and on testament evidence of Hellenistic legal usage. We have summarized suggestions for a religious background of the concept of adoption of the period, from Hellenistic mystery cult usage to Jewish theological imagery, especially from Philo.

Any of these sources may reflect the basis of Paul's selection of the term *huiothesia*, but it is not clear that there is a direct dependence upon any of them. In order to further interpret the use Paul makes of this term, we need to go more deeply into the way the concept of the adoption of believers functions within the understanding of the Pauline church groups, the people with whom Paul is communicating. We need to come to an understanding of the purpose or role of adoption terminology. How did the concept of the adoption of believers into a fictive kinship relationship function within the Pauline church faction?

The Function of Adoption Terminology

Adoption, as Paul uses the term, describes the believer by way of a theological metaphor. This metaphor orders or organizes the world of the believer, providing a rationale for specific behavioral patterns. Given the background of the term, it carries multiple literary, theological, and legal images. The term functions within the Pauline church faction to integrate conflicting concerns for incorporation and equality.

In asking about the function of a theological construct like *huiothesia*, we are asking a new question, one that is different from the question of its background. We are seeking to understand a theological image or idea used by the earliest church by examining the way it successfully or unsuccessfully integrates the experience of the believers. We are less interested in the antecedents of the term—that is, cause-and-effect relationships— than in comparisons.

Our knowing the place in the history of thought, the ideological background, of Paul's use of the term *huiothesia* is less important to a functional analysis than our understanding the use he makes of it in interpreting the experience of those who participate in the Pauline church. If we better understand the function of adoption terminology, we enhance our ability to interpret Paul's message as it applied to his local church audience and to our own. Identifying a historical background—by way of contrast—helps us to interpret what those outside the faction might have thought of Paul's message.

Using sociological terms to interpret a theological concept is a new way of asking the hermeneutical question. This means using social science models for interpreting the behavior of participants in the Pauline church. There is no clear historic antecedent that explains Paul's use of *huiothesia*. To question Paul's motivation for using an image like adoption to describe believers is to ask about the function of the term. It also provides a basis for translating a theological image used by Paul into an image that speaks in today's world.

Adoption Terminology within the Pauline Cosmology

Three categories describe the values and beliefs of the Pauline church: the dimensional, interactional, and emergent categories; each offers insight into the function of adoption terminology used by Paul. We take up each of these descriptions in turn, focusing on the egalitarian cultural bias that is the context of the use of the adoption concept.

This description of the use of the term does not answer the question of the provenance of adoption imagery for Paul, but it may provide historical clues. We are more interested in the way his understanding and use of the term is correlated with his cultural bias. For our purpose, the term *huiothesia* may have come from anywhere. By defining the function, we explore the fields of meaning of the concept of the adoption of all Christians by God that were available to the Pauline church. The issues we are concerned with are those that reflect the Pauline cultural bias—Quadrant D cosmology.

Dimensional Categories. The dimensional categories are made up of two parts considered independently: the group level and the grid level. The Pauline church is highly invested in group issues but weak in grid strength.

Adoption terminology, like other related images—those concerning the body (Rom. 12:4–5) and horticultural grafting (Rom. 11:24)—is used by Paul as a metaphor of inclusion. The disparate cultural backgrounds and social levels of the participants in the Pauline church presented a complex problem to the early church. Paul justifies his participation and the participation of Jewish and Gentile Christians by using adoption terminology. Salvation is conceived in the context of participation in the church and in the promises of God. The function of adoption is to explain group participation.

Adoption terminology is used by Paul without a sense of hierarchy in this fictive kinship of Christians. The gifts of the Spirit are distributed to those who are siblings in Christ. In this way the metaphor of adoption confers a spiritual equality among the participants in the Pauline church faction, an equality that extends to a lack of constraint on interactions between individuals. Paul justifies his related concern for the righteousness (that is, the purity) of the individual by using adoption terminology. Salvation is expressed in individual terms: by faith alone. The function of adoption is to explain this concern for the individual.

Integrating Conflicting Levels of Grid and Group Strength. For Paul, *huiothesia* is a metaphor for inclusion, not hierarchy. Conflicting grid and group strengths result in an unstable social situation. *Huiothesia* is a particularization of the unstable interactional diagonal. Adoption imagery functions to integrate conflicting levels of grid and group strength in the Pauline church, emphasizing participation rather than disintegration, equality rather than hierarchy.

The metaphor of adoption simplifies the relationships of those involved in the Pauline church faction, though Paul does not elaborate on these relationships. Adoption imagery provides a contrast with those outside the religious faction who do not participate in this fictive kinship. Paul explains the relationship with nature and outside society in the literary context of future expectation and anticipation, together with present signs and preparations.

Emergent Pattern: A Small, Millennialist Group and Adoption. Paul's choice of the word for adoption is not occasioned by any technical sense of the term *huiothesia,* but by the appropriateness of the image to his egalitarian, small-group, millennialist ideology. The adoption of all Christians puts all participants into the same classification of operational time and space without internal boundaries or classifications. Adoption functions to explain inclusion into the group of disparate people who are awaiting a sudden intervention from outside the social order. This intervention will result in a reversal of value and roles. It will be apparent to everyone, especially those who have chosen not to follow.

Parallel Findings in the Sociology of Narrative

Norman R. Petersen embarks on a daunting journey in his award-winning book *Rediscovering Paul: Philemon and the Sociology of Paul's Narrative World.* He sets his course early by identifying himself with

Clifford Geertz's interpretive ethnography, and the thesis that faith is sustained by symbolic forms and social arrangements.[53] He journeys out to find the crossroads of literary and sociological criticism of the Bible and, more particularly, the letters of Paul. In line with the social theories of Emile Durkheim, he believes that there is a conjunction of faith or patterns of belief with social forms or patterns of behavior. The narrative structure of Paul's world—revealed in his letters—correlates with the way Paul organizes or structures his understanding of events around him, and this correlation ultimately affects his behavior.

Two concepts in the title of Petersen's book represent two paths of scholarship he believes intersect. The literary-critical path of scholarship is represented by his focus on the narrative world of Paul's letters. Because of this focus, Petersen cannot assume that the meaning of a text is the same as the message of the letter. He explores the narrative story— the referential world—implied or described in the text to identify a narrative world—the "reality" described by the writer. The meaning of the text is informed by this reality. The social scientific path is represented by Petersen's sociological analysis of Paul's referential world revealed in literary analysis. He describes the social facts of *the lives of the actors who inhabit the narrative world.* This intersection is quite distinct from reconstructing the "historical narrative" or sequence of events that surrounded the writing of each letter and assuming that these events somehow explain or interpret the content of the letters. Petersen does not attempt a social scientific or positivist reconstruction of Paul's historical situation.

Each of the concepts with which he works is itself quite difficult to grasp. Petersen is one step removed even behind these because he is looking for their intersection: the sociology of a referential world. He does not mean only to describe and analyze the social forms—the rituals, patterned behaviors, hierarchies, and role relationships—of the actors in Paul's letters. He is seeking in his sociological study of Paul's narrative world to find clues to understanding the relationship of Paul's symbolic system to the social world.

Paul had a particular way of viewing and understanding the world in which he lived. We can glimpse something of that particular vision by reading his letters. If we were to have a source of information concerning everything there is to know about the events surrounding the writing of his letters—if we had biographical information about every person Paul knew—if information about the controversies and situations that occasioned Paul's letters was available to us from independent observers—even *then,* with complete information about the context of Paul's letters available to us, we still would have to infer Paul's "narrative point of view." Our actual situation is that we have little of these kinds of observations. In general, we must infer from Paul's letters themselves the contextual history of the letters. In other words, we are forced to work at understanding Paul's point of view and the role it plays in coloring or influencing his description of the world before we begin to infer any historical context for the letters.

If we agree to provisionally exclude information about the contextual history of Paul's letters and if we work from observations made entirely from within the context of Paul's narrative world, we can then proceed with an analysis of Paul's narrative point of view—we can begin to understand the cultural bias that colors Paul's letters. Unless we agree to provisionally exclude the question of contextual history, we will be trapped in the circle of unknowns: What influence does Paul's symbolic universe have on our reconstruction of Paul's social universe? The conjunction of symbolic universe and social forms is the concern of social anthropology. The description of Paul's narrative world is the concern of literary criticism.

Petersen sets out to describe in sociological terms the world Paul narrates. He analyzes the complex relationships of the actors in the story a literary critic finds in Paul's letter to Philemon. In so doing he describes the cultural bias that enables Paul to interpret and interact with his social world. This endeavor is exactly parallel to the purpose and intent of a grid-group analysis of Paul's letters. Because the method is different—while the social-anthropological concern remains the same—Petersen's work constitutes an important test for the results of our analysis of Paul.

With Petersen's method, we agree to exclude information about the social context of Paul's letters from the discussion. This means that inferences about the socially patterned behavior of participants of Paul's church is less interesting than inferences about social relationships in the referential world of the letters. With grid-group analysis, using a differing ethnographic method, we agree to provisionally exclude explicitly theological or ideological statements from the discussion. This means that observations of the patterned behavior of the participants of Paul's church faction that we can infer from his letters are more interesting than inferences concerning Paul's statements about the church. Since different categories of data are excluded from the observed set, Petersen's work constitutes a research test of the conclusions of a grid-group analysis of Paul's social world.

The key finding of our grid-group analysis is the mapping of Paul and the Pauline church in the low grid, high group Quadrant "D." The cultural bias of this quadrant is unstable, with competing interests in grid and group concerns. We have found this instability reflected in the ambiguity of the combination of a concern for a strong group boundary with little concern for internal division or hierarchy. In discussing Paul's symbolic universe and social relations, Petersen notes the presence of *two* opposing organizational systems: "There is . . . no question *that* the kinship and master-slave systems are related in Paul's symbolic universe through the notion of the children of God, but there still remains the question of exactly *how* the two systems are related to form a single system."[54]

Petersen identifies adoption as the process by which these two organizing systems of Paul's symbolic universe are related. Adoption terminology represents not a secondary, systematic reflection upon a preexisting knowledge or understanding—Paul is not theologizing—but, rather, a reference to a process of mediation within Paul's symbolic system—a metaphor that distinguishes the believer from a kinship relationship founded on biological descent.[55] Similarly, we have found in our grid-group analysis that adoption functions to distinguish between conferred status outside the church and achieved status within the church. Adoption identifies the believer within the church faction without implying an organizational hierarchy.

Petersen identifies the master-slave relationship and the kinship relationship as the two "organizing principles" of Paul's symbolic universe. The relationship between these is temporal: "the master-slave system coincides with the limited duration of the superordinacy of Christ, God's son. Because in social terms being 'in the Lord' is synonymous with being 'in Christ,' the believer is, in the interim between baptism and the eschatological redemption from the physical body, a slave to Christ Jesus the Lord."[56]

Adoption functions—in terms used by Petersen—to mediate the radical opposition of the master-slave and kinship relationships. This opposition is given concrete example in the conflict between Paul's use of the language of "appeals" rather than commands in the letter to Philemon.[57] In the terms of our grid-group analysis, it is at the point of proximity to group boundary concerns (purity and identity) that Paul's appeals become commands. Either operating through public utterance and peer pressure (Petersen's language) or through Paul's own presence, Paul presents himself within the frame of the symbolic universe described by the group boundary. Petersen says that *"Paul's rhetorical style serves to mediate the paradox that the egalitarian social structure of Paul's churches is complemented by a hierarchical axis."*[58] This mediation must occur because "ultimately . . . the two views [the master-slave and kinship systems] come together because social existence always takes place within a symbolic universe."[59]

There is a parallel between the symbolic universe to which Petersen refers and the cultural bias identified by Mary Douglas. Douglas begins her work in ethnography—the systematic observation and recording of social behavior. Petersen begins in a literary analysis of the text. Both are informed by the theories of Emile Durkheim: In society, that which is— that is, the behavior we can observe—matches that which ought to be— that is, the organizing principles or justifications of a society or social unit. In other words, the world we know—as well as the world Paul knew—is socially constructed. Neither Petersen nor Douglas attempts an analysis of change—theories of dissonance—nor an analysis that proceeds in reverse—from that which ought to be to that which is, from cultural bias or symbolic universe to an inference of observed behavior or narrative structure.

The parallel findings of Petersen's work and this one confirm both. These mutually supportive conclusions are arrived at using distinct methods and sets of data.

Conclusion

Paul's use of adoption terminology is both structurally and functionally a centerpiece of his understanding of what it is to be a follower of Christ and a participant in the Pauline church. Adoption, as used by Paul, is a theological concept or metaphor that functions to integrate conflicting or opposing elements of Paul's experience and the experience of the

Pauline church. *Huiothesia* performs its integrative function by incorporating both the concepts of equality and of interactive participation among the members of the Pauline church faction.

The results of our grid-group analysis using a modified ethnographic method are confirmed in two ways. (1) The results help to describe Paul and the Pauline church faction in such a way as to mediate historic conflicts between theological and historical interpretations of Paul's letters (Stendahl and Käsemann). (2) Independent confirmation is provided by Norman R. Petersen's work in that the results of differing methods result in parallel conclusions.

Although there is no lexical background to support the conclusion that Paul's was a technical use of the term *huiothesia,* several elements of the background of the concept of adoption may have partly informed Paul's use. Paul's use of the term *huiothesia* is not derived from the transactional image of Roman law, which would bring in concepts of *patria potestas;* concepts of social hierarchy do not apply. Inheritance, however, does play a part in Paul's imagery. Concepts of filial relationships among members from the mystery cult usage apply to Paul's imagery. The whole story of salvation history, the promises of God and fictive kinship relationships from the covenantal history of Israel apply. None of these wholly explains Paul's usage, but each offers a partial background.

The modern interpreter of the biblical text needs to be aware that there is discontinuity between the cosmology represented in the literary remains of this small-group Quadrant D early Christian faction and that of contemporary society. This discontinuity is not simply the variation in technology or physical sciences that nineteen centuries have brought to the West. The discontinuity is also and more profoundly the variation in cultural bias found in differing social mappings.

Each contemporary interpreter of Paul's letters must determine for herself or himself the cultural bias of the audience for which the letter is being interpreted. Interpretation itself is an art, not a science. The interpreter helps us cross powerful cultural boundaries.

The ambiguity of conflicting grid and group strengths is not "worked out" in Paul's letters because ambiguity correctly reflects Paul's social world. If the interpreter's social world cannot tolerate ambiguity, Paul's imagery will need to be interpreted with greater artistic license if meaning, and not just words, is to be communicated.

In an entrepreneurial social world—the dominant cultural bias of the

West—emphasis is placed on competition, achievement, logic, and social rules that "level the playing field" for some, not all, competitors. With this cultural bias, Paul's concern for purity and for group boundary is automatically read as a concern for the rules of fair social and economic contract. His concern for an egalitarian community without internal social boundary is inevitably read as a moral concern for equal access to the means of achieving individual success, interpreted as power, influence, and wealth in the community. His concern for individual righteousness and faith—as a marker for participation in the salvation story—is read as a description of the means to achieve individual status and prestige.

The contemporary interpreter of Paul's letters who is conscious of the great difference between Paul's social world and her or his own is provided with the opportunity for social comment and critique. The attempt to provide late-twentieth-century western hearers of Paul's words with appropriate analogies and explanations requires both sensitivity and creativity. Most of us do not live in egalitarian communities; therefore, we must identify and describe images from our world that offer comparisons and contrasts.

For example—and this is only an example of the interpretive art and not the exegesis of Paul—in the summer of 1989 Pete Rose received the "death sentence" from professional baseball in the United States: he is no longer allowed to participate in the game in any professional or managerial role. This coercive sanction was applied for his "sin" of gambling—placing a wager on the outcome of a game in which his own team was involved. The interpreter of Paul's letters might use the situation of Pete Rose to provide an analogy to the concern for purity and group boundary. Americans can understand professional baseball as the group and contact with gambling as the pollution that brings death—the coercive sanction.

The pollution that resulted in coercive sanctions was a perceived breach of the fairness rules of contract. These rules represent a different world than that confronted by an egalitarian church faction to which Paul wrote. The analogy of Pete Rose helps open up interpretively the concept of group boundary implied in Paul's use of adoption language. But at this point we must turn and notice the other—contrasting—ideological value of the egalitarian community: a limitation on ascribed hierarchy or internal social boundaries. We should note that the coercive sanction is not applied by professional baseball for examples of racist or sexist behavior. Or we might take notice of that most telling of elitisms which makes a game between the "National" league and the "American" league into a "World" series.

When Paul is confronting the question of who is a participant in the Pauline church faction, he confronts directly the conflicting strengths of grid and of group within his social network. It is possible for Paul's language to challenge us where we are when we hear him as he is; this is far better than reinterpreting his language to fit our cosmology. Each of the impressions noted above in regard to Paul's use of the term *huiothesia* has its ideological context in Quadrant D cosmology and Paul's expression of that cosmology. We need to have these in mind as we go about the business of interpreting Paul for our contemporary hearers.

We return now to interpret the several impressions we gathered in our review of Paul's use of the term *huiothesia*. Paul's metaphor of adoption functions within its context to mediate or integrate conflicting images of hierarchy and group strength within Paul's social world. *Huiothesia* is related to future inheritance and to present status. The term provides for a temporal mediation between conflicting priorities of unequal social status and egalitarianism.

Huiothesia refers to a fictive kinship relationship offering the advantages of privileges of future inheritance and present status. This kinship relationship defines or justifies the demand for group participation. Purity and identity are issues whose strength is a measure of proximity to the boundaries of the group. There is a commonality in the background of those who enter this fictive kinship. This commonality is represented by the hierarchical social environment from which the participants come and that dominates their conflicts.

Huiothesia is linked to baptism and to gifts of the Spirit. The confirmation of participation is in the rituals of the small factional group. These rituals are the patterns that confirm and order the experience of the world for the participants.

Huiothesia combines incorporation and faith as signs of participation. The cultural bias of an egalitarian community is confirmed in Paul's use of this term. Conflicting strengths of grid and group are integrated in one image.

Notes

Foreword

1. James G. Flanagan and Steve Rayner, *Rules, Decisions, and Inequality in Egalitarian Societies* (U.K. and Vermont: Gower, 1988).
2. Mary Douglas, *How Institutions Think* (Syracuse: Syracuse University Press, 1986).
3. Jonathan L. Gross and Steve Rayner, *Measuring Culture: A Paradigm for the Analysis of Social Organization* (New York: Columbia University Press, 1985).
4. Aaron Wildavsky, *The Nursing Father: Moses as a Political Leader* (University, Ala.: University of Alabama Press, 1984).
5. Vincent Descombes, *Proust, Philosophic du Roman* (Paris: Editions de Minuit, 1987).
6. Rosabeth Moss Kanter, *Commitment and Community: Communes and Utopias in Sociological Perspective* (Cambridge, Mass.: Harvard University Press, 1972).

1. The Social World of Paul

1. Norman K. Gottwald, *The Tribes of Yahweh: A Sociology of the Religion of Liberated Israel, 1250–1050 B.C.E.* (Maryknoll, N.Y.: Orbis Books, 1979), p. 912, quoted by Aaron Wildavsky, *The Nursing Father: Moses as a Political Leader* (University, Ala.: University of Alabama Press, 1984), p. 2.

2. Wayne Meeks, *The First Urban Christians: The Social World of the Apostle Paul* (New Haven: Yale University Press, 1983), pp. 2–3. See also Derek Tidball, *The Social Context of the New Testament: A Sociological Analysis* (Grand Rapids, Mich.: Academie Books, Zondervan, 1984), for the perspective of an evangelical.

3. See the excellent short summary of "Contextual Methodology" by Graydon F. Snyder, *Ante Pacem: Archaeological Evidence of Church Life before Constantine* (Macon, Ga.: Mercer University Press, 1985), pp. 7–11.

4. Bruce J. Malina, *The New Testament World: Insights from Cultural Anthropology* (Atlanta, Ga.: John Knox Press, 1981), p. 3.

5. A sample bibliography: Gerd Theissen, *The Social Setting of Pauline Christianity: Essays on Corinth,* trans. John H. Schütz (Philadelphia: Fortress Press, 1982); Abraham Malherbe, *Social Aspects of Early Christianity* (Baton Rouge: Louisiana State University Press, 1977); Howard Clark Kee, *Christian Origins in Sociological Perspective: Methods and Resources* (Philadelphia: Westminster Press, 1980); Edwin A. Judge, *The Social Pattern of Christian Groups in the First Century* (London: Tyndale, 1960); Bengt Holmberg, *Paul and Power: The Structure of Authority in the Primitive Church as Reflected in the Pauline Epistles* (Lund: CWK Gleerup, 1978); Bruce J. Malina, *Christian Origins and Cultural Anthropology: Practical Models for Biblical Interpretation* (Atlanta, Ga.: John Knox Press, 1986); John G. Gager, *Kingdom and Community: The Social World of Early Christianity* (Englewood Cliffs, N.J.: Prentice-Hall, 1975); Ronald F. Hock, *The Social Context of Paul's Ministry: Tentmaking and Apostleship* (Philadelphia: Fortress Press, 1980); Martin Hengel, *Property and Riches in the Early Church: Aspects of a Social History of Early Christianity* (London: SCM Press, 1974); John Elliot, "Social-Scientific Criticism of the New Testament and Its Social World: More on Method and Models," *Semeia* 35 (1986): 1–34; Jerome Neyrey; "Body Language in I Corinthians: The Use of Anthropological Models for Understanding Paul and His Opponents," *Semeia* 35 (1986): 129–70; Norman R. Petersen, *Rediscovering Paul: Philemon and the Sociology of Paul's Narrative World* (Philadelphia: Fortress Press, 1985); Robert Jewett, *The Thessalonian Correspondence: Pauline Rhetoric and Millenarian Piety* (Philadelphia: Fortress Press, 1986); Meeks, *First Urban Christians.*

6. Jonathan Z. Smith, "The Social Description of Early Christianity," *Religious Studies Review* 1 (1975): 19–25.

7. Carolyn Osiek, *What Are They Saying about the Social Setting of the New Testament?* (Ramsey, N.J.: Paulist Press, 1984).

8. See the distinction between models and methods well laid out by Elliot, "Social-Scientific Criticism of the New Testament," pp. 1–31, esp. 5: "the model is *consciously structured* and *systematically arranged* in order to serve as a *speculative instrument* for the purpose of organizing, profiling, and interpreting a complex welter of detail."

9. Wayne Meeks, *The Moral World of the First Christians* (Philadelphia: Westminster Press, 1986).

10. Meeks, *First Urban Christians*, pp. 6f.

11. Wayne Meeks, "Social Functions of Apocalyptic Language in Pauline Christianity," in *Apocalypticism in the Mediterranean World and the Near East*, ed. David Hellholm, pp. 687–705, Proceedings of the International Colloquium on Apocalypticism, Uppsala, August 12–17, 1979 (Tübingen: J. C. B. Mohr [Paul Siebeck], 1983).

12. Albert Schweitzer, *The Mysticism of the Apostle Paul* (New York: Seabury Press, 1968).

13. Gager, *Kingdom and Community*, pp. 35f. and 80ff.

14. Meeks, "Social Functions," p. 703.

15. Meeks, *First Urban Christians*, p. 6. This is a very important methodological statement.

16. Meeks, "Social Functions," p. 688; *First Urban Christians*, pp. 6–8, 172–73.

17. Meeks, *First Urban Christians*, p. 50.

18. Vincent Jeffries and H. Edward Ransford, *Social Stratification: A Multiple Hierarchy Approach* (Boston: Allyn and Bacon, 1980), present this synthetic approach for integrating the analysis of multiple hierarchies including class, ethnology, sex, and age. See also Aloys Funk, *Status und Rollen in den Paulusbriefen: Eine inhaltsanalytische Untersuchung zur Religionssoziologie*, Innsbrucker Theologische Studien 7 (Innsbruck: Tyrolia, 1981), and the review by Bruce Malina, *Catholic Biblical Quarterly* 49 (1987): 143–44.

19. Meeks, *First Urban Christians*, p. 55.

20. Ibid., p. 73.

21. Meeks would seem to be describing the contemporary phenomenon known as "Yuppies." Bruce Malina rightly criticizes patterns of observation that result from biblical scholars' failure to place filters when they are doing cross-cultural studies. See his review of *First Urban Christians* in *Journal of Biblical Literature* 104 (1985): 346–49.

22. Wayne Meeks, *First Urban Christians*, p. 73.

23. Theissen, "Social Stratification in the Corinthian Community: A Contribution to the Sociology of Early Hellenistic Christianity," *The Social Setting of Pauline Christianity*, pp. 69–119.

24. See also Robert Banks, *Paul's Idea of Community: The Early House Churches in Their Historical Setting* (Grand Rapids, Mich.: William B. Eerdmans, 1980); Lloyd Michael White, "*Domus Ecclesiae—Domus Dei*: Adaptation and Development in the Setting for Early Christian Assembly" (Ph.D. diss., Yale University, 1982), esp. vol. 1, and Snyder, *Ante Pacem*, pp. 67–118.

25. Meeks, *First Urban Christians*, p. 75.

26. Ibid., p. 76.

27. Beryl Rawson, "The Roman Family," *The Family in Ancient Rome: New Perspectives* (Ithaca, N.Y.: Cornell University Press, 1986), pp. 1–57, describes the term *paterfamilias* and discusses its importance for understanding Roman society.

28. Abraham Malherbe, *Social Aspects of Early Christianity*, pp. 87–91. See also Judge, *Social Pattern of Christian Groups in the First Century*, pp. 40–48. See Meeks, *First Urban Christians*, p. 221, no. 16, and also J. Paul Sampley, *Pauline Partnership in Christ: Christian Community and Commitment in Light of Roman Law* (Philadelphia: Fortress Press, 1980).

29. Meeks, *First Urban Christians*, p. 78.

30. Ibid., p. 82. See also E. A. Judge, "The Early Christians as Scholastic Community," *Journal of Religious History* 1 (1960): 4–15, 125–37.

31. Meeks, *First Urban Christians*, p. 85. It is curious that at two points Meeks has offered hypotheses about organizational structures that he then uses to structure his understanding of the evidence: "In order to persist, a social organization must have boundaries, must maintain structural stability as well as flexibility, and must create a unique culture" (p. 84 and so again at p. 111). Since we have no assurance that the local churches Paul founds have any continuity, the appeal to persistence is premature. Malherbe, *Social Aspects of Early Christianity*, p. 11, offers this advice: "we should be aware of excessive enthusiasm. For example, although it is not at all clear that Paul and his co-workers were primarily responsible for the growth of the church in the first century, it is not immediately obvious that the communities apart from their leaders will provide us with the information we seek about early Christianity."

32. Meeks, *First Urban Christians*, p. 87. He notes the use of the concept of adoptive brotherhood in inscriptions related to worship of *theos hupsistos* in the Bosporus region without comment on dependence. This evidence serves to provide similarity to another Hellenistic factional group.

33. Ibid., p. 88.

34. Ibid., pp. 91–93.

35. Ibid., pp. 95–96.

36. Ibid., p. 97. Emphasis added.

37. Ibid., p. 103. Though Paul does indeed throw out the structure of the Jewish law, and he does not allow the social norms of differential classes in the Corinthian church to pervade the celebration of the eucharist, this does not necessarily mean that there was no remaining structure to the resultant community. The "new man" who appeared in the baptismal rite and who shared the eschatological meal was bounded by the demand that he wait patiently for the Lord.

38. Ibid., p. 105.

39. Ibid., p. 107. These two ideas, missionary zeal and acceptable social interactions, should be kept separate. There is no demand in Paul's letters that the new Christians go out and make new disciples, as there is at the close of the Gospel according to Matthew. Only the reference to the example of the Thessalonians for Macedonia and the possibility of a husband's or wife's saving the spouse give a hint that such a mission was even possible.

40. Ibid., pp. 106–110.

41. Ibid., p. 111. The assumption that the Pauline church developed a hierarchy of roles has yet to be demonstrated. Meeks seems to assume that within the Pauline church a system of social stratification and the institutionalization of offices has already developed because concern for these is required by the concern for group preservation.

42. Holmberg, *Paul and Power.*

43. Meeks, *First Urban Christians,* p. 113.

44. Ibid., p. 122. See here John H. Schütz, *Paul and the Anatomy of Apostolic Authority,* Society for New Testament Studies Monograph Series 26 (Cambridge: Cambridge University Press, 1975), pp. 9–14. See also George A. Kennedy, *New Testament Interpretation through Rhetorical Criticism* (Chapel Hill: University of North Carolina Press, 1984), and Jewett, *The Thessalonian Correspondence,* pp. 71–72. See also the collected essays *The Romans Debate,* ed. Karl Donfried (Minneapolis, Minn.: Augsburg Publishing House, 1977).

45. Schütz, *Paul and the Anatomy of Apostolic Authority,* discusses the ideology of authority in the Pauline church; Holmberg, *Paul and Power,* discusses the sociological concepts of power.

46. Meeks, *First Urban Christians,* pp. 136–39. These categories are similar to the pattern found by Holmberg, noted above. See also Carolyn Osiek, *What Are They Saying about the Social Setting of the New Testament?,* pp. 67–69.

47. Legitimacy norms are defined in the context of the sociology of apostolic authority; Schütz, *Paul and the Anatomy of Apostolic Authority,* pp. 249ff. Holmberg, *Paul and Power,* discusses the ambiguity and inconsistency that resulted from Paul's "self-chosen limitation" of his authority in rationalizing his instructions and admonitions with reference to the sacred *ratio,* pp. 189f. The conflict represented by 2 Cor. 10–13 is an example of this ambiguity (p. 190).

48. Meeks, *First Urban Christians,* pp. 137f.

49. Ibid., p. 139.

50. Ibid., p. 142, where he notes the difficulties of working with the presuppositions of Emile Durkheim. When one hypothesizes a kernel within the onion and attempts to peel away the outside to reveal it, there is the possibility that the whole will be thrown away and no meaning will be left.

51. Mary Douglas, "Pollution," in *Implicit Meanings: Essays in Anthropol-*

ogy (London: Routledge & Kegan Paul, 1975; rpt. 1979), pp. 47–59, where she describes the difficulty with Durkheim's treatment of sacred contagion.

52. Mary Douglas, "Introduction to the *a priori* in Nature," in ibid., p. 207.

53. Meeks, *First Urban Christians*, p. 161.

54. Ibid., p. 159. See Theissen, *The Social Setting of Pauline Christianity*, the bibliography on pp. 25–26.

55. Meeks, *First Urban Christians*, pp. 161f.

56. Meeks has an excellent summary of the state of research that provides reconstructions of the liturgy of the Pauline church; ibid., p. 237, n. 44.

57. Ibid., p. 151. He notes that the practice of putting on new white clothes after baptism was probably an innovation that occurred later than the Pauline text, p. 237, n. 50.

58. Ibid., pp. 150–57.

59. Ibid., p. 157. Victor Turner, *The Ritual Process: Structure and Anti-Structure* (Ithaca, N.Y.: Cornell University Press, 1977), links the liminal state to death and to being in the womb, p. 95. The state of communitas is first visible within the liminal period. It refers to the socially unstructured liminal state in which only the general authority of the ritual elders is recognized. This is a transitory egalitarian social world, pp. 96–97.

60. Meeks, *First Urban Christians*, pp. 161–62.

61. Ibid., pp. 5–7. In this section Meeks discusses the issue of method. Although he notes that the advantage of an explicitly stated theory is its falsifiability, he goes on, with reasons stated, to use an eclectic approach. The dangers of using specific categories for arranging the evidence include the problem of using implied or manifest theological categories as an interpretive framework.

62. Ibid., p. 174.

63. Ibid., pp. 190–92. See especially the middle of p. 191; after referring to the observed status inconsistency of Pauline church participants, he says: "Would, then, the intimacy of the Christian groups become a welcome refuge, the emotion-charged language of family and affection and the image of a caring, personal God powerful antidotes, while the master symbol of the crucified savior crystallized a believable picture of the way the world seemed really to work?"

64. One concern of grid-group analysis is precisely this distinction: Mary Douglas, *Cultural Bias,* Occasional Paper 35 of the Royal Anthropological Institute of Great Britain and Ireland (London: Royal Anthropological Institute, 1978), pp. 7f. It is also the concern of functional analysis: Robert Merton, "Manifest and Latent Functions," in *Social Theory and Social Structure*, enlarged ed. (New York: Free Press, 1968), pp. 105 and 114–18.

65. Meeks, *First Urban Christians*, p. 6.

66. Ibid., p. 7.

67. Ibid., p. 5.

2. Anthropology and Biblical Criticism

1. George E. Marcus and Michael M. J. Fischer, *Anthropology as Cultural Critique: An Experimental Moment in the Human Sciences* (Chicago: University of Chicago Press, 1986), pp. 19–20.

2. Ibid., p. 24.

3. Bronislaw Malinowski, *A Scientific Theory of Culture and Other Essays* (Chapel Hill: University of North Carolina Press, 1944), p. 71.

4. Robert C. Ulin, *Understanding Cultures: Perspectives in Anthropology and Social Theory* (Austin: University of Texas Press, 1988), summarizes the rationality debates. See his introduction.

5. Peter L. Berger describes this conflict more eloquently than I in his introductory essay "Sociology and Freedom," in *Facing Up to Modernity: Excursions in Society, Politics, and Religion* (New York: Basic Books, 1977), pp. x–xix.

6. Ulin, *Understanding Cultures*, p. 92.

7. Marcus and Fischer, *Anthropology as Cultural Critique*, p. 29.

8. James Clifford and George E. Marcus, *Writing Culture: The Poetics and Politics of Ethnography* (Berkeley and Los Angeles: University of California Press, 1986). See also the critique by P. Steven Sangren, "Rhetoric and the Authority of Ethnography: Postmodernism and the Social Reproduction of Texts," *Current Anthropology* 29 (1988): 405–35.

9. Talal Asad, "The Concept of Cultural Translation in British Social Anthropology," in *Writing Culture,* ed. Clifford and Marcus, pp. 141–64. See also the response to Sangren's critique by James Clifford, *Current Anthropology* 29 (1988): 425.

10. Vincent Jeffries, "Supporting Ideologies," chap. 9 of Vincent Jeffries and H. Edward Ransford, *Social Stratification: A Multiple Hierarchy Approach* (Boston: Allyn and Bacon, 1980), pp. 338–72. The identification of categories of social stratification, power, privilege, and prestige are discussed on pp. 64–73. For the New Testament perspective, see also Gerd Theissen, "Theoretische Probleme Religionssoziologischer Forschung und die Analyze des Urchristentums," in *Studien zur Soziologie des Urchristentums,* Wissenschaftliche Untersuchungen zum Neuen Testament 19, 2nd expanded ed. (Tübingen: J. C. B. Mohr [Paul Siebeck], 1983), pp. 55–76.

11. Jeffries, "Basic Concepts and Theories of Class Stratification," in *Social Stratification,* pp. 57–64.

12. See the review by Carol Owen, *Contemporary Sociology* 10 (1981): 591–92.

13. Jeffries, "Basic Concepts and Theories of Class Stratification," in *Social Stratification,* p. 60.

14. Jeffries, "Supporting Ideologies," in ibid., pp. 345f.

15. Emile Durkheim, *The Division of Labor in Society* (Glencoe, Ill.: Free Press, 1960), and Herbert Spencer, *On Social Evolution* (Chicago: University of Chicago Press, 1972).

16. Jeffries, "Basic Concepts and Theories of Class Stratification," in *Social Stratification,* p. 58.

17. Jeffries, "Supporting Ideologies," in ibid., p. 348.

18. Herbert Blumer, *Symbolic Interactionism* (Englewood Cliffs, N.J.: Prentice-Hall, 1969).

19. Jeffries, "Basic Concepts and Theories of Class Stratification," in *Social Stratification,* pp. 61f.

20. Jeffries, "Supporting Ideologies," in ibid., p. 350.

21. Jeffries, "Basic Concepts and Theories of Class Stratification," in ibid., pp. 60f.

22. Max Weber, *The Theory of Social and Economic Organization* (Glencoe, Ill.: Free Press, 1947).

23. Jeffries, "Supporting Ideologies," in *Social Stratification,* p. 349.

24. Jeffries, "Basic Concepts and Theories of Class Stratification," in ibid., pp. 60f.

25. J. M. Robinson and Helmut Koester, *Trajectories through Early Christianity* (Philadelphia: Fortress Press, 1979), pp. 120f.

26. Hans von Campenhausen, *Ecclesiastical Office and Spiritual Power in the Church in the First Three Centuries* (Stanford, Calif.: Stanford University Press, 1969), p. 3.

27. Ibid., p. 29.

28. Ernst Käsemann, "Paul and Early Catholicism," in *New Testament Questions of Today* (Philadelphia: Fortress Press, 1969), pp. 236–51.

29. Ibid., p. 237.

30. Ibid., p. 243.

31. Ibid., p. 247 (emphasis added).

32. Ibid., p. 248.

33. Robinson and Koester, *Trajectories,* p. 34. The "protognostic fanatics" are synonymous with Käsemann's enthusiasts.

34. Ibid., pp. 36f. See here also Hans von Campenhausen, *Polykarp von Smyrna und die Pastoralbriefe* (Heidelberg: C. Winter, 1951), pp. 49–51.

35. Jeffries and Ransford, *Social Stratification,* define the multiple hierarchy model in chap. 1, pp. 3–13.

36. John G. Gager, "Some Notes on Paul's Conversion," *New Testament Studies* 27 (1981): 697–704, esp. p. 702.

37. For an example of this distinction, please see Bengt Holmberg, "Sociological versus Theological Analysis of the Question Concerning a Pauline Church Order," in *Die Paulinische Literatur und Theologie,* ed. Sigfred Pedersen (Göttingen: Vandenhoeck & Ruprecht, 1980), pp. 187–200.

38. John G. Gager, *Kingdom and Community: The Social World of Early Christianity* (Englewood Cliffs, N.J.: Prentice-Hall, 1975), pp. 10f.

39. Ibid., p. 21.

40. Gerd Theissen, *Sociology of Early Palestinian Christianity,* trans. John Bowen (Philadelphia: Fortress Press, 1978), p. 93. See also his study of methodology appropriate to the study of primitive (Palestinian) Christianity, "Theoretische Probleme Religionssoziologischer Forschung und die Analyze des Urchristentums," in *Studien zur Soziologie,* pp. 55–76.

41. Gager, *Kingdom and Community,* p. 87.

42. Ibid., p. 88.

43. Bruce J. Malina, *The New Testament World: Insights from Cultural Anthropology* (Atlanta, Ga.: John Knox Press, 1981), p. iv.

44. Susan R. Garrett, "Review of *Christian Origins and Cultural Anthropology: Practical Models for Biblical Interpretation* by Bruce J. Malina. Atlanta, Ga.: John Knox, 1986," *Journal of Biblical Literature* 107 (1988): 532–34.

45. Marcus and Fischer, *Anthropology as Cultural Critique.*

46. Bruce J. Malina, *Christian Origins and Cultural Anthropology: Practical Models for Biblical Interpretation* (Atlanta, Ga.: John Knox Press, 1986), pp. 29–30.

47. Please see the introduction of ibid.

48. Mary Douglas, *Cultural Bias,* Occasional Paper 35 of the Royal Anthropological Institute of Great Britain and Ireland (London: Royal Anthropological Institute, 1978), pp. 2–3.

49. Garrett, "Review of *Christian Origins and Cultural Anthropology,*" p. 533.

50. Susan R. Garrett, *The Demise of the Devil: Magic and the Demonic in Luke's Writings* (Minneapolis: Fortress Press, 1989), pp. 32–36. See also Jerome H. Neyrey and Bruce J. Malina, "Jesus the Witch: Witchcraft Accusations in Matthew 12," in their *Calling Jesus Names: The Social Value of Labels in Matthew* (Sonoma, Calif.: Polebridge Press, 1988), pp. 3–32, and Jerome H. Neyrey, "Witchcraft Accusations in 2 Cor. 10–13: Paul in Social Science Perspective," *Listening* 21 (1986): 160–70.

51. Marcus and Fischer, *Anthropology as Cultural Critique,* pp. 44–45.

52. Ibid., p. 42.

53. John Van Maanen, *Tales of the Field: On Writing Ethnography* (Chicago: University of Chicago Press, 1988), pp. 130f.

54. Ernest Gellner, "Concepts and Society," reprinted in *Sociological Theory and Philosophical Analysis,* ed. Dorothy Emmet and Alasdair Macintyre (London: Macmillan, 1970), pp. 115–49, see esp. section 6, pp. 121–23.

55. In open discussion in the section on Social Sciences and New Testament Interpretation at the Society of Biblical Literature meeting in Chicago, November 19, 1988.

56. Michael Thompson, Richard Ellis, and Aaron Wildavski, "Cultural Theory, or, Why All That Is Permanent Is Bias" (typescript, August 1989), chap. 15, p. 19. See Jürgen Habermas, *Legitimation Crisis* (Boston: Beacon Press, 1975), and *Communication and the Evolution of Society* (Boston: Beacon Press, 1979).

57. Reprinted in Malinowski, *A Scientific Theory of Culture and Other Essays*, pp. 145–76.

58. Robert K. Merton, "Manifest and Latent Functions," in *Social Theory and Social Structure*, enlarged ed. (New York: Free Press, 1968), pp. 104–109.

59. Ibid., p. 104.

60. Ibid., p. 108, n. 55. He points out that the orientation toward the interpretation of the data helps determine which data set is included and which is excluded as it is collected by the researcher. This paradigm is intended to help *sensitize* the researcher.

61. Ibid., p. 109. The titles of each section correspond to Merton's.

62. J. J. Finkelstein, "Mesopotamian Historiography," *Proceedings of the American Philosophical Society* 107 (1963): 461–72.

63. Robert Merton, "Manifest and Latent Functions," in *Social Theory*, p. 104.

64. Ibid., p. 104.

65. Ibid., p. 114. This listing summarizes the discussion of pp. 109–114, "Items Subjected to Functional Analysis." Note, for example, the alternatives to baptism that are noted by Wayne Meeks in his functionalist description of the early cultic practice, *The First Urban Christians: The Social World of the Apostle Paul* (New Haven: Yale University Press, 1983), pp. 152–53.

66. Meeks provides a good example of description by examining alternative patterns as he describes early Christian baptism, *First Urban Christians*, pp. 152–53.

67. Meeks's description of the progression of baptism, including "some liminal elements," is an example of the slippery nature of the inclusion of psychological motivations; ibid., p. 156f.

68. This is Merton's term; "Manifest and Latent Functions," in *Social Theory*, p. 114.

69. Despite the many suggestions for punctuation and reinterpretation, this passage is to be taken to mean some form of vicarious baptism. See here Meeks's discussion of Baptism in *First Urban Christians*, pp. 150–57, and Hans Conzelmann, *1 Corinthians: A Commentary on the First Epistle to the Corinthians*, trans. J. Leitch, A Hermeneia Series Commentary (Philadelphia: Fortress Press, 1975), pp. 275–77 (see the notes there).

70. Robert Merton, "Manifest and Latent Functions," in *Social Theory*, p. 114.

71. Ibid., p. 105.

72. Ibid., p. 117.

73. See, e.g., Keith F. Nickle, *The Collection: A Study in Paul's Strategy*, Studies in Biblical Theology 49 (Naperville, Ill.: Alec R. Allenson, 1966). This is a study of the intended and unintended consequences of the collection in Paul's work. Nickle identifies the latent social function of the collection for the poor in Jerusalem as unity in the church, but the manifest function in the letters of Paul as an act of charity motivated by Christian love (pp. 142, 154).

74. Meeks, *First Urban Christians*, pp. 72f.

75. Stephen Benko, *Pagan Rome and the Early Christians* (Bloomington: Indiana University Press, 1984); see esp. the chapter on the problems caused by the holy kiss, pp. 79–102.

76. The literature on millenarian movements, sometimes called cargo cults, is wide. The point is the concern for survival, which shifts to the future situation and new beginnings rather than the present and past development. See John G. Gager, *Kingdom and Community: The Social World of Early Christianity* (Englewood Cliffs, N.J.: Prentice-Hall, 1975), and especially Kenelm Burridge, *New Heaven, New Earth: A Study of Millenarian Activities* (Oxford: Basil Blackwell, 1969), pp. 97ff.

77. Contrary to Meeks's study, which uses the concern for survival *in society* to order the protocol of observation. Meeks uses terms like "in order to persist" and "no group can persist" in *First Urban Christians*, pp. 84, 111, to organize major sections of his work. It is not certain that survival in this sense motivated either Paul or the local churches at this early stage, or provided the functional requirement for the evaluation of objective consequences of patterned behavior.

78. Robert Merton, "Manifest and Latent Functions," in *Social Theory*, p. 106.

79. Ibid., p. 110.

80. Robert Merton's examples of social mechanisms are "role-segmentation, insulation of institutional demands, hierarchic ordering of values, social division of labor, ritual and ceremonial enactments, etc." Ibid., p. 106.

81. Ibid., p. 106.

82. Robinson and Koester, *Trajectories*.

83. John H. Schütz, *Paul and the Anatomy of Apostolic Authority*, Society for New Testament Studies Monograph Series 26 (Cambridge: Cambridge University Press, 1975), p. 16.

84. Ibid., p. 257.

85. Gager, *Kingdom and Community*, pp. 43ff., proposes that cognitive dissonance caused by the delay of the Parousia motivated mission, a substitution of a functional alternative. See also Bruce J. Malina, "Normative Dissonance and Christian Origins," *Social-Scientific Criticism of the New Testament and Its Social World: Semeia* 35 (1986): 35–59.

86. Robert Merton, "Manifest and Latent Functions," in *Social Theory*, p. 106.

87. Ibid., p. 103.

88. Mary Douglas, *Cultural Bias*, pp. 5–6.

89. Robert Merton, "Manifest and Latent Functions," in *Social Theory*, p. 105.

90. Ibid., p. 107.

91. Ibid., p. 108.

92. Meeks, *First Urban Christians*, p. 7.

93. Ibid., pp. 55–63.

94. Ibid., p. 150.

95. Jonathan L. Gross and Steve Rayner, *Measuring Culture: A Paradigm for the Analysis of Social Organization* (New York: Columbia University Press, 1985).

96. E. P. Sanders, *Paul and Palestinian Judaism: A Comparison of Patterns of Religion* (Philadelphia: Fortress Press, 1977), offers insight into the relationship of ideology and the study of Paul in his introduction, pp. 1–12.

97. Marcus and Fischer, *Anthropology as Cultural Critique*, pp. 17–25.

98. Robert Merton, "Manifest and Latent Functions," in *Social Theory*, p. 108.

99. Meeks, *First Urban Christians*, p. 164, attempts to begin interpreting the sociological data by correlating it with stated beliefs. He says he intends to avoid "strong theoretical assumptions," but in so doing he offers no organization for the discussion other than that which occurs to him at the moment.

100. Mary Douglas, "Pollution," in *Implicit Meanings: Essays in Anthropology* (London: Routledge & Kegan Paul, 1975; rpt. 1979), p. 51.

101. Several models are discussed by R. Wuthnow, J. D. Hunter, A. Bergesen, and E. Kurzweil, *Cultural Analysis: The Work of Peter L. Berger, Mary Douglas, Michel Foucault, and Jürgen Habermas* (Boston: Routledge & Kegan Paul, 1984).

3. The Grid-Group Model

1. For clarity in this study, this description of Mary Douglas's work follows the outline of *Cultural Bias*, Occasional Paper 35 of the Royal Anthropological Institute of Great Britain and Ireland (London: Royal Anthropological Institute, 1978). The title page of this monograph incorrectly says this is occasional paper no. 34. Other works of Mary Douglas are quoted in support of this outline.

2. Aaron Wildavsky, *The Nursing Father: Moses as a Political Leader* (University, Ala.: University of Alabama Press, 1984).

3. Nicholas David, Judy Sterner, and Kodozo Gavua, "Why Pots are Decorated," *Current Anthropology* 29 (1988): 365–89, and Aaron Wildavsky, "Choosing Preferences by Constructing Institutions: A Cultural Theory of Preference Formation," *American Political Science Review* 81 (1987).

4. Mary Douglas and Aaron Wildavsky, *Risk and Culture* (Berkeley and Los Angeles: University of California Press, 1982).

5. Joan M. Morris, "Images of Community in Scientific Texts: A Grid/Group Approach to the Analysis of Journal Editorials," *Sociological Inquiry* 58 (1988): 240–60.

6. Bruce J. Malina, *Christian Origins and Cultural Anthropology: Practical Models for Biblical Interpretation* (Atlanta, Ga.: John Knox Press, 1986).

7. E. E. Evans-Pritchard, *Social Anthropology* (London: Cohen & West, 1951), p. 117.

8. Mary Douglas, *E. E. Evans-Pritchard* (Sussex: Harvester Press, 1980).

9. Peter Berger and Thomas Luckmann, *The Social Construction of Reality: A Treatise in the Sociology of Knowledge* (Garden City, N.Y.: Doubleday, 1966), pp. 3, 172. See also the critique by Peter Hamilton, *Knowledge and Social Structure: An Introduction to the Classical Argument in the Sociology of Knowledge* (London: Routledge & Kegan Paul, 1974), pp. 137–46, where he finds the necessity of distinguishing between interpretive and explicative theory.

10. See the summary of R. Wuthnow, J. D. Hunter, A. Bergesen, and E. Kurzweil, *Cultural Analysis: The Work of Peter L. Berger, Mary Douglas, Michel Foucault, and Jürgen Habermas* (Boston: Routledge & Kegan Paul, 1984), pp. 109–32.

11. See the introduction of Mary Douglas, *Natural Symbols, Explorations in Cosmology* (New York: Pantheon Books, 1982), for a complete definition of the term "cosmology" within the grid-group model.

12. See the definition offered by Bruce J. Malina, *Christian Origins and Cultural Anthropology*, p. 26.

13. Historical-critical research has tended to define the situation-in-life in largely religious terms. John G. Gager, *Kingdom and Community: The Social World of Early Christianity* (Englewood Cliffs, N.J.: Prentice-Hall, 1975), pp. 9f.

14. Wayne Meeks, "The Social Context of Pauline Theology," *Interpretation* 37 (July 1982): 266–77. In this article Meeks examines the theological implications of some observations taken from his larger work, *The First Urban Christians: The Social World of the Apostle Paul* (New Haven: Yale University Press, 1983).

15. Meeks, "The Social Context of Pauline Theology," p. 267.

16. Ibid., p. 267.

17. This hypothesis is found in the work of Emile Durkheim. See *The Elementary Forms of the Religious Life*, trans. Joseph Swain (New York: Macmillan, 1915), esp. the article on the secondary subject of study, p. 10.

18. Werner G. Kümmel, *The New Testament: The History of the Investigation of Its Problems,* trans. S. MacLean Gilmour and Howard Clark Kee (Nashville: Abingdon Press, 1972), pp. 327–41.

19. E. A. Judge, "The Social Identity of the First Christians: A Question of Method in Religious History," *Journal of Religious History* 11 (1980): 201–217, offers an introduction to the concern for social study of the early church. Jonathan L. Gross and Steve Rayner, *Measuring Culture: A Paradigm for the Analysis of Social Organization* (New York: Columbia University Press, 1985), note that "general claims that social environment affects behavior and attitudes are unassailable" (p. x). See also John Dewey, "Introduction," *Reconstruction in Philosophy,* enlarged ed. (Boston: Beacon Press, 1957), pp. v–xli. There is great difficulty in defining the exact causal relationship between the justifications a person uses for actions and the actions themselves. See below concerning Mary Douglas and also Gross and Rayner, *Measuring Culture,* pp. 1–5.

20. Mary Douglas, "Social Preconditions of Enthusiasm and Heterodoxy," *Forms of Symbolic Action,* ed. Robert F. Spencer, Proceedings of the 1969 Annual Spring Meeting of the American Ethnological Society (Seattle: University of Washington Press, 1969), p. 79.

21. Meeks, "The Social Context of Pauline Theology," p. 267.

22. Douglas, *Cultural Bias.*

23. Ibid., p. 3.

24. Her word, which she uses to emphasize the artificial nature of the model; ibid., p. 7.

25. Mary Douglas, *Natural Symbols* (1970, 1973, 1982). The three editions of this book are significantly different in their explanation of this important correlation. See James V. Spickard, "A Guide to Mary Douglas's Three Versions of 'Grid/Group' Theory" (privately published: James V. Spickard, 414 Rose Ave., Box 406, Aromas, Calif. 95004, January 1987) and presented before the Society of Biblical Literature section on Social Sciences and New Testament Interpretation in November 1987. See also his dissertation, "Relativism and Cultural Comparison in the Anthropology of Mary Douglas: A Meta-Theoretical Evaluation of Her Grid/Group Theory" (Ph.D. diss., Graduate Theological Union, 1984).

26. Mary Douglas, *Purity and Danger: An Analysis of the Concepts of Pollution and Taboo* (Baltimore: Pelican Books, 1970), p. 12. Another example is her elegant essay "Deciphering a Meal," in *Implicit Meanings: Essays in Anthropology* (London: Routledge & Kegan Paul, 1975; rpt. 1979), pp. 249–75.

27. This emphasis on the individual is the basis of criticism of the use of grid-group analysis for New Testament work. James V. Spickard has voiced these objections in his privately published "Guide to Mary Douglas's Three Versions of 'Grid/Group' Theory," pp. 34ff.

28. Mary Douglas uses an analogy from the ecology of foxes and rabbits in the English countryside in her "Introduction to Grid-Group Analysis," *Essays in the Sociology of Perception* (London: Routledge & Kegan Paul, 1982), pp. 1–13. The two, the availability of rabbits and the ease or difficulty of hunting them, keep the numbers of foxes and rabbits in a balance that only appears to be static. Robert Merton uses the (quite Pauline!) analogy of a living organism in his paradigm of functional analysis in sociology. A tensile structure is a construct in which weight is born by an entire system of interlocking supports that share the load. Damage to one member of the structure affects the entire structure. The best example of this type of structure is R. Buckminster Fuller's geodesic dome.

29. Aaron Wildavsky, "Choosing Preferences by Constructing Institutions: A Cultural Theory of Preference Formation," p. 16.

30. Douglas, *Cultural Bias*, p. 6.

31. Ibid., pp. 1–3.

32. Claude Levi-Strauss, *Structural Anthropology*, trans. Claire Jacobson and Brooke Grundfest Schoepf (New York: Basic Books, 1963).

33. She notes especially Margaret Mead, *Sex and Temperament* (New York: William Morrow, 1963).

34. Gross and Rayner, *Measuring Culture*, p. xiii.

35. Many commentators use this model to interpret Paul's situation in Galatians. Paul negotiates more or less successfully between Hellenistic Christian enthusiasm (5:13ff.) and renewed Jewish Christian legalism (3:6ff) in the context of apocalyptic theology. See here Wilhelm Lütgert, *Gesetz und Geist: eine Untersuchung zur Vorgeschichte des Galaterbriefes* (Gütersloh: C. Bertelsmann, 1919), and J. H. Ropes, *The Singular Problem of the Epistle to the Galatians*, Harvard Theological Studies 14 (Cambridge: Harvard University Press, 1929). Robert Jewett, "Agitators and the Galatian Congregation," *New Testament Studies* 17 (1970–71): 198–212, provides an overview of various hypotheses relating to the opponents of Paul in Galatians and comes up with a new hypothesis in which a "pneumatic libertine" congregation is attracted to circumcision and a cultic calendar.

36. See here David Ostrander, "One- and Two-Dimensional Models of the Distribution of Beliefs," in *Essays in the Sociology of Perception*, ed. Mary Douglas (London: Routledge & Kegan Paul, 1982), pp. 14–24, for a discussion of the way social environments may act as the basis of comparison in single- and multi-dimensional models.

37. Michael Thompson, "A Three-Dimensional Model," in ibid., pp. 31–36.

38. "Cosmology" is defined above as the explanations or justifications with which a society or group describes its behavior. It is the manifest "meaning" attached to behavior. "Social accountability" is the basis for understanding this

term, following Mary Douglas, *In the Active Voice* (London: Routledge & Kegan Paul, 1982), pp. 190, 201, and Spickard, "A Guide to Mary Douglas's Three Versions of 'Grid/Group' Theory," p. 28.

39. The standard text in this field is Robert R. Blake and Jane S. Mouton, *The New Managerial Grid* (Houston, Tex.: Gulf Publishing, 1978).

40. Mary Douglas, *Natural Symbols*, p. 98.

41. Douglas, *Cultural Bias*, p. 13.

42. Ibid., p. 6.

43. Harold Garfinkel, *Studies in Ethnomethodology* (Englewood Cliffs, N.J.: Prentice-Hall, 1967); Douglas, *Natural Symbols* (1982 ed.).

44. Douglas, *Cultural Bias*, p. 6. The word "plastic" implies "moldable" and therefore is a metaphor for the lack of rigidity in culture. "Dynamic" implies action or force and is a metaphor for the power of change.

45. Bruce J. Malina explains the relationship of social mapping to "cultural scripts" with the analogy of games and with reference to the four generalized symbolic media of social interaction: chap. 4 of *Christian Origins and Cultural Anthropology*, pp. 68–97.

46. Douglas, *Cultural Bias*, pp. 7f.

47. Thompson, "Three-Dimensional Model," p. 32.

48. Malina, *Christian Origins and Cultural Anthropology*, pp. 18–20, offers an extended description of group categories from the perspective of a New Testament scholar.

49. Gross and Rayner, *Measuring Culture*, pp. 5f.

50. Douglas, *Cultural Bias*, p. 38.

51. Malina, *Christian Origins and Cultural Anthropology*, pp. 17f., offers an extended description of grid categories with reference to the match between the individual's and society's symbolic system. This idiosyncratic definition of grid reflects the definition of the "stable diagonal" used in this study.

52. Douglas, *Cultural Bias*, p. 8.

53. Ibid., p. 14.

54. Mary Douglas, "Introduction," in Gross and Rayner, *Measuring Culture*, pp. xxii–xxiii.

55. Gross and Rayner, *Measuring Culture*, p. x.

56. This confusion is a product of changing theory. See Spickard, "Guide to Mary Douglas's Three Versions of 'Grid/Group' Theory," pp. 2ff.

57. Gross and Rayner, *Measuring Culture*. The distinction among weak group categories is blurred by changes in the description offered by Douglas. See Spickard, "Relativism and Cultural Comparison in the Anthropology of Mary Douglas."

58. Malina, *Christian Origins and Cultural Anthropology*, pp. 45–54, describes the weak group, low grid cultural script with New Testament period examples. Malina's descriptions of weak group, low grid and of weak group, high

grid are reversed from the ones employed here. This is because of his use of the 1973 edition of *Natural Symbols* and variations in his interpretation of Mary Douglas's work.

59. Douglas, *Cultural Bias*, p. 24; Gross and Rayner, *Measuring Culture*, pp. 7f.; and Ostrander, "One- and Two-Dimensional Models of the Distribution of Beliefs," p. 27.

60. Malina, *Christian Origins and Cultural Anthropology*, pp. 55–61, describes the weak group, high grid cultural script with New Testament period examples. Again, it must be noted that the definitions of Quadrants A and B are reversed in Malina's work.

61. Douglas, *Cultural Bias*, p. 24; Gross and Rayner, *Measuring Culture*, pp. 8f.; and Ostrander, "One- and Two-Dimensional Models of the Distribution of Beliefs," p. 27.

62. Malina, *Christian Origins and Cultural Anthropology*, pp. 29–37, describes the strong group, high grid cultural script with New Testament period examples.

63. Douglas, *Cultural Bias*, pp. 23f.; Gross and Rayner, *Measuring Culture*, pp. 9f.; and Ostrander, "One- and Two-Dimensional Models of the Distribution of Beliefs," pp. 28f.

64. Douglas, *Cultural Bias*, p. 23.

65. Hence the name for this quadrant used in this study, "small group." Malina, *Christian Origins and Cultural Anthropology*, pp. 37–44, describes the strong group, low grid cultural script with New Testament period examples.

66. Douglas, *Cultural Bias*, pp. 22f.; Gross and Rayner, *Measuring Culture*, pp. 10ff.; and Ostrander, "One- and Two-Dimensional Models of the Distribution of Beliefs," p. 29.

67. Ostrander, "One- and Two-Dimensional Models of the Distribution of Beliefs," pp. 14–30.

68. Ibid., p. 25.

69. Ibid., p. 28. There are other models; see Malina, *Christian Origins and Cultural Anthropology*, where he combines several social science models under the rubric of the grid-group map to identify useful distributions of behavioral rules and patterns of belief.

70. Ostrander, "One- and Two-Dimensional Models of the Distribution of Beliefs," p. 25.

71. Gross and Rayner, *Measuring Culture*, p. x.

72. Ibid., pp. 4–5.

4. A Social Accounting of the Pauline Church

1. These questions occur as one seeks to find clues to the ways the behavior functions or dysfunctions for the group. Robert Merton has summarized these

questions succinctly; *Social Theory and Social Structure*, enlarged ed. (New York: Free Press, 1968), p. 112. Merton's paradigmatic model for functional analysis is discussed in chap. 2.

2. Robert Merton, "Manifest and Latent Functions," in ibid., p. 110.

3. Clifford Geertz, *The Interpretation of Culture: Selected Essays* (New York: Basic Books, 1973).

4. See Chapter Two for notes on Robert Merton's paradigm for functional analysis and the way it may inform New Testament research.

5. This procedure is not to be confused with content analysis. Content analysis makes inferences by objectively counting specifically identifiable characteristics of communications; e.g., Aloys Funk, *Status und Rollen in den Paulusbriefen: Eine inhaltsanalystische Untersuchung zur Religionssoziologie* (Innsbruck: Tyrolia, 1981), and the review by Bruce J. Malina, *Catholic Biblical Quarterly* 49 (1987): 143f. In contrast, the concern here is to make as clear a distinction as possible between various categories of data inferred from the content of the communication.

6. In this study the words "faction" and "factionalism" have been used for identifying social entities that occupy the D Quadrant and for the movement down group. See Bruce J. Malina, "Normative Dissonance and Christian Origins," *Social-Scientific Criticism of the New Testament and Its Social World: Semeia* 35 (1986): 35–59, esp. pp. 35f., for a definition of the term "faction" and the reason for its use.

7. Wayne Meeks, *The First Urban Christians: The Social World of the Apostle Paul* (New Haven: Yale University Press, 1983), pp. 142, 150, 157, 162.

8. Lloyd Michael White, "*Domus Ecclesiae—Domus Dei*: Adaptation and Development in the Setting for Early Christian Assembly" (Ph.D. diss., Yale University, 1982). Robert Banks, *Paul's Idea of Community: The Early House Churches in Their Historical Setting* (Grand Rapids, Mich.: William B. Eerdmans, 1980).

9. Keith F. Nickle, *The Collection: A Study in Paul's Strategy*, Studies in Biblical Theology 49 (Naperville, Ill.: Alec R. Allenson, 1966). We will find, contrary to expectation, that the collection for the saints actually functions to define group categories, not to increase hierarchical social structure nor to increase Big-Man status.

10. John H. Schütz, *Paul and the Anatomy of Apostolic Authority*, Society for New Testament Studies Monograph Series 26 (Cambridge: Cambridge University Press, 1975), and also Bengt Holmberg, *Paul and Power: The Structure of Authority in the Primitive Church as Reflected in the Pauline Epistles* (Lund: CWK Gleerup, 1978). Authority categories relate to the limitations on choices an individual can make. See also Bruce J. Malina, *Christian Origins and Cultural Anthropology: Practical Models for Biblical Interpretation* (Atlanta, Ga.: John Knox Press, 1986), esp. chap. 6.

11. This is Merton's term; "Manifest and Latent Functions," in *Social Theory*, p. 114. This means that inference from the letter itself, not its content, is extremely powerful evidence for the activity of the Pauline mission.

12. Meeks, *First Urban Christians*, pp. 84–96.

13. Jonathan L. Gross and Steve Rayner, *Measuring Culture: A Paradigm for the Analysis of Social Organization* (New York: Columbia University Press, 1985).

14. Ibid., p. 59.

15. Ibid., pp. 71–85.

16. Ibid., p. 88.

17. Tendency and its cognates will be the technical term for the estimation of value for a predicate. Estimating a value for a polythetic predicate is a straightforward process. It is simply a sum of the variables, weighted according to the manner in which they interact. See H. D. Brunk, *An Introduction to Mathematical Statistics* (Boston: Ginn, 1960), esp. pp. 130f., 136, and 146ff., for the method of statistical "maximum likelihood estimators" and "decision rules."

18. Gross and Rayner, *Measuring Culture*, pp. 83–84.

19. Brunk, *An Introduction to Mathematical Statistics*, p. 147. The extended discussion of statistical decision theory and the work of A. Wald, *Statistical Decision Functions* (New York: John Wiley, 1950), is helpful.

20. Gross and Rayner, *Measuring Culture*, p. 64.

21. Ibid., p. 72.

22. Ibid., p. 61. "One should first construct a precise mathematical model of the processes being observed and then define the predicates in terms of properties of the model, rather than of the actual collection of observed entities."

23. Mary Douglas, "Introduction," to ibid., p. xxv, indicates the need for adaptation of the model to the situation.

24. Ibid., pp. 73–75.

25. Various collections of the names of participants in the Pauline church exist. E. Earle Ellis, "Paul and His Co-Workers," *New Testament Studies* 17 (1971): 437–52, identifies those who are mentioned in the context of various titles. See also Edwin A. Judge, *The Social Pattern of Christian Groups in the First Century* (London: Tyndale, 1960), and "The Social Identity of the First Christians: A Question of Method in Religious History," *Journal of Religious History* 11 (1980): 201–217. Wayne Meeks collects prosopographic data in *First Urban Christians*, pp. 55–63. See also F. F. Bruce, *The Pauline Circle* (Grand Rapids, Mich.: William B. Eerdmans, 1985), for a description of the inner circle of Paul's associates.

26. Gross and Rayner, *Measuring Culture*, pp. 75–77.

27. Ibid., pp. 77–78.

28. Ibid., p. 78.

29. Ibid., p. 79.

30. Ibid., pp. 78–79.

31. Gross and Rayner call these measures "Commonality of Experience"; ibid., p. 79.

32. Mary Douglas, "Pollution," in *Implicit Meanings: Essays in Anthropology* (London: Routledge & Kegan Paul, 1975; rpt., 1979), p. 51.

33. 2 Cor. 6:14: "Do not be mismated with unbelievers. For what partnership have righteousness and iniquity? Or what fellowship has light with darkness?" This quote is a statement of group separation. Though it may not be authentically Pauline, it is a good example of the concern for separation between the believer and the rest of the world.

34. The literature on purity and danger is extensive. Important insights in the field follows Mary Douglas's *Purity and Danger: An Analysis of Concepts of Pollution and Taboo* (Baltimore: Pelican Books, 1970) and *Natural Symbols: Explorations in Cosmology* (New York: Pantheon, 1982). Her essay "Pollution," found in *Implicit Meanings,* pp. 47–59, is a functional analysis of pollution concepts. The concept of the division of sanctions is derived from this essay, pp. 54–55.

35. The primary physical distinction between ritual washing and Christian baptism is that ritual washing is done each time pollution is encountered, baptism only once.

36. Mary Douglas, "Pollution," in *Implicit Meanings,* p. 56.

37. Mary Douglas, *Cultural Bias,* Occasional Paper 35 of the Royal Anthropological Institute of Great Britian and Ireland (London: Royal Anthropological Institute, 1978), p. 8.

38. Mary Douglas, "Pollution," in *Implicit Meanings,* p. 55.

39. Gross and Rayner, *Measuring Culture,* pp. 79–82. The language of this paragraph comes from this passage.

40. Mary Douglas and Jonathan L. Gross, "Food and Culture: Measuring the Intricacy of Rule Systems," *Social Science Information* 20 (1981): 1–35. Jonathan L. Gross, "Measurement of Calendric Information in Food-taking Behavior," *Food in the Social Order: Studies of Food and Festivities in Three American Communities,* ed. Mary Douglas (New York: Russell Sage Foundation, 1984); "Graph-theoretical Model of Social Organization," *Annals of Discrete Mathematics* 13 (1982): 81–88; and "Information-theoretic Scales for Measuring Cultural Rule Systems," in *Sociological Methodology 1983–1984* (San Francisco: Jossey-Bass, 1983), pp. 248–71.

41. Gross and Rayner, *Measuring Culture,* pp. 79–80. The language of this paragraph comes from this passage.

42. Gross, "Graph-theoretical Model of Social Organization," p. 85.

43. These qualities of office are gleaned from Holmberg, *Paul and Power,* p. 111. He cites Ulrich Brockhaus, *Charisma und Amt: Die paulinischen Charis-*

menlehre auf dem Hintergrund der frühchristlichen Gemeindefunktionen, 2d ed. (Wuppertal: Brockhaus, 1975), pp. 24, 123.

44. Social networks are defined by David A. Snow, Louis A. Zurcher, Jr., and Sheldon Ekland-Olson, "Social Networks and Social Movements: A Microstructural Approach to Differential Recruitment," *American Sociological Review* 45 (1980): 787–801.

45. These will be taken up under the grid predicate "authority."

46. In the presence of decreasing insulation, autonomy, control, and competition represent different kinds of individual freedom. See Douglas, *Cultural Bias,* p. 16.

47. Gross and Rayner, *Measuring Culture,* p. 70.

48. Ibid., pp. 80–81.

49. Holmberg, in his *Paul and Power,* discusses asymmetric relationships of authority among members of the early church. (See esp. his conclusions, pp. 196–98.) The behavior of the Pauline church itself is ambiguous. Holmberg notes the "self-imposed limitation of apostolic authority" (p. 197) that Paul places upon himself. Whatever the ideological reasoning, Paul's behavior is contradictory in a social environment in which we could expect him to exercise legal or rational domination.

50. David Ostrander, "One- and Two-Dimensional Models of the Distribution of Beliefs," in *Essays in the Sociology of Perception,* ed. Mary Douglas (London: Routledge & Kegan Paul, 1982), pp. 14–30. See esp. "the unstable diagonal," pp. 26–27.

51. Ralph W. Nicholas, "Factions: A Comparative Analysis," in *Friends, Followers, and Factions: A Reader in Political Clientelism* (Berkeley and Los Angeles: University of California Press, 1977), pp. 55–58, offers a sociological definition of factions that focuses on their existence as political groups. The words "faction" and "factionalism" have been used in this study to avoid the problem of ethnocentrism implicit in the use of the words "cult" and "denominationalism" applied to the Pauline church. See Malina, "Normative Dissonance and Christian Origins," pp. 35–59, esp. pp. 35f., for a definition of the term "faction" and the reason for its use.

52. Douglas, *Cultural Bias,* pp. 16–17. Control is one of the three signs of individual freedom in society: autonomy, control, and competition. Control is translated into concern for authority because of the possibility of high group investment in the Pauline church.

53. Holmberg, *Paul and Power,* p. 119.

54. Ibid., pp. 124–35.

55. Gross and Rayner, *Measuring Culture,* p. 81.

56. Douglas, *Cultural Bias,* p. 16.

57. Ibid., pp. 16–17. Again, as with the category control, because of the pos-

sibility of a high investment in group, competition—a word related to Quadrant A—is translated into the category "initiative" for the sake of clarity.

58. Ibid., p. 17.

59. These tests are drawn directly from Douglas's discussion of increasing individual freedom, ibid., pp. 16–17.

60. Gross and Rayner, *Measuring Culture*, pp. 81–82.

61. Ibid., p. 82.

62. Douglas, *Cultural Bias*, pp. 16–17.

63. Ibid., p. 16.

64. These tests come directly from the discussion of grid autonomy in ibid., p. 16, quoted above. Malina has outlined three levels of the linguistic symbol "freedom." He cautions us to beware of limiting the term to simply the removal of obstacles or restraints. The freedom to pursue or attain some goal or value is also a part of Paul's perspective. See his article, "Freedom: A Theological Inquiry into the Dimensions of a Symbol," *Biblical Theology Bulletin* 8 (1978): 62–76.

65. Gross and Rayner, *Measuring Culture*, p. 72.

5. A Social Accounting: Group

1. This chapter follows the proposal for grid-group analysis outlined by Mary Douglas, *Cultural Bias*, Occasional Paper 35 of the Royal Anthropological Institute of Great Britain and Ireland (London: Royal Anthropological Institute, 1978); it is structured by Jonathan L. Gross and Steve Rayner, *Measuring Culture: A Paradigm for the Analysis of Social Organization* (New York: Columbia University Press, 1985), and is restated as a working hypothesis in the preceding chapter.

2. Douglas's word, *Cultural Bias*, p. 8.

3. E. Earle Ellis, "Paul and His Co-workers," *New Testament Studies* 17 (1971): 438.

4. Bengt Holmberg, *Paul and Power: The Structure of Authority in the Primitive Church as Reflected in the Pauline Epistles* (Lund: CWK Gleerup, 1978), pp. 58–71.

5. Lloyd Michael White, "*Domus Ecclesiae—Domus Dei*: Adaptation and Development in the Setting for Early Christian Assembly (Ph.D. diss., Yale University, 1982), is especially helpful in anticipating the primitive form of the house church meeting.

6. Robert Banks, *Paul's Idea of Community: The Early House Churches in Their Historical Setting* (Grand Rapids, Mich.: William B. Eerdmans, 1980), p. 42. White, "*Domus Ecclesiae—Domus Dei,*" pp. 560ff. Wayne Meeks, *The*

First Urban Christians: The Social World of the Apostle Paul (New Haven: Yale University Press, 1983), p. 143.

7. Meeks, *First Urban Christians,* p. 109. The letters themselves, which Paul's coworkers carried, function to provide connections between threesomes.

8. This is as we would intuitively expect. Increased interaction between people in Paul's mission and the local cluster of house churches would tend to increase group awareness.

9. Holmberg, *Paul and Power,* pp. 35–50.

10. Please note that we are not interested in the content of that which the participants *say* about their involvement, but in the evidences for that which they do. In other words, we are interested in what is said not for its content but for its form and that which we can infer from its content about the participants' actions.

11. Meeks, *First Urban Christians,* pp. 75f. White, *"Domus Ecclesiae— Domus Dei,"* pp. 482f.

12. Norman R. Petersen, *Rediscovering Paul: Philemon and the Sociology of Paul's Narrative World* (Philadelphia: Fortress Press, 1985). In Chapter Eight we will return to this study to confirm the results of this grid-group analysis.

13. Ibid., p. 301.

14. Meeks, *First Urban Christians,* p. 77.

15. Gerd Theissen, *The Social Setting of Pauline Christianity: Essays on Corinth,* trans. John H. Schütz (Philadelphia: Fortress Press, 1982).

16. Meeks, *First Urban Christians,* pp. 72–73.

17. Ibid., pp. 95 and 105–107.

18. Commonality of experience is accounted in the section so titled.

19. Banks, *Paul's Idea of Community,* p. 89. See also Nils Alstrup Dahl, "Paul and Possessions," in *Studies in Paul: Theology for the Early Christian Mission* (Minneapolis, Minn.: Augsburg Publishing House, 1977), pp. 22–39.

20. Hans Dieter Betz, *2 Corinthians 8 and 9: A Commentary on Two Administrative Letters of the Apostle Paul* (Philadelphia: Fortress Press, 1985).

21. The group boundary score is considered in the section so titled.

22. Meeks, *First Urban Christians,* p. 95. He lists examples of these as: Gal. 3:23ff., 4:3–5, 4:8f.; Eph. 2:1–10, 2:11–22; Rom. 6:17–22, 7:5f., 11:30; Col. 1:21f.; 2:13f. He gets the term "soteriological contrast pattern" from Nils Alstrup Dahl, "Form-critical Observations on Early Christian Preaching," in *Jesus in the Memory of the Early Church* (Minneapolis, Minn.: Augsburg Publishing House, 1976), pp. 30–36.

23. Gerd Theissen, "The Strong and the Weak in Corinth: A Sociological Analysis of a Theological Quarrel" and "Social Stratification in the Corinthian Community: A Contribution to the Sociology of Early Hellenistic Christianity," both in *The Social Setting of Pauline Christianity.*

24. Meeks, *First Urban Christians,* p. 73.

25. Ibid., p. 150–57. See also Nils Alstrup Dahl, "The Origin of Baptism," *Interpretationes ad Vetus Testamentum Pertinentes Sigmundo Mowinckel Septuagenario Missae*, ed. Nils A. Dahl and A. S. Kapelrud (Oslo: Land og Kirke, 1955), pp. 36–52.

26. Banks, *Paul's Idea of Community*, pp. 89–91, suggests that Paul may be metaphorically referring to conversion in using the term "baptism." Even if this is true, the conversion experience would become then the mark of division between the pre- and postmembership status.

27. Banks offers examples of "physical expressions of fellowship" as baptism, the laying on of hands, the common meal, the exchange of kisses, and the sharing of possessions. Ibid., pp. 80–90.

28. Meeks, *First Urban Christians*, pp. 84–94.

29. Ibid., pp. 94–103. See also under "Boundary Score."

30. Stephen Benko, *Pagan Rome and the Early Christians* (Bloomington: Indiana University Press, 1984), see esp. the chapter on the problems caused by the kiss, pp. 79–102.

31. Ibid., p. 98.

32. Banks, *Paul's Idea of Community*, pp. 89–91.

33. Meeks, *First Urban Christians*, p. 102.

34. This list is from ibid., p. 154.

35. See above, "soteriological contrast pattern," under the discussion of the predicate "Commonality of Experience." The type of marker of the division between the old state and the new is exemplified by 2 Cor. 5:17: "Therefore, if any one is in Christ, he is a new creation; the old has passed away, behold the new has come."

36. Meeks, *First Urban Christians*, p. 100.

37. Hans Conzelmann, *I Corinthians: A Commentary on the First Epistle to the Corinthians*, trans. J. Leitch, A Hermeneia Series Commentary (Philadelphia: Fortress Press, 1975), pp. 170–71. See also his note to Hans von Soden, "Sakrament und Ethik bei Paulus," *Das Paulusbild in der neueren Deutschen Forschung*, ed. Karl Heinrich Rengstorf, Weg der Forschung 24 (Darmstadt: Wissenschaftliche Buchgesellschaft, 1964), pp. 338–79.

38. Hans Dieter Betz, *Galatians: A Commentary on Paul's Letter to the Churches in Galatia*, A Hermeneia Series Commentary (Philadelphia: Fortress Press, 1979), p. 261.

39. Meeks, *First Urban Christians*, pp. 105ff.

40. Theissen, "Legitimation and Substance," in *The Social Setting of Pauline Christianity*, pp. 27–67.

41. Meeks, *First Urban Christians*, pp. 105ff.

42. Robert Jewett, *The Thessalonian Correspondence: Pauline Rhetoric and Millenarian Piety* (Philadelphia: Fortress Press, 1986), pp. 105f. Jewett examines

Wilhelm Lütgert's suggestion that a libertinistic movement was active among the Christians in Thessalonica. He concludes that Paul is indeed "countering an effort in Thessalonica to challenge" the traditional Jewish view of marriage, p. 106.

43. William David Moore, "The Origin of 'Porneia' Reflected in I Cor. 5–6 and Its Implications to an Understanding of the Fundamental Orientation of the Corinthian Church," (Ph.D. diss., Baylor University, 1978).

44. Mary Douglas, "Pollution," in *Implicit Meanings: Essays in Anthropology* (London: Routledge & Kegan Paul, 1975; rpt. 1979), pp. 47–59, esp. p. 57.

45. Ernst Käsemann, *Essays on New Testament Themes* (Naperville, Ill.: Alec R. Allenson, 1964), pp. 123ff., and Conzelmann, *I Corinthians,* p. 203.

46. This is characteristic of sanctions applied when the offender is a member of the group and the group is entrusted with the protection of the member's interests. See Douglas, "Pollution," in *Implicit Meanings,* p. 54.

47. Authority itself will be discussed in the sections that deal with measures of grid.

48. Ronald F. Hock, *The Social Context of Paul's Ministry: Tentmaking and Apostleship* (Philadelphia: Fortress Press, 1980), and "Paul's Tentmaking and the Problem of His Social Class," *Journal of Biblical Literature* 97 (1978): 555–64.

49. Meeks, *First Urban Christians,* pp. 117ff.

50. Theissen, "Legitimation and Substance" in *The Social Settings of Pauline Christianity,* pp. 27–67.

51. Ibid., p. 28.

52. Holmberg, *Paul and Power,* p. 112. See also his reference to Ulrich Brockhaus, *Charisma und Amt: Die paulinischen Charismenlehre auf dem Hintergrund der frühchristlichen Gemeindefunktionen,* 2nd ed. (Wuppertal: Brockhaus, 1975), pp. 102f., against K. Andrew Kirk, "Did 'Officials' in the New Testament Church Receive a Salary?" *Evangelical Times* 84 (1972/3): 108. Kirk argues that a regular compensation for the teaching task is not implied in the Galatian text.

6. A Social Accounting: Grid

1. Since Paul's letters were saved and there is a progression in the concerns of the Corinthian correspondence, we can assume that Paul's letters must have met at least some of their objectives and therefore tell us something of the structure of the Pauline churches. See Wayne Meeks, *The First Urban Christians: The Social World of the Apostle Paul* (New Haven: Yale University Press, 1983), p. 118.

2. Ibid., pp. 89–90. Robert Jewett, "The Sexual Liberation of the Apostle

Paul," *Journal of the American Academy of Religion* 47 Supplement (1979): 55–87. Jewett traces three stages in the development of Paul's understanding of equality in relation to the sexes. This is one example of the pressure on social understanding that cultural bias exerts. Paul comes naturally to adapt his thinking and his way of adjusting to his world.

3. Ralph P. Martin, *The Spirit and the Congregation: Studies in I Cor. 12–15* (Grand Rapids, Mich.: William B. Eerdmans, 1984); Gerhard Dautzenberg, *Urchristliche Prophetie: ihre Erforschung ihre Voraussetzungen im Judentum und ihre Structure im ersten Korintherbrief* (Stuttgart: W. Kohlhammer, 1975).

4. Bengt Holmberg, *Paul and Power: The Structure of Authority in the Primitive Church as Reflected in the Pauline Epistles* (Lund: CWK Gleerup, 1978), pp. 97–104, reviews the secondary literature to conclude that specific titles and tasks like prophecy and teaching were limited to closed sets of individuals.

5. Ibid., pp. 98–102, cites Heinrich Greeven, "Propheten, Lehrer, Vorsteher bei Paulus. Zur Frage der 'Ämter' im Urchristentum," *Zeitschrift fur die Neutestamentliche Wissenschaft* 44 (1952/53): 1–43.

6. Jonathan L. Gross and Steve Rayner, *Measuring Culture: A Paradigm for the Analysis of Social Organization* (New York: Columbia University Press, 1985), p. 82.

7. Holmberg, *Paul and Power*, chap. 3, pp. 96–123. Although the tests of the predicate grid role distribution have been inferred on the basis of Douglas's statement that insulation is the primary grid category, the side-effects of insulation— places in the society to categorize individuals, specific descriptions of role that occupy the individual, sanctions that result from failure to accomplish the task, an order to the hierarchy, however byzantine or simple, and specific individuals who do participate in these categories—these are the very topics Holmberg treats in this important chapter (although in a different order).

8. Ibid., p. 97.

9. Ibid., p. 110.

10. Ibid., pp. 112–13.

11. Ibid., p. 113. See also p. 159, where he contrasts the situation found in the letters of Ignatius. He says that only "personal social influences of an ordinary kind" result in what authority the *proïstamenoi* exhibit.

12. Ibid., pp. 97–104.

13. Ibid., pp. 107–108.

14. Ibid., p. 63, offers this description: "These same three principles for apostolic work: to receive no support from the church but to work for one's living, to maintain good relations with the church in Jerusalem and to maintain a law-free Gentile church were adopted by Paul, who elaborated them theologically and kept to them faithfully all his life. This indicates that there was a time when Paul was taught by Barnabas and learned the 'trade' of being a missionary to the Gentiles."

15. Robert Banks, *Paul's Idea of Community: The Early House Churches in Their Historical Setting* (Grand Rapids, Mich.: William B. Eerdmans, 1980), p. 139 (emphasis added). He notes esp. 1 Cor. 11:33–34a, 14:39–40, and 16:2–3 in this context. See also the discussion of "dialectical authority" in Holmberg, *Paul and Power*, pp. 118–20.

16. Holmberg offers a listing of related citings in Paul's letters: *Paul and Power*, p. 80. See also the power of the term "father" in Roman society: Beryl Rawson, "The Roman Family," and W. K. Lacey, *"Patria Potestas,"* in *The Family in Ancient Rome: New Perspectives*, ed. Beryl Rawson (Ithaca, N.Y.: Cornell University Press, 1986).

17. Holmberg, *Paul and Power*, pp. 120–22.

18. Ibid., p. 120.

19. Ibid., p. 123.

20. Ibid., p. 121.

21. Ibid., p. 66. See also the discussion of Titus and his rank, pp. 60–61.

22. Ibid., p. 110. He cites Pierre Grelot, "Sur l'origine des ministères dans les églises pauliniennes," *Istina* 16 (1971): 459.

23. The developmental sequence outlined by Holmberg, *Paul and Power* (see various references in Part II), follows Max Weber's categories for understanding power and authority in culture.

24. Mary Douglas, *Cultural Bias,* Occasional Paper 35 of the Royal Anthropological Institute of Great Britain and Ireland (London: Royal Anthropological Institute, 1978), p. 17.

25. John H. Schütz, *Paul and the Anatomy of Apostolic Authority,* Society for New Testament Studies Monograph Series 26 (Cambridge: Cambridge University Press, 1975), p. 275.

26. Holmberg, *Paul and Power*, pp. 150ff., and Gerd Theissen, "Legitimation and Subsistence," in *The Social Setting of Pauline Christianity: Essays on Corinth,* trans. John H. Schütz (Philadelphia: Fortress Press, 1982), pp. 27–67, esp. pp. 40ff.

27. Hans Conzelmann, *I Corinthians: A Commentary on the First Epistle to the Corinthians,* trans. J. Leitch, A Hermeneia Series Commentary (Philadelphia: Fortress Press, 1975), pp. 103–106, notes the contrast between outsiders—called unrighteous—and the saints as the only grounds for judgment. This is a result of a concern for group boundary. See his comments on 1 Cor. 5:10, p. 100.

28. Paul does make it clear with the introduction to chapter 5 (1 Cor. 5:1) that he has information about "immoral" or impure behavior among Corinthian Christians. This chapter is a parallel to chapter 6 in the themes of *porneia* and *pleoneksia*. See Conzelmann, *I Corinthians*, p. 104, n. 9. Therefore, the inclusion of this concern *may* have been a literary device. But it still would describe the negative situation (no Christian option for the adjudication of participants' rights existed at Corinth).

29. In 2 Cor. 13:1b Paul invokes the requirement of the Torah (Deut. 19:15) that two or three witnesses must be produced for any evidence. The invocation of this forensic device suggests an unidentified group process of consensus; so Meeks, *First Urban Christians*, p. 124.

30. Holmberg cautions that we must be careful when universalizing the Corinthian experience as regards the development of leadership: *Paul and Power*, p. 114.

31. Ibid., p. 87.

32. Norman R. Petersen, *Rediscovering Paul: Philemon and the Sociology of Paul's Narrative World* (Philadelphia: Fortress Press, 1985), pp. 132–33.

33. Holmberg, *Paul and Power*, chap. 1, pp. 14–57, esp. p. 27: "the Gentile Mission of Antioch (Paul and Barnabas) is in fact dependent on what decision is taken by the Jerusalem authorities."

34. Meeks, *First Urban Christians*, p. 113.

35. Holmberg, *Paul and Power*, pp. 117–18. See also p. 159. Note also Paul's effect on the group proximity score. The loss of Paul can be predicted to have a major impact on the sociology of the Pauline church faction.

36. Holmberg lists five cases where Paul leaves choices open for individuals to decide on their own: (1) 1 Cor. 7:3–6, sexual relations in marriage; (2) 1 Cor. 8:8–10, 10:25–28, Rom. 14:13–23, food offered to idols; (3) 1 Cor. 7:8f, 28, 38, abstaining from marriage; (4) 2 Cor. 8:8–10, giving to the collection; (5) Philem. 8–10, 17, 21f., treating Onesimus as a brother; ibid., p. 84.

37. Conzelmann, *I Corinthians*, pp. 170–71, quoted above.

38. These essays of Theissen's are collected and translated into English in *The Social Setting of Pauline Christianity*.

39. Holmberg, *Paul and Power*, p. 106.

40. Meeks, *First Urban Christians*, pp. 121–22. See also Holmberg, Paul and Power, pp. 114–15.

41. Holmberg, *Paul and Power*, p. 116.

42. Theissen, "Legitimation and Subsistence," in *The Social Setting of Pauline Christianity*, p. 43. See also his *Sociology of Early Palestinian Christianity*, trans. John Bowen (Philadelphia: Fortress Press, 1978).

43. Conzelmann, *I Corinthians*, p. 154, esp. n. 28.

44. Meeks, *First Urban Christians*, p. 115.

45. Hans Dieter Betz, *Galatians: A Commentary on Paul's Letter to the Churches in Galatia*, A Hermeneia Series Commentary (Philadelphia: Fortress Press, 1979), p. 24.

46. Ibid., p. 25.

47. Ibid., p. 28.

48. Ibid., pp. 28–29.

49. These terms—"strong" and "weak"—used by Paul refer to sociological,

not theological or ideational categories. Theissen, *The Social Setting of Pauline Christianity,* pp. 69–119. Theissen's conclusions from several related articles are summarized by Holmberg, *Paul and Power,* pp. 104–106.

50. We are less concerned here with the issue of the leadership of the entire Christian church negotiated between the pillars and Barnabas and Paul, which Paul cites for evidence, than we are with pattern behavior that involved Paul in controversy with the Galatians. See here the outline of the letter summarized by Betz, *Galatians,* pp. 16–23.

51. Holmberg, *Paul and Power,* p. 128.

52. See here ibid., pp. 191–92. Holmberg concludes, "It cannot be excluded that Paul participated in the institutionalization of intra-church authority even during the initial stage, but this assumption represents only an educated guess."

53. Holmberg's word; ibid., p. 128.

54. Ibid., p. 155.

55. Ibid., p. 142.

56. Ibid., pp. 113–18 and 191–95.

57. The relationship of patron and client is asymmetrical. S. N. Eisenstadt and L. Roniger have summarized the core analytical characteristics of the asymmetry of the patron-client relationship: *Patrons, Clients and Friends: Interpersonal Relations and the Structure of Trust in Society* (Cambridge: Cambridge University Press, 1984), pp. 48f.

58. Meeks, *First Urban Christians,* p. 119.

59. William Baird, "Visions, Revelation, and Ministry: Reflections on 2 Cor. 12:1–5 and Gal. 1:11–17," *Journal of Biblical Literature* 104 (1985): 651–62.

60. Ibid., p. 661.

61. Holmberg notices that Paul "chooses" to limit his exercise of authority: in the interest of fostering Christian maturity (*Paul and Power,* pp. 82–88), and in the controversy over the "rights of apostleship" (pp. 89–95). He concludes that this choice is a part of Paul's manipulation of the process of the legitimization of authority in the local situation (pp. 186–95, esp. p. 189). This choice results in conflict (p. 190).

62. Discussed in the previous chapter, under "Deferential Involvement," in conjunction with Petersen, *Rediscovering Paul.*

63. Douglas, *Cultural Bias,* pp. 16–17. See also the discussion of entitlement above in Chapter Four.

64. See Holmberg, *Paul and Power,* p. 107.

65. Ibid., pp. 107–110.

66. See ibid., pp. 107ff. Paul encourages those who work in the faction; see above.

67. Douglas, *Cultural Bias,* p. 17. See also Holmberg's discussion of this incident, *Paul and Power,* pp. 14–34.

68. See Theissen, *The Social Setting of Pauline Christianity*, pp. 121–43.

69. Theissen, *Sociology of Early Palestinian Christianity* and *The Social Setting of Pauline Christianity*.

70. Holmberg, *Paul and Power*, p. 84.

71. Theissen, *The Social Setting of Pauline Christianity*.

72. Conzelmann, *I Corinthians*, pp. 181–91.

73. Jewett, "The Sexual Liberation of the Apostle Paul," argues that Paul develops over time in his understanding of equality in relation to the sexes. This developmental theme *could* imply that Paul's theology was in the process of catching up to the reality of the experience of the church.

74. Conzelmann, *I Corinthians*, pp. 184–85.

75. See Chapter Three for a description of grid-group analysis and the social environment of the D Quadrant.

7. Quadrant D Mapping

1. This mapping on the basis of typology was first suggested by Mary Douglas in conversation with me in June 1985. The following sections describe the argument and answer her proposed initial mapping.

2. The "New Guinea Big Man" has been described in several anthropological studies. The relevant characteristics of New Guinea culture include: (1) opportunism: enslavement to fashion, (2) individualism: free social contracting in an open social marketplace, (3) secularity: many secular rituals. Anthony Forge, "Prestige, Influence and Society, a New Guinea Example," chap. 12 in *Witchcraft Confessions and Accusations*, ed. Mary Douglas, Association of Social Anthropologists Monograph Series 9 (London: Tavistock Publications, 1970). Peter Lawrence and M. J. Meggitt, eds., *Gods, Ghosts and Men in Melanesia: Some Religions of Australian New Guinea and the New Hebrides* (Melbourne: Oxford University Press, 1965), esp. R. M. Berndt, pp. 94–95, and P. Lawrence, pp. 218ff. Important field work has been done by Andrew Strathern, *The Rope of Moka: Big-men and Ceremonial Exchange in Mount Hagen, New Guinea* (Cambridge: Cambridge University Press, 1971), and also Ongka, *Ongka: A Self Account by a New Guinea Big Man*, trans. Andrew Strathern (New York: St. Martin's Press, 1979). Margaret Mead, ed., *Cooperation and Competition among Primitive Peoples*, rev. paperback ed. (Boston: Beacon Press, 1967), esp. chap. 9. Paula Brown, *The Chimbu: A Study of Change in the New Guinea Highlands* (Cambridge, Mass.: Schenkman, 1972). L. Pospisil, *The Kapauku Papuans of Western New Guinea* (New York: Holt Rinehart Winston, 1963), and L. Pospisil, *Kapauku Papuans and Their Law* (New Haven: Yale University Press, 1963).

3. Mary Douglas, *Cultural Bias,* Occasional Paper 35 of the Royal Anthropological Institute of Great Britain and Ireland (London: Royal Anthropological Institute, 1978), p. 11. The article by Anthony Forge to which reference is made is "Prestige, Influence and Society, a New Guinea Example," noted above.

4. Gerd Theissen, "Legitimation and Subsistence: An Essay on the Sociology of Early Christian Missionaries," in *The Social Setting of Pauline Christianity: Essays on Corinth,* trans. John H. Schütz (Philadelphia: Fortress Press, 1982), pp. 27–67, esp. pp. 40–41, 53–54.

5. Paul may be interpreted as saying here: "I shall go to the Gentiles, that is, to the diaspora, you will go to the circumcision, that is, to Palestine." This interpretation fits the pattern of contractual negotiations over "Long Yams" between Big Men from neighboring villages. Bengt Holmberg, *Paul and Power: The Structure of Authority in the Primitive Church as Reflected in the Pauline Epistles* (Lund: CWK Gleerup, 1978), discusses the "Antioch Incident" from the perspective of Paul's report (pp. 14–34) and concludes that there is a hierarchical relationship of authority in the negotiations between Paul and the Jerusalem apostles (pp. 56–57).

6. The problem of appropriate categories of evidence is discussed in Chapter Two, on sociological studies of the Pauline church. We are concerned with the actions, not the explanations of the participants. The problem of circularity, arguing from theological categories to sociological categories and back to theological ones, is avoided by keeping categories of evidence separate. Jonathan L. Gross and Steve Rayner, *Measuring Culture: A Paradigm for the Analysis of Social Organization* (New York: Columbia University Press, 1985), p. 91.

7. Ibid., p. 61.

8. For example, the approach of Bruce J. Malina, *Christian Origins and Cultural Anthropology: Practical Models for Biblical Interpretation* (Atlanta, Ga.: John Knox Press, 1986), in which he uses a technique he terms "kitbashing" to combine selected models of social interaction. He concludes his work with examples of insights obtained and proposals for study. He says in his introduction: "In this way the purpose of such models can be better realized since they are meant to generate more explicit, articulate, testable understanding" (p. v).

9. The results of using David Ostrander's model for deriving a typological cosmology from grid-group categories have been described in Chapter Three above. The article that describes this method is David Ostrander, "One- and Two-Dimensional Models of the Distribution of Beliefs," in *Essays in the Sociology of Perception,* ed. Mary Douglas (London: Routledge & Kegan Paul, 1982), pp. 14–30. The method has been adapted in what follows for the purpose of defining the particular cosmology of Paul and the Pauline church. Mary Douglas's works, *Natural Symbols: Explorations in Cosmology* (New York: Pantheon Books, 1970, 1973 and 1982), and her programatic study *Cultural Bias,* offer important insights and are quoted in defining small group, Quadrant D ty-

pological cosmology. The term "small group" refers to the inherent tendency of Quadrant D factions to divide.

10. Ostrander, "One- and Two-Dimensional Models of the Distribution of Beliefs," p. 29.

11. Ibid., pp. 25–26. See also Mary Douglas's summary of the general social requirements of ritualism and "effervescence," *Natural Symbols* (1970), pp. 73–74.

12. The issue here is not authority, as is pointed out by Wayne Meeks, *The First Urban Christians: The Social World of the Apostle Paul* (New Haven: Yale University Press, 1983), pp. 84 and 111, but the object of symbolic action in the group. See here, Douglas, *Natural Symbols* (1970), pp. 57, 142, and Ostrander, "One- and Two-Dimensional Models of the Distribution of Beliefs," p. 25: "The focus of symbolic action in high-group environments is on the preservation and continuity of the group."

13. Wayne Meeks, *The Moral World of the First Christians* (Philadelphia: Westminster Press, 1986), p. 136.

14. Nils Alstrup Dahl, "The Doctrine of Justification: Its Social Function and Implications," in *Studies in Paul: Theology for the Early Christian Mission* (Minneapolis, Minn.: Augsburg Publishing House, 1977), p. 110.

15. Krister Stendahl, "The Apostle Paul and the Introspective Conscience of the West," in *Paul among Jews and Gentiles* (Philadelphia: Fortress Press, 1976), pp. 78–96. See J. M. Espy, "Paul's 'Robust Conscience' Re-examined," *New Testament Studies* 31 (1985): 161–88, for criticism of Stendahl's exegesis.

16. Ernst Käsemann, "Justification and Salvation History in the Epistle to the Romans," in *Perspectives on Paul* (Philadelphia: Fortress Press, 1971), pp. 60–78.

17. Ibid., p. 74.

18. Stendahl, "The Apostle Paul and the Introspective Conscience of the West," in *Paul among Jews and Gentiles*, pp. 86, 130f.

19. Ibid., p. 86.

20. Ostrander, "One- and Two-Dimensional Models of the Distribution of Beliefs," p. 26, and Steve Rayner, "The Perceptions of Time and Space in Egalitarian Sects: A Millenarian Cosmology," in *Essays in the Sociology of Perception*, ed. Mary Douglas (London: Routledge & Kegan Paul, 1982), pp. 247–74. See esp. pp. 256–63.

21. Käsemann, "Justification and Salvation History in the Epistle to the Romans," in *Perspectives on Paul*, p. 63.

22. Ibid., p. 67.

23. Ibid., p. 72.

24. Stendahl, "The Apostle Paul and the Introspective Conscience of the

West," in *Paul among Jews and Gentiles,* pp. 84f., asserts that Paul dealt with the issue he faced: defining a place for Gentiles in the church.

25. See Käsemann's forceful and personal statement of the importance of reformation theology: Ernst Käsemann, "Justification and Salvation History in the Epistle to the Romans," in *Perspectives on Paul,* pp. 63–65.

26. Douglas, *Natural Symbols,* pp. 57–59.

27. Robert Jewett, "Romans as an Ambassadorial Letter," *Interpretation* 36 (1982): 5–20, uses the term "flexibility" to describe Paul's internalized ambassadorial qualities (p. 11; see notes there).

28. Hans Conzelmann, *I Corinthians: A Commentary on the First Epistle to the Corinthians,* trans. J. Leitch, A Hermeneia Series Commentary (Philadelphia: Fortress Press, 1975), pp. 176–79, questions whether the "informant" is a pagan or a weak brother for the sake of whose conscience one should refrain from eating. The weak brother is not mentioned in this passage but is inferred from 8:9–10. High group, low grid mapping places emphasis on the relationship of chapter 8 to 10:23–30. We conclude that Paul is concerned about the scruples of the weaker brother.

29. Robert Jewett, "The Redaction of I Corinthians and the Trajectory of the Pauline School," *Journal of the American Academy of Religion* 44 (1978): 389–444. See also Bruce J. Malina, "Freedom: A Theological Inquiry into the Dimensions of a Symbol," *Biblical Theology Bulletin* 8 (1987): 62–68.

30. Meeks, *First Urban Christians,* p. 166: "For Paul's circle as for Philo, the desired social expression of faith in the one God is the exclusive unity of the worshippers."

31. Wayne Meeks, "The Social Context of Pauline Theology," *Interpretation* 37 (July 1982): 271.

32. Dahl, "The One God of Jews and Gentiles," in *Studies in Paul,* pp. 188–91. W. S. Campbell, "Romans III as a Key to the Structure and Thought of the Letter," *Novum Testamentum* 23 (1981): 22–40.

33. Theissen's studies on the Corinthian church, collected in *The Social Setting of Pauline Christianity,* describe this situation.

34. Norman R. Petersen, *Rediscovering Paul: Philemon and the Sociology of Paul's Narrative World* (Philadelphia: Fortress Press, 1985), p. 301.

35. These categories are summarized from the description offered by David Ostrander, "One- and Two-Dimensional Models of the Distribution of Belief," pp. 26–27.

36. Again, these categories are taken directly from the description offered in ibid., pp. 26–27.

37. Meeks, *First Urban Christians,* pp. 165–70.

38. Conzelmann, *I Corinthians,* pp. 70–78.

39. Meeks, *Moral World of the First Christians,* pp. 124–36, points to the mediating image of Christ crucified as the ideology Paul uses to justify his dialectical "strong, weak, Pauline" position.

40. Jewett, "Romans as an Ambassadorial Letter," p. 19.

41. Ernest Best, *A Commentary on the First and Second Epistles to the Thessalonians* (London: Adam & Charles Black, 1972), p. 135.

42. Ostrander, "One- and Two-Dimensional Models of the Distribution of Beliefs," pp. 25–26.

43. Ibid., p. 27.

44. Against Meeks, *First Urban Christians,* p. 107, where he identifies the missionary task as the motive for dropping the obvious impediments to social intercourse with outsiders.

45. See the excellent discussion of the problem of the phrase "law of Christ" in Hans Dieter Betz, *Galatians: A Commentary on Paul's Letter to the Churches in Galatia,* A Hermeneia Series Commentary (Philadelphia: Fortress Press, 1979), pp. 298–301.

46. Gerd Theissen in "Legitimation and Subsistence: An Essay on the Sociology of Early Christian Missionaries," in *The Social Setting of Pauline Christianity,* pp. 37–49, describes the renunciation of the privilege of support from the Christian community by Paul. This renunciation incurred problems for him, so it must have held significance.

47. Ostrander, "One- and Two-Dimensional Models of the Distribution of Beliefs," pp. 26–27.

48. Ibid., p. 28.

49. Steve Rayner, "The Perceptions of Time and Space in Egalitarian Sects," p. 248.

50. Ibid., p. 247.

51. Relative Deprivation theory: David F. Aberle, "A Note on Relative Deprivation Theory as Applied to Millenarian and Other Cult Movements," *Millennial Dreams in Action: Essays in Comparative Study,* ed. S. L. Thrupp (The Hague: Mouton, 1962), pp. 209–214. Kenelm Burridge, *New Heaven, New Earth: A Study of Millenarian Activities* (Oxford: Basil Blackwell, 1969).

52. Cognitive dissonance theory: Bryan R. Wilson, *Religion in Sociological Perspective* (Oxford: Oxford University Press, 1982).

53. Steve Rayner, "The Perceptions of Time and Space in Egalitarian Sects," p. 251. Robert Jewett, *The Thessalonian Correspondence: Pauline Rhetoric and Millenarian Piety* (Philadelphia: Fortress Press, 1986), pp. 161ff.

54. Steve Rayner, "The Perceptions of Time and Space in Egalitarian Sects," p. 252.

55. Robert Jewett, *The Thessalonian Correspondence,* pp. 161ff., offers many

helpful notes and a review of the literature, including: Yonina Talmon, "Pursuit of the Millennium: The Relation between Religious and Social Change," *Archives Europëennes de Sociologie* 3 (1962): 125–48; "Millenarian Movements," in ibid. 7 (1966): 159–200; "Millenarism," *International Encyclopedia of the Social Sciences* 10 (New York: Free Press, 1968): 349–62. Peter Worsley, *The Trumpet Shall Sound: A Study of "Cargo" Cults in Melanesia*, 2nd ed. (New York: Schocken Books, 1968), and Kenelm Burridge in *New Heaven, New Earth* and in *Mambu* (London: Methuen, 1960), describe the Melanesian cargo cults.

56. Jewett, *The Thessalonian Correspondence*, pp. 168ff.

57. Rayner, "The Perceptions of Time and Space in Egalitarian Sects," p. 258.

58. Ibid., p. 259.

59. Ibid., p. 257.

60. Ibid., p. 263.

61. Ibid., p. 265.

62. Jewett, *The Thessalonian Correspondence*, pp. 176ff.

63. Meeks, *First Urban Christians*, p. 176; his translations and emphasis.

64. Ibid., p. 179.

65. Ibid., p. 179.

66. Ibid., pp. 97 and 100.

67. Ibid., p. 98.

68. Ibid., pp. 183–89.

69. Ibid., p. 189.

70. Ostrander, "One- and Two-Dimensional Models of the Distribution of Beliefs," p. 26. See above for a definition of personalized symbolic action.

71. Jouette Bassler, *Divine Impartiality: Paul and a Theological Axiom*, S.B.L. Dissertation Series 59 (Chico, Calif.: Scholars Press, 1982), p. 185; emphasis added.

72. Ibid., p. 173.

73. Wayne Meeks, "Social Functions of Apocalyptic Language in Pauline Christianity," in *Apocalypticism in the Mediterranean World and the Near East*, ed. David Hellholm, Proceedings of the International Colloquium on Apocalypticicism, Uppsala, August 12–17, 1979 (Tübingen: J. C. B. Mohr [Paul Siebeck], 1983), p. 694.

74. John G. Gager, *Kingdom and Community: The Social World of Early Christianity* (Englewood Cliffs, N.J.: Prentice-Hall, 1975), p. 36.

75. Douglas, *Natural Symbols* (1970), p. 142.

76. Bassler, *Divine Impartiality*, p. 187; emphasis added.

77. Meeks, *First Urban Christians*, p. 188. The reference to Theissen is: Gerd Theissen, "Soteriologische Symbolik in den paulinischen Schriften: Ein strukturalistischer Beitrag," *Kerygma und Dodma* 20 (1974): 282–304, esp. p. 300.

78. Mary Douglas, "Deciphering a Meal," *Implicit Meanings: Essays in Anthropology* (London: Routledge & Kegan Paul, 1975; rpt. 1979), pp. 249–75, discusses the relationship of cognition and behavior.

8. Paul's Use of *Huiothesia*

1. John G. Gager, *Kingdom and Community: The Social World of Early Christianity* (Englewood Cliffs, N.J.: Prentice-Hall, 1975), pp. 3f. He quotes Yonina Talmon, "Pursuit of the Millennium: The Relation between Religious and Social Change," *Archives Europëenes de Sociologie* 3 (1962): 127.

2. Gager, *Kingdom and Community*, p. 3.

3. Brendan Byrne, *"Sons of God"—"Seed of Abraham"*: *A Study of the Idea of the Sonship of God of All Christians in Paul against the Jewish Background*, Analecta Biblica 83 (Rome: Biblical Institute Press, 1979). This doctoral dissertation (Oxford, 1977) provides the basis for the following discussion of *huiothesia*. Another thesis published in the series Analecta Biblica contains an extended discussion of divine sonship in Old Testament, intertestamental, and Hellenistic literature (including Philo): Matthew Vellanickal, *The Divine Sonship of Christians in the Johannine Writings*, Analecta Biblica 72 (Rome: Biblical Institute Press, 1977). Between these two works, the wider semantic field of *huiothesia* has been described fully. This study is interested in the more limited goal of observing the various options available for interpreting *huiothesia* in its ideological and literary context.

4. Byrne, *"Sons of God"—"Seed of Abraham,"* pp. 80 and 126f.

5. Ibid., pp. 85ff. and 127ff. See also C. E. B. Cranfield, *A Critical and Exegetical Commentary on the Epistle to the Romans*, International Critical Commentary (Edinburgh: T. & T. Clark, vol. 1, 1975; vol. 2, 1979), pp. 27ff., for an outline of Romans with comments. See also Ernst Käsemann, *Commentary on Romans*, trans. and ed. Geoffrey W. Bromiley (Grand Rapids, Mich.: William B. Eerdmans, 1980), pp. 253–56, for a clear statement of the theological concerns related to this transition and the unity of the letter.

6. Hans Dieter Betz, *Galatians: A Commentary on Paul's Letter to the Churches in Galatia*, A Hermeneia Series Commentary (Philadelphia: Fortress Press, 1979), pp. 20 and 202ff.

7. Ibid., pp. 19f.

8. Byrne, *"Sons of God"—"Seed of Abraham,"* pp. 1 and 174ff.

9. Ibid., pp. 1ff. Cranfield, *Commentary on the Epistle to the Romans*, following Karl Barth, finds a linkage between the inheritance and ethical concerns for the behavior of believers, (pp. 371, 400f.). He also points out that this linkage

does not claim that the faithful are children of God, but rather are fictively related to Abraham (pp. 405f.).

10. Byrne, *"Sons of God"—"Seed of Abraham,"* pp. 2, 108f., discusses the textual problems.

11. Käsemann, *Commentary on Romans,* p. 237, points out the theological dialectic between the now present and now future in Paul's characterization of the gift of salvation.

12. Cf. 1 Cor. 2:12 for a parallel construction. See Cranfield, *Commentary on the Epistle to the Romans,* p. 396. Byrne, *"Sons of God"—"Seed of Abraham,"* pp. 98f.

13. See Käsemann, *Commentary on Romans,* p. 227; Cranfield, *Commentary on the Epistle to the Romans,* p. 396; Byrne, *"Sons of God"—"Seed of Abraham,"* pp. 98f. There is uniformity in seeing a "liturgical event" behind vv. 15 and 16. (See Käsemann, *Commentary on Romans,* p. 227.)

14. Byrne, *"Sons of God"—"Seed of Abraham,"* pp. 108f.

15. C. K. Barrett, *A Commentary on the Epistle to the Romans* (London: A. & C. Black, 1971), p. 163, and Byrne, *"Sons of God"—"Seed of Abraham,"* pp. 99f. and 215.

16. See Käsemann, *Commentary on Romans,* pp. 226f., for his detailed comments.

17. Cranfield, *Commentary on the Epistle to the Romans,* p. 419.

18. Byrne, *"Sons of God"—"Seed of Abraham,"* pp. 99ff. He cites Otto Michel, *Der Brief an die Römer,* Meyer Commentary IV (Göttingen: Vandenhoeck & Ruprecht, 1966), p. 197.

19. Byrne, *"Sons of God"—"Seed of Abraham,"* pp. 81ff. Cranfield calls the arrangement of the list consciously artistic: *Commentary on the Epistle to the Romans,* p. 459f. Käsemann calls it rhetorical and carefully structured: *Commentary on Romans,* p. 258.

20. Byrne, *"Sons of God"—"Seed of Abraham,"* pp. 81 and 216.

21. Ibid., p. 83; Michel, *Der Brief an die Römer,* p. 228.

22. Käsemann, *Commentary on Romans,* pp. 257, 260, esp. p. 258.

23. Cranfield, *Commentary on the Epistle to the Romans,* p. 397, n. 1. See also Byrne, *"Sons of God"—"Seed of Abraham,"* pp. 184f.

24. Byrne, *"Sons of God"—"Seed of Abraham,"* p. 178.

25. Betz, *Galatians,* p. 202. See also Byrne, *"Sons of God"—"Seed of Abraham,"* pp. 174ff.

26. Betz, *Galatians,* p. 209.

27. Ibid., p. 186; emphasis added.

28. L. Wenge and A. Oepke, "Adoption," *Reallexikon für Antike und Christentum,* vol. 1, col. 100. Also in Liddell, Scott, and Jones, *"huiothesia," A Greek-English Lexicon* with supplement 1968 (Oxford: Oxford University Press, 1977).

29. Nicolaus Damascenus, *bios kaisaros* 55 = Frag. 130.5 = Felix Jacoby, in Felix Jacoby, *Die Fragmente der Griechischen Historiker* (Berlin: Weidmannsche, 1926), vol. IIA, p. 401, ll. 17–25.

30. Appian, *Civil Wars* III ii and Cassius Dio Cocceianus XLV iii 1–3. At other points, where one might reasonably expect the use of *huiothesia*, Appianus uses *thetos . . . pais* (*Civil Wars* II 143) and Cassius Dio uses *huion pepoiaetai* (XLIV xxxv 2).

31. Archie C. Bush, *Studies in Roman Social Structure* (Washington, D.C.: University Press of America, 1982), is a structuralist study of marriage patterns in the Roman republic and early Roman empire. The transactional basis of kinship and marriage is diagrammed with examples. Adoption is used to ensure equivalency of a son for succession in the Julio-Claudian line (p. 93).

32. Vellanickal, *The Divine Sonship of Christians*, p. 71. (But corrected to citations in C. T. Lewis and C. Short, *A Latin Dictionary* [Oxford: Clarendon Press, 1969]). See also *"Adoptio," Oxford Classical Dictionary* (London: Oxford University Press, 1949).

33. See the citings under *"Adoptio"* in Lewis and Short, *A Latin Dictionary*, and *"Adoptio"* in the *Oxford Classical Dictionary*.

34. See inscriptions from Delphi and Crete, cited above.

35. W. v. Martitz, *"huiothesia," Theological Dictionary of the New Testament* (Grand Rapids, Mich.: William B. Eerdmans, 1975), 8: 398.

36. W. K. Lacey, *"Patria Potestas,"* in Beryl Rawson, ed., *The Family in Ancient Rome: New Perspectives* (Ithaca, N.Y.: Cornell University Press, 1986), pp. 121–44; see esp. the summary from which this argument is taken, pp. 123–34.

37. See also the first article in the anthology *The Family in Ancient Rome: New Perspectives*, "The Roman Family" by Beryl Rawson, pp. 1–57, esp. p. 8.

38. W. K. Lacey, *"Patria Potestas,"* in *The Family in Ancient Rome*, p. 123. See also p. 140.

39. Ibid., p. 133.

40. Ibid., pp. 134–37.

41. Francis Lyall, "Roman Law in the Writings of Paul—Adoption," *Journal of Biblical Literature* 88 (1969): 466.

42. Ibid., p. 466.

43. Betz, *Galatians*, p. 209.

44. Ibid., pp. 185–86.

45. Wayne Meeks, *First Urban Christians: The Social World of the Apostle Paul* (New Haven: Yale University Press, 1983), p. 87. See also A. D. Nock, "The Historical Importance of Cult-Associations," *Classical Review* 38 (1924): 105–109. The inscriptions are *Corpus Inscriptionum Regni Bosporani* 1281, 1283, 1285, 1286.

46. Meeks, *First Urban Christians*, p. 88.

47. Byrne, *"Sons of God"—"Seed of Abraham."* The lack of adoption in the Bible may have been the result of an effective alternative strategy for inheritance found in the institution of levirate marriage: Jack Goody, *The Development of the Family and Marriage in Europe,* Past and Present Publications (Cambridge: Cambridge University Press, 1983), pp. 68ff.

48. William H. Rossell, "New Testament Adoption—Greco-Roman or Semitic?" *Journal of Biblical Literature* 71 (1952): 233–34.

49. For further contradictory arguments on the applicability of Nuzi documents for Old Testament study: John van Seters, "The Problem of Childlessness in Near Eastern Law and the Patriarchs of Israel," *Journal of Biblical Literature* 87 (1968): 401–408.

50. Adolph von Harnack, *Die Terminologie der Wiedergeburt und verwandter Erlebnisse in der Ältesten Kirche,* in *Texte und Untersuchungen,* vol. 42, pt. 3 (Leipzig: J. C. Hinrich, 1918), p. 103.

51. Gerhard von Rad, *Old Testament Theology* (Evanston: Harper & Row, 1962), pp. 130–31. Von Rad has here also an excellent summary of the history of the conception of the covenant with reference to Mendenhall's work on Hittite treaties.

52. Please see the extended discussion of the wider semantic field in Vellanickal, *The Divine Sonship of Christians,* pp. 45–52.

53. Norman R. Petersen, *Rediscovering Paul: Philemon and the Sociology of Paul's Narrative World* (Philadelphia: Fortress Press, 1985), p. 1. See especially pp. 1–42 (the introduction to the book) for a very helpful discussion of Petersen's goals.

54. Ibid., p. 208.

55. Ibid., p. 217.

56. Ibid., p. 211.

57. Ibid., pp. 93–109, esp. pp. 104f., and pp. 131–51 for a discussion of Paul's rhetorical referent.

58. Ibid., p. 133. Emphasis is Petersen's.

59. Ibid., p. 204.

Bibliography

Aberle, David F. "A Note on Relative Deprivation Theory as Applied to Millenarian and Other Cult Movements." In *Millennial Dreams in Action: Essays in Comparative Study,* edited by S. L. Thrupp, pp. 209–214. The Hague: Mouton, 1962.

Asad, Talal. "The Concept of Cultural Translation in British Social Anthropology." In *Writing Culture: The Poetics and Politics of Ethnography,* edited by James Clifford and George E. Marcus, pp. 141–64. Berkeley and Los Angeles: University of California Press, 1986.

Baird, William. "Visions, Revelation, and Ministry: Reflections on 2 Cor. 12:1–5 and Gal. 1:11–17." *Journal of Biblical Literature* 104 (1985): 651–62.

Banks, Robert. *Paul's Idea of Community: The Early House Churches in Their Historical Setting.* Grand Rapids, Mich.: William B. Eerdmans, 1980.

Barrett, C. K. *A Commentary on the Epistle to the Romans.* London: A. & C. Black, 1971.

Bassler, Jouette. *Divine Impartiality: Paul and a Theological Axiom,* S.B.L. Dissertation Series 59. Chico, Calif.: Scholars Press, 1982.

Benko, Stephen. *Pagan Rome and the Early Christians.* Bloomington: Indiana University Press, 1984.

Berger, Peter L. *Facing Up to Modernity: Excursions in Society, Politics, and Religion.* New York: Basic Books, 1977.

Berger, Peter, and Thomas Luckmann. *The Social Construction of Reality: A Treatise in the Sociology of Knowledge.* Garden City, N.Y.: Doubleday, 1966.

Best, Ernest. *A Commentary on the First and Second Epistles to the Thessalonians.* London: Adam & Charles Black, 1972.

Betz, Hans Dieter. *Galatians: A Commentary on Paul's Letter to the Churches in Galatia.* A Hermeneia Series Commentary. Philadelphia: Fortress Press, 1979.
———. *2 Corinthians 8 and 9: A Commentary on Two Administrative Letters of the Apostle Paul.* Philadelphia: Fortress Press, 1985.
Blake, Robert R., and Jane S. Mouton. *The New Managerial Grid.* Houston, Tex.: Gulf Publishing, 1978.
Blumer, Herbert. *Symbolic Interactionism.* Englewood Cliffs, N.J.: Prentice-Hall, 1969.
Brockhaus, Ulrich. *Charisma und Amt: Die paulinischen Charismenlehre auf dem Hintergrund der frühchristlichen Gemeindefunktionen.* 2d ed. Wuppertal: Brockhaus, 1975.
Brown, Paula. *The Chimbu: A Study of Change in the New Guinea Highlands.* Cambridge, Mass.: Schenkman, 1972.
Bruce, F. F. *The Pauline Circle.* Grand Rapids, Mich.: William B. Eerdmans, 1985.
Brunk, H. D. *An Introduction to Mathematical Statistics.* Boston: Ginn, 1960.
Burridge, Kenelm. *Mambu.* London: Methuen, 1960.
———. *New Heaven, New Earth: A Study of Millenarian Activities.* Oxford: Basil Blackwell, 1969.
Bush, Archie C. *Studies in Roman Social Structure.* Washington, D.C.: University Press of America, 1982.
Byrne, Brendan. *"Sons of God"—"Seed of Abraham": A Study of the Idea of the Sonship of All Christians in Paul against the Jewish Background.* Analecta Biblica 83. Rome: Biblical Institute Press, 1979.
Campbell, W. S. "Romans III as a Key to the Structure and Thought of the Letter." *Novum Testamentum* 23 (1981): 22–40.
Campenhausen, Hans von. *Ecclesiastical Office and Spiritual Power in the Church in the First Three Centuries.* Stanford, Calif.: Stanford University Press, 1969.
———. *Polykarp von Smyrna und die Pastoralbriefe.* Heidelberg: C. Winter, 1951.
Clifford, James, and George E. Marcus. *Writing Culture: The Poetics and Politics of Ethnography.* Berkeley and Los Angeles: University of California Press, 1986.
Conzelmann, Hans. *I Corinthians: A Commentary on the First Epistle to the Corinthians,* translated by J. Leitch. A Hermeneia Series Commentary. Philadelphia: Fortress Press, 1975.
Cranfield, C. E. B. *A Critical and Exegetical Commentary on the Epistle to the Romans.* International Critical Commentary. Edinburgh: T. & T. Clark, vol. 1, 1975; vol. 2, 1979.
Dahl, Nils Alstrup. *Jesus in the Memory of the Early Church.* Minneapolis, Minn.: Augsburg Publishing House, 1976.

———. "The Origin of Baptism." In *Interpretationes ad Vetus Testamentum Pertinentes Sigmundo Mowinckel Septuagenario Missae,* edited by Nils A. Dahl and A. S. Kapelrud, pp. 36–52. Oslo: Land og Kirke, 1955.

———. "Paul and the Church at Corinth According to I Corinthians 1:10–4:21." In *Christian History and Interpretation,* Studies presented to John Knox, edited by W. R. Farmer, C. F. D. Moule, R. R. Neibuhr, pp. 313–35. Cambridge: Cambridge University Press, 1967.

———. *Studies in Paul: Theology for the Early Christian Mission.* Minneapolis, Minn.: Augsburg Publishing House, 1977.

Dautzenberg, Gerhard. *Urchristliche Prophetie: ihre Erforschung ihre Voraussetzungen im Judentum und ihre Structure im ersten Korintherbrief.* Stuttgart: W. Kohlhammer, 1975.

David, Nicholas, Judy Sterner, and Kodozo Gavua. "Why Pots are Decorated." *Current Anthropology* 29 (1988): 365–89.

Descombes, Vincent. *Proust, Philosophie du Roman.* Paris: Editions de Minuit, 1987.

Dewey, John. *Reconstruction in Philosophy.* Enlarged ed. Boston: Beacon Press, 1957.

Donfried, Karl, ed. *The Romans Debate.* Minneapolis, Minn.: Augsburg Publishing House, 1977.

Douglas, Mary. *Cultural Bias.* Occasional Paper 35 of the Royal Anthropological Institute of Great Britain and Ireland. London: Royal Anthropological Institute, 1978.

———. *E. E. Evans-Pritchard.* Sussex: Harvester Press, 1980.

———. *How Institutions Think.* Syracuse: Syracuse University Press, 1986.

———. *Implicit Meanings: Essays in Anthropology.* London: Routledge & Kegan Paul, 1975; reprint, 1979.

———. *In the Active Voice.* London: Routledge & Kegan Paul, 1982.

———. "Introduction to Grid-Group Analysis." *Essays in the Sociology of Perception.* London: Routledge & Kegan Paul, 1982.

———. *Natural Symbols: Explorations in Cosmology.* New York: Pantheon, 1970, 1973, and 1982.

———. *Purity and Danger: An Analysis of the Concepts of Pollution and Taboo.* Baltimore: Pelican Books, 1970.

———. "Social Preconditions of Enthusiasm and Heterodoxy." *Forms of Symbolic Action,* edited by Robert F. Spencer. Proceedings of the 1969 Annual Spring Meeting of the American Ethnological Society. Seattle: University of Washington Press, 1969.

Douglas, Mary, and Jonathan L. Gross. "Food and Culture: Measuring the Intricacy of Rule Systems." *Social Science Information* 20 (1981): 1–35.

Douglas, Mary, and Aaron Wildavsky. *Risk and Culture.* Berkeley and Los Angeles: University of California Press, 1982.

Durkheim, Emile. *The Division of Labor in Society.* Glencoe, Ill.: Free Press, 1960.

————. *The Elementary Forms of The Religious Life,* translated by Joseph Swain. New York: Macmillan, 1915.

Eisenstadt, S. N., and L. Roniger. *Patrons, Clients and Friends: Interpersonal Relations and the Structure of Trust in Society.* Cambridge: Cambridge University Press, 1984.

Elliot, John. "Social-Scientific Criticism of the New Testament and Its Social World: More on Method and Models." *Semeia* 35 (1986): 1–34.

Ellis, E. Earle. "Paul and His Co-Workers." *New Testament Studies* 17 (1971): 437–52.

Espy, J. M. "Paul's 'Robust Conscience' Re-examined." *New Testament Studies* 31 (1985): 161–88.

Evans-Pritchard, E. E. *Social Anthropology.* London: Cohen & West, 1951.

Finkelstein, J. J. "Mesopotamian Historiography." *Proceedings of the American Philosophical Society* 107 (1963): 461–72.

Flanagan, James G., and Steve Rayner. *Rules, Decisions, and Inequality in Egalitarian Societies.* Brookfield, Vt.: Gower, 1988.

Forge, Anthony. "Prestige, Influence and Society, A New Guinea example." In *Witchcraft Confessions and Accusations,* edited by Mary Douglas. Association of Social Anthropologists monograph series 9. London, New York: Tavistock Publications, 1970.

Funk, Aloys. *Status und Rollen in den Paulusbriefen: Eine inhaltsanalytische Untersuchung zur Religionssoziologie.* Innsbrucker Theologische Studien 7. Innsbruck: Tyrolia, 1981.

Gager, John G. *Kingdom and Community: The Social World of Early Christianity.* Englewood Cliffs, N.J.: Prentice-Hall, 1975.

————. "Some Notes on Paul's Conversion." *New Testament Studies* 27 (1981): 697–704.

Garfinkel, Harold. *Studies in Ethnomethodology.* Englewood Cliffs, N.J.: Prentice-Hall, 1967.

Garrett, Susan R. *The Demise of the Devil: Magic and the Demonic in Luke's Writings.* Minneapolis: Fortress Press, 1989.

————. "Review of *Christian Origins and Cultural Anthropology: Practical Models for Biblical Interpretation* by Bruce J. Malina. Atlanta, Ga.: John Knox, 1986." *Journal of Biblical Literature* 107 (1988): 532–34.

Geertz, Clifford. *The Interpretation of Culture: Selected Essays.* New York: Basic Books, 1973.

Gellner, Ernest. "Concepts and Society." In *Sociological Theory and Philosophical Analysis,* edited by Dorothy Emmet and Alasdair Macintyre, pp. 115–49. London: Macmillan, 1970.

Goodenough, E. R. *Jewish Symbols in the Greco-Roman Period.* 13 vols. New York: Pantheon Books, 1953–68.

Goody, Jack. *The Development of the Family and Marriage in Europe.* Past and Present Publications. Cambridge: Cambridge University Press, 1983.

Gottwald, Norman K. *The Tribes of Yahweh: A Sociology of the Religion of Liberated Israel, 1250–1050 B.C.E.* Maryknoll, N.Y.: Orbis Books, 1979.

Grelot, Pierre. "Sur l'origine des ministères dans les églises pauliniennes." *Istina* 16 (1971): 459.

Greeven, Heinrich. "Propheten, Lehrer, Vorsteher bei Paulus. Zur Frage der 'Ämter' im Urchristentum." *Zeitschrift fur die Neutestamentliche Wissenschaft* 44 (1952-53): 1–43.

Gross, Jonathan L. "Graph-theoretical Model of Social Organization." *Annals of Discrete Mathematics* 13 (1982): 81–88.

———. "Information-theoretic Scales for Measuring Cultural Rule Systems." In *Sociological Methodology 1983–1984,* pp. 248–71. San Francisco: Jossey-Bass, 1983.

———. "Measurement of Calendric Information in Food-taking Behavior." In *Food in the Social Order: Studies of Food and Festivities in Three American Communities,* edited by Mary Douglas. New York: Russell Sage Foundation, 1984.

Gross, Jonathan L., and Steve Rayner. *Measuring Culture: A Paradigm for the Analysis of Social Organization.* New York: Columbia University Press, 1985.

Habermas, Jürgen. *Communication and the Evolution of Society.* Boston: Beacon Press, 1979.

———. *Legitimation Crisis.* Boston: Beacon Press, 1975.

Hamilton, Peter. *Knowledge and Social Structure: An Introduction to the Classical Argument in the Sociology of Knowledge.* London: Routledge & Kegan Paul, 1974.

Hanson, A. T. "The Domestication of Paul: A Study in the Development of Early Christian Theology." *Bulletin of the John Rylands University Library of Manchester* 62, no. 2 (1981): 402–18.

Harnack, Adolph von. *Die Terminologie der Wiedergeburt und verwandter Erlebnisse in der Ältesten Kirche.* In *Texte und Untersuchgen,* 42: 3. Leipzig: J. C. Hinrich, 1918.

Hengel, Martin. *Property and Riches in the Early Church: Aspects of a Social History of Early Christianity.* London: SCM Press, 1974.

Hester, James D. *Paul's Concept of Inheritance: A Contribution to the Understanding of Heilsgeschichte.* Scottish Journal of Theology Occasional Papers No. 14. Edinburgh: Oliver & Boyd, 1968.

Hock, Ronald F. "Paul's Tentmaking and the Problem of His Social Class." *Journal of Biblical Literature* 97 (1978): 555–64.

————. *The Social Context of Paul's Ministry: Tentmaking and Apostleship.* Philadelphia: Fortress Press, 1980.

Holmberg, Bengt. *Paul and Power: The Structure of Authority in the Primitive Church as Reflected in the Pauline Epistles.* Lund: CWK Gleerup, 1978.

————. "Sociological versus Theological Analysis of the Question Concerning a Pauline Church Order." In *Die Paulinische Literatur und Theologie,* edited by Sigfred Pedersen, pp. 187–200. Göttingen: Vandenhoeck & Ruprecht, 1980.

Jacoby, Felix. *Die Fragmente der Griechischen Historiker.* Berlin: Weidmannsche, 1926.

Jeffries, Vincent, and H. Edward Ransford. *Social Stratification: A Multiple Hierarchy Approach.* Boston: Allyn and Bacon, 1980.

Jewett, Robert. "Agitators and the Galatian Congregation." *New Testament Studies* 17 (1970–71): 198–212.

————. *A Chronology of Paul's Life.* Philadelphia: Fortress Press, 1979.

————. *Paul's Anthropological Terms: A Study of Their Use in Conflict Settings.* Leiden: E. J. Brill, 1971.

————. "The Redaction of I Corinthians and the Trajectory of the Pauline School." *Journal of the American Academy of Religion* 44 (1978): 389–444.

————. "Romans as an Ambassadorial Letter." *Interpretation* 36 (1982): 5–20.

————. "The Sexual Liberation of the Apostle Paul." *Journal of the American Academy of Religion* 47 Supplement (1979): 55–87.

————. *The Thessalonian Correspondence: Pauline Rhetoric and Millenarian Piety.* Philadelphia: Fortress Press, 1986.

Judge, Edwin A. "The Early Christians as Scholastic Community." *Journal of Religious History* 1 (1960): 4–15, 125–37.

————. "The Social Identity of the First Christians: A Question of Method in Religious History." *Journal of Religious History* 11 (1980): 201–217.

————. The *Social Pattern of Christian Groups in the First Century.* London: Tyndale, 1960.

Käsemann, Ernst. *Commentary on Romans.* Translated by Goeffrey W. Bromiley. Grand Rapids, Mich.: William B. Eerdmans, 1980.

————. *Essays on New Testament Themes.* Naperville, Ill.: Alec R. Allenson, 1964.

————. *New Testament Questions of Today.* Philadelphia: Fortress Press, 1969.

————. *Perspectives on Paul.* Philadelphia: Fortress Press, 1971.

Kee, Howard Clark. *Christian Origins in Sociological Perspective: Methods and Resources.* Philadelphia: Westminster Press, 1980.

Kennedy, George A. *New Testament Interpretation through Rhetorical Criticism.* Chapel Hill: University of North Carolina Press, 1984.

Kirk, K. Andrew. "Did 'Officials' in the New Testament Church Receive a Salary?" *Evangelical Times* 84 (1972/3): 108.

Kümmel, Werner G. *The New Testament: The History of the Investigation of Its Problems.* Translated by S. MacLean Gilmour and Howard Clark Kee. Nashville: Abingdon Press, 1972.

Lampe, G. W. H. "Church Discipline and the Interpretation of the Epistles to the Corinthians." In *Christian History and Interpretation: Studies Presented to John Knox,* edited by W. R. Farmer, C. F. D. Moule, R. R. Neibuhr, pp. 337–61. Cambridge: Cambridge University Press, 1967.

Lawrence, Peter, and M. J. Meggitt, eds. *Gods, Ghosts and Men in Melanesia: Some Religions of Australian New Guinea and the New Hebrides.* Melbourne: Oxford University Press, 1965.

Levi-Strauss, Claude. *Structural Anthropology.* Translated by Claire Jacobson and Brooke Grundfest Schoepf. New York: Basic Books, 1963.

Lüdemann, Gerd. *Paul Apostle to the Gentiles: Studies in Chronology.* Translated by F. Stanley Jones. Philadelphia: Fortress Press, 1984.

Lütgert, Willhelm. *Gesetz und Geist: Eine Untersuchung zur Vorgeschichte des Galaterbriefes.* Gütersloh: C. Bertelsmann, 1919.

Lyall, Francis. "Roman Law in the Writings of Paul—Adoption." *Journal of Biblical Literature* 88 (1969).

Malherbe, Abraham. *Social Aspects of Early Christianity.* Baton Rouge: Louisiana State University Press, 1977.

Malina, Bruce J. *Christian Origins and Cultural Anthropology: Practical Models for Biblical Interpretation.* Atlanta, Ga.: John Knox Press, 1986.

———. "Freedom: A Theological Inquiry into the Dimensions of a Symbol." *Biblical Theology Bulletin* 8 (1978): 62–76.

———. *The New Testament World: Insights from Cultural Anthropology.* Atlanta, Ga.: John Knox Press, 1981.

———. "Normative Dissonance and Christian Origins." *Social-Scientific Criticism of the New Testament and Its Social World: Semeia* 35 (1986): 35–59.

———. "Review of Aloys Funk, *Status und Rollen in den Paulusbriefen: Eine inhaltsanalytische Untersuchung zur Religionssoziologie,* Innsbrucker Theologische Studien 7 (Tyrolia: Tyrolia-Verlag, 1981)." *Catholic Biblical Quarterly* 49 (1987): 143–44.

———. "Review of Wayne Meeks, *The First Urban Christians: The Social World of the Apostle Paul* (New Haven: Yale University Press, 1983)." *Journal of Biblical Literature* 104 (1985): 346–49.

Malinowski, Bronislaw. *A Scientific Theory of Culture and Other Essays.* Chapel Hill: University of North Carolina Press, 1944.

Marcus, George E., and Michael M. J. Fischer. *Anthropology as Cultural Critique: An Experimental Moment in the Human Sciences.* Chicago: University of Chicago Press, 1986.

Martin, Ralph P. *The Spirit and the Congregation: Studies in I Cor. 12–15.* Grand Rapids, Mich.: William B. Eerdmans, 1984.

Martitz, W. v. *"Huiothesia."* *Theological Dictionary of the New Testament,* vol. 8. Grand Rapids, Mich.: William B. Eerdmans, 1975.

Mead, Margaret. *Sex and Temperament.* New York: William Morrow, 1963.

Mead, Margaret, ed. *Cooperation and Competition Among Primitive Peoples.* Rev. paperback ed. Boston: Beacon Press, 1967.

Meeks, Wayne. *The First Urban Christians: The Social World of the Apostle Paul.* New Haven: Yale University Press, 1983.

———. *The Moral World of the First Christians.* Philadelphia: Westminster Press, 1986.

———. "The Social Context of Pauline Theology." *Interpretation* 37 (July 1982): 266–77.

———. "Social Functions of Apocalyptic Language in Pauline Christianity." In *Apocalypticism in the Mediterranean World and the Near East,* edited by David Hellholm, pp. 687–705. Proceedings of the International Colloquium on Apocalypticism, Uppsala, August 12–17, 1979. Tübingen: J. C. B. Mohr (Paul Siebeck), 1983.

Merton, Robert K. *Social Theory and Social Structure.* Enlarged ed. New York: Free Press, 1968.

Michel, Otto. *Der Brief an die Römer.* Meyer Commentary 4. Göttingen: Vandenhoeck & Ruprecht, 1966.

Moore, William David. "The Origin of 'Porneia' Reflected in I Cor. 5–6 and Its Implications to an Understanding of the Fundamental Orientation of the Corinthian Church." Ph.D. diss., Baylor University, 1978.

Morris, Joan M. "Images of Community in Scientific Texts: A Grid/Group Approach to the Analysis of Journal Editorials." *Sociological Inquiry* 58 (1988): 240–60.

Moss Kanter, Rosabeth. *Commitment and Community: Communes and Utopias in Sociological Perspective.* Cambridge, Mass.: Harvard University Press, 1972.

Neyrey, Jerome H. "Body Language in I Corinthians: The Use of Anthropological Models for Understanding Paul and His Opponents." *Semeia* 35 (1986): 129–70.

———. "Witchcraft Accusations in 2 Cor. 10–13: Paul in Social Science Perspective." *Listening* 21 (1986): 160–70.

Neyrey, Jerome H., and Bruce J. Malina. "Jesus the Witch: Witchcraft Accusations in Matthew 12." In *Calling Jesus Names: The Social Value of Labels in Matthew,* edited by Jerome H. Neyrey and Bruce J. Malina. Sonoma, Calif.: Polebridge Press, 1988, pp. 3–32.

Nicholas, Ralph W. "Factions: A Comparative Analysis." In *Friends, Followers, and Factions: A Reader in Political Clientelism.* Berkeley and Los Angeles: University of California Press, 1977.

Nickle, Keith F. *The Collection: A Study in Paul's Strategy.* Studies in Biblical Theology 49. Naperville, Ill.: Alec R. Allenson, 1966.

Nock, A. D. "The Historical Importance of Cult-Associations." *Classical Review* 38 (1924): 105–109.

Ongka. *Ongka: A Self Account by a New Guinea Big Man.* Translated by Andrew Strathern. New York: St. Martin's Press, 1979.

Osiek, Carolyn. *What Are They Saying about the Social Setting of the New Testament?* Ramsey, N.J.: Paulist Press, 1984.

Ostrander, David. "One- and Two-Dimensional Models of the Distribution of Beliefs." In *Essays in the Sociology of Perception,* edited by Mary Douglas, pp. 14–24. London: Routledge & Kegan Paul, 1982.

Owen, Carol. "Book Review of Jeffries, Vincent and Ransford, H. Edward. *Social Stratification: A Multiple Hierarchy Approach.* Boston: Allyn and Bacon, Inc., 1980." *Contemporary Sociology* 10 (1981): 591–92.

Petersen, Norman R. *Rediscovering Paul: Philemon and the Sociology of Paul's Narrative World.* Philadelphia: Fortress Press, 1985.

Pospisil, L. *Kapauku Papuans and Their Law.* New Haven: Yale University Press, 1963.

———. *The Kapauku Papuans of Western New Guinea.* New York: Holt Rinehart Winston, 1963

Rad, Gerhard von. *Old Testament Theology.* Evanston, Ill.: Harper & Row, 1962.

Rayner, Steve. "The Perceptions of Time and Space in Egalitarian Sects: A Millenarian Cosmology." In *Essays in the Sociology of Perception,* edited by Mary Douglas, pp. 247–74. London: Routledge & Kegan Paul, 1982.

Rawson, Beryl, ed. *The Family in Ancient Rome: New Perspectives.* Ithaca, N.Y.: Cornell University Press, 1986.

Robinson, J. M., and Helmut Koester. *Trajectories through Early Christianity.* Philadelphia: Fortress Press, 1979.

Rossell, William H. "New Testament Adoption—Greco-Roman or Semitic?" *Journal of Biblical Literature* 71 (1952): 233–34.

Sampley, J. Paul. *Pauline Partnership in Christ: Christian Community and Commitment in Light of Roman Law.* Philadelphia: Fortress Press, 1980.

Sanders, E. P. *Paul and Palestinian Judaism: A Comparison of Patterns of Religion.* Philadelphia: Fortress Press, 1977.

Sangren, P. Steven. "Rhetoric and the Authority of Ethnography: Postmodernism and the Social Reproduction of Texts." *Current Anthropology* 29 (1988): 405–435.

Schütz, John H. *Paul and the Anatomy of Apostolic Authority.* Society for New Testament Studies Monograph Series 26. Cambridge: Cambridge University Press, 1975.

Schweitzer, Albert. *The Mysticism of the Apostle Paul.* New York: Seabury Press, 1968.

Seters, John van. "The Problem of Childlessness in Near Eastern Law and the Patriarchs of Israel." *Journal of Biblical Literature* 87 (1968): 401–408.

Smith, Jonathan Z. "The Social Description of Early Christianity." *Religious Studies Review* 1 (1975): 19–25.

Snow, David A., Louis A. Zurcher, Jr., and Sheldon Ekland-Olson. "Social Networks and Social Movements: A Microstructural Approach to Differential Recruitment." *American Sociological Review* 45 (1980): 787–801.

Snyder, Graydon F. *Ante Pacem: Archaeological Evidence of Church Life before Constantine.* Macon, Ga.: Mercer University Press, 1985.

Soden, Hans von. "Sakrament und Ethik bei Paulus." In *Das Paulusbild in der neueren Deutschen Forschung,* edited by Karl Heinrich Rengstorf, Weg der Forschung 24, pp. 338–79. Darmstadt: Wissenschaftliche Buchgesellschaft, 1964.

Spencer, Herbert. *On Social Evolution.* Chicago: University of Chicago Press, 1972.

Spickard, James V. "A Guide to Mary Douglas's Three Versions of 'Grid/Group' Theory." Privately published: James V. Spickard, 414 Rose Ave., Box 406, Aromas, Calif. 95004, January 1987.

———. "Relativism and Cultural Comparison in the Anthropology of Mary Douglas: A Meta-Theoretical Evaluation of Her Grid/Group Theory." Ph.D. diss., Graduate Theological Union, 1984.

Stendahl, Krister. *Paul Among Jews and Gentiles.* Philadelphia: Fortress Press, 1976.

Strathern, Andrew. *The Rope of Moka, Big-men and Ceremonial Exchange in Mount Hagen, New Guinea.* Cambridge: Cambridge University Press, 1971.

Talmon, Yonina. "Millenarian Movements." *Archives Européennes de Sociologie* 7 (1966): 159–200.

———. "Millenarism." *International Encyclopedia of the Social Sciences,* vol. 10, pp. 349–62. New York: Free Press, 1968.

———. "Pursuit of the Millennium: The Relation between Religious and Social Change." *Archives Européennes de Sociologie* 3 (1962): 125–48.

Theissen, Gerd. *The Social Setting of Pauline Christianity: Essays on Corinth.* Translated by John H. Schütz. Philadelphia: Fortress Press, 1982.

———. *Sociology of Early Palestinian Christianity.* Translated by John Bowen. Philadelphia: Fortress Press, 1978.

———. "Soteriologische Symbolik in den paulinischen Schriften: Ein strukturalistischer Beitrag." *Kerygma und Dogma* 20 (1974): 282–304.

———. *Studien Zur Soziologie des Urchristentums.* Wissenschaftliche Untersuchungen zum Neuen Testament 19. 2nd expanded ed. Tübingen: J. C. B. Mohr (Paul Siebeck), 1983.

Thompson, Michael. "A Three-Dimensional Model." In *Essays in the Sociology of Perception,* edited by Mary Douglas, pp. 31–63. London: Routledge & Kegan Paul, 1982.

Tidball, Derek. *The Social Context of the New Testament: A Sociological Analysis.* Grand Rapids, Mich.: Academie Books, Zondervan, 1984.

Turner, Victor. *The Ritual Process: Structure and Anti-Structure.* Ithaca, N.Y.: Cornell University Press, 1977.

Ulin, Robert C. *Understanding Cultures: Perspectives in Anthropology and Social Theory.* Austin: University of Texas Press, 1988.

Van Maanen, John. *Tales of the Field: On Writing Ethnography.* Chicago: University of Chicago Press, 1988.

Vellanickal, Matthew. *The Divine Sonship of Christians in the Johannine Writings.* Analecta Biblica 72. Rome: Biblical Institute Press, 1977.

Wald, A. *Statistical Decision Functions.* New York: John Wiley, 1950.

Weber, Max. *The Theory of Social and Economic Organization.* Glencoe, Ill.: Free Press, 1947.

Wenge, L., and A. Oepke. "Adoption." *Reallexikon für Antike und Christentum: Sachworerbuch zur Auseinandersetzung des Christentums mit der antiken Welt,* vol. 1, col. 100. Stuttgart: Hiersemann, 1950.

White, Lloyd Michael. "*Domus Ecclesiae—Domus Dei:* Adaptation and Development in the Setting for Early Christian Assembly." Ph.D. diss., Yale University, 1982.

Wildavsky, Aaron. "Choosing Preferences by Constructing Institutions: A Cultural Theory of Preference Formation." *American Political Science Review* 81 (1987).

———. *The Nursing Father: Moses as a Political Leader.* University, Ala.: University of Alabama Press, 1984.

Wilson, Bryan R. *Religion in Sociological Perspective.* Oxford: Oxford University Press, 1982.

Worsley, Peter. *The Trumpet Shall Sound: A Study of "Cargo" Cults in Melanesia.* 2nd augmented ed. New York: Schocken Books, 1968.

Wuthnow, R., J. D. Hunter, A. Bergesen, and E. Kurzweil. *Cultural Analysis: The Work of Peter L. Berger, Mary Douglas, Michel Foucault, and Jürgen Habermas.* Boston: Routledge & Kegan Paul, 1984.

Author–Subject Index

Scripture Index